These I

Each Time

A Collection of jokes compiled and gathered
from here and there over time by

J P Landahl

To Tammy
Here is to miles of smiles

J.P. Landahl

Preface

There are jokes that are funny to some and to others go flat for humor. Through sixty years of listening to, reading jokes in paperback joke books, perusing internet joke sites and telling jokes, a collection was compiled of those that made me laugh every time. I found that many jokes were the same with possibly that the subject of the joke was changed from a blonde to Pollock to hillbilly but the joke was the same. From gathering material for speeches and wanting to add humor to enlighten a possible boring subject, I would change the joke to fit the occasion by dropping in personal names adding a bit of laughter helping bring attention to the talk. Then there were the clown acts that needed jokes for the kids which made them feel good. Of course, my comedy routines needed that extra moment after moment of keeping the crowd laughing. The audience would be asked to name a subject and the comedic response had to be with an appropriate bit of humor. It is hoped that you will laugh the first time and every time thereafter reading these humor selections. Some are funnier than others but that is to be expected. This collection of jokes includes poking fun at each and everyone with no exclusions to race, color, religion, politics, and well, look at the contents page to see just about every part of life has been covered.

Enjoy

Forward

The 1964 Christmas show given by Bob Hope in Vinh Long, Vietnam will always be in my memories. It was my job to see that the performers were taken care of and set up for giving the show before everyone returned from a joint mission in the Northern part of Vietnam.

The unit commanders prepared a plaque with the unit's insignia noting our appreciation to Bob Hope and all the performers for spending Christmas with us. After Mr. Hope was presented the plaque, he brought the plaque back giving it to his son, Tony. He said to Tony, "Keep this in a special place" and was visually emotionally moved. He spoke to Tony and I was standing there with Tony. The man spoke from his heart and was truly moved by our actions.

Jill St John concluded the show by singing "Silent Night". As she was singing, the men began singing along with her. It was so moving that it brought her to tears and she had to leave the stage.

Anita Bryant wore a fatigue jacket and had added patches from each of the units that they had visited. She came over to me and said that she had been told that I was in charge of the "straight arrow" pins. A straight arrow was a soldier that was true to his wife or girlfriend while in Vietnam and did not fool around with the Vietnamese women. I had designed and had made an arrow pin that went out circled around making a loop. Getting a pin was more of a joke than an honor. However, I personally pinned two "straight arrow" pins on her jacket; each on the flap of the two front pockets. I told her that she was officially a "straight arrow" but not giving her the background of the designation. At a show later that day at another location, she pointed to her two "straight arrow pins" pointing out the fact that she was officially a "straight arrow;" it brought the troops to an extreme roar. Mr. Hope commented by saying something like, "who wrote that line for her?" I saw that in the re-run of the show some years later and knew that I was the reason for that line. It was funny to the men at the time and it was even funnier to me when I saw it because I set it up.

Posted by J P Landahl on March 22, 2010 to an online posting for Mr. Hope "Thanks for the Memories" remembering Mr. Hope.

Table of Contents

Adult XXX
(Warning - these are very suggestive)

99 Condoms

A guy walks into a local pharmacy and walks up to the counter where a lady pharmacist is filling prescriptions. When she finally gets around to helping him he says, "I'd like 99 condoms please". With a surprised look on her face the pharmacist says, "99 Condoms!?! Fuck me!" to which the guy replies, "Make it 100 then..."

A Blind Man Ordering Diner

A blind man walks into a restaurant and sits down. The waiter, who is also the owner, walks up to the blind man and hands him a menu. "I'm sorry sir, but I am blind and can't read the menu. Just bring me a dirty fork from the previous customer, I'll smell it and order from there."

A little confused, the owner walks over to the dirty dish pile and picks up a greasy fork. He returns to the blind man's table and hands it to him. The blind man puts the fork to his nose and takes in a deep breath.

"Ah, yes that's what I'll have, meatloaf and mashed potatoes." Unbelievable, the owner says to himself as he walks towards the kitchen. The cook happens to be the owner's wife and he tells her what had just happened. The blind man eats his meal and leaves. Several days later the blind man returns and the owner mistakenly brings him a menu again.

"Sir, remember me? I'm the blind man." "I'm sorry, I didn't recognize you. I'll go get you a dirty fork." The owner again retrieves a dirty fork and brings it to the blind man.

After another deep breath, the blind man says, "That smells great, I take the Macaroni and cheese with broccoli. Once again walking away in disbelief, the owner thinks the blind man is screwing around with him and tells his wife that the next time the blind man comes in he's going to test him.

The blind man eats and leaves. He returns the following week, but this time the owner sees him coming and runs to the kitchen. He tells his wife, "Mary rub this fork around your vagina before I take it to the blind man." Mary complies and hands her husband the fork back.

As the blind man walks in and sits down, the owner is ready and waiting. "Good afternoon sir, this time I remembered you and I already have the fork ready for you." The blind man puts the fork to his nose, takes a deep whiff and says, "Hey I didn't know that Mary worked here?"

A Husband and Wife Were Sitting Watching TV

A husband and wife were sitting watching a TV program about psychology and explaining the phenomenon of "mixed emotions". The husband turned to his wife and said, "Honey, that is a bunch of crap. I bet you can't tell me anything that will make me happy and sad at the same time.

She said: "Out of all your friends, you have the biggest dick".

A Man Hopelessly Lost in China

A man is out in the Chinese wilderness and he's hopelessly lost. It's been nearly three weeks since he's eaten anything besides what he could forage and he's been reduced to sleeping in caves and under trees. One afternoon he comes upon an old mansion in the woods. It has vines covering most of it and the man can't see any other buildings in the area. However, he sees smoke coming out of the chimney implying someone is home.

He knocks on the door and an old man answers, with a beard almost down to the ground. The old man squints his eyes and says "What do you want?"

The man says "I've been lost for the past three weeks and haven't had a decent meal or sleep since that time. I would be most gracious if I could have a meal and sleep in your house for tonight"

The old Chinese man says "I'll let you come in on one condition: You cannot mess around with my granddaughter"

The man, exhausted and hungry readily agrees, saying "I promise I won't cause you any trouble. I'll be on my way tomorrow morning"

The old Chinese man counters "Ok, but if I do catch you then I'll give you the three worst Chinese torture tests ever known to man."

"Ok, Ok" the man said as he entered the old house. Besides, he thought to himself, what kind of woman would live out in the wilderness all her life?

Well, that night, when the man came down to eat (after showering), he saw how beautiful the granddaughter was. She was an absolute pearl, and while he had only been lost three weeks, it had been many, many months without companionship. And the girl had only seen the occasional monk besides her grandfather and well, they both couldn't keep their eyes off each other throughout the meal.

That night, the man snuck into the girls' bedroom and they had quite a time, but had kept the noise down to a minimum. The man crept back to his room later that night thinking to himself, "Any three torture tests would be worth it after that experience."

Well, the next morning the man awoke to find a heavy weight on his chest. He opened his eyes and there was this huge rock on his chest. On the rock was a sign saying "1st Chinese torture test: 50 kg rock on your chest".

"What a lame torture test" the man thought to himself as he got up and walked over to the window. He opened the shutter and threw the rock out. On the backside of the rock is another sign saying "2nd worst Chinese torture test: Rock tied to RIGHT testicle".

The man, seeing the rock was too far out the window to be grabbed, jumps out the window after the rock. Outside the window is a third sign saying "3rd worst Chinese torture test: LEFT testicle tied to bedpost".

A Pure Wife

There was a man who wanted a pure wife. So he started to attend church to find a woman. He met a gal who seemed nice so he took her home. When they got there, he whips out his manhood and asks "What's this?" She replies "A cock." He thinks to himself that she is not pure enough.

A couple of weeks later he meets another gal and soon takes her home. Again, he pulls out his manhood and asks the question. She replies "A cock". He is pissed because she seemed more pure than the first but oh well.

A couple of weeks later he meets a gal who seems real pure. She won't go home with him for a long time but eventually he gets her to his house. He whips it out and asks, "What is this?" She giggles and says "A pee-pee" He thinks to himself that he has finally found his woman.

They get married but after several months every time she sees his member she giggles and says "That's your pee-pee." He finally breaks down and says "Look this is not a pee-pee, it is a cock."

She laughs and says "No it's not, a cock is ten inches long and black."

All Ears

Bill rents an apartment in Chicago, and goes to the lobby to put his name on the group mailbox. While he was there, an attractive young lady comes out of the apartment next to the mailboxes wearing a robe. Bill smiles at the young girl, so she strikes up a conversation with him.

As they talk, her robe slips open, and it's quite obvious that she has nothing on under the robe. Poor Bill breaks out into a sweat trying to maintain eye contact. After a few minutes, she places her hand on his arm and says, "Let's go to my apartment. I hear someone coming..."

Bill follows her into the apartment. Once inside, she leans against the wall allowing her robe to fall off completely. Now completely nude, she purrs, "What would you say is my best feature?"

The flustered, embarrassed Bill stammers, clears his throat several times, and finally squeaks out, "Oh, your best feature has to be your ears!"

She's astounded! "Why my ears? Looks at these breasts! They're full, they don't sag, and they're 100% natural! My butt is firm and doesn't sag, and have no cellulite! So, why in the world would you say my ears are my best feature?"

Clearing his throat once again, Bill stammers, "Because, when we were in the hallway you said you heard someone coming... that was me!"

Bob Joins a Nudist Colony

Bob joins a very exclusive nudist colony. On his first day he takes off his clothes and starts wandering around. A gorgeous petite blonde walks by him and the man immediately gets an erection. The woman notices his erection, comes over to him grinning sweetly and says: "Sir, did you call for me?" Bob replies: "No, what do you mean?" She says: "You must be new here; let me explain. It's a rule here that if I give you an erection, it implies you called for me." Smiling, she then leads him to the side of a pool, lays down on a towel, eagerly pulls him to her and happily lets him have his way with her.

Bob continues exploring the facilities. He enters a sauna, sits down, and farts. Within a few seconds a huge, horribly corpulent, hairy man with a firm erection lumbers out of the steam towards him. The Huge Man says: "Sir, did you call for me?" Bob replies: "No, what do you mean?" The Huge Man: "You must be new here; it is a rule that when you fart, it implies you called for me." The huge man then easily spins Bob around, bends him over the bench and has his way with him.

Bob rushes back to the colony office. He is greeted by the smiling naked receptionist: "May I help you?"

Bob says: "Here is your card and key back. You can keep the $500 joining fee."

Receptionist: "But Sir, you've only been here a couple of hours; you only saw a small fraction of our facilities....."

Bob replies: "Listen lady, I am 58 years old, I get a hard-on twice a month, but I fart 15 times a day. No thanks."

Cut Off 4 Inches

A guy's eating in a restaurant and spots a gorgeous woman sitting all alone. He calls over his waiter and says, "Send that woman a bottle of your most expensive champagne, on me." The waiter quickly brings the champagne over to the woman, and says, "Ma'am, this is from the gentleman over there." She says to the waiter, "Please tell him that for me to accept this champagne, he better have a Mercedes in his garage, a million dollars in the bank, and eight inches in his pants." The waiter delivers the message, and the guy says, "Please go back and tell her I have two Mercedes in my garage, three million dollars in the bank, but I haven't even met her...so why the fuck would I cut off four inches?"

Edward walks out of a bar...

Edward walks out of a bar, stumbling back and forth with a key in his hand. A cop on the beat sees him and approaches "Can I help you, fella?", asks the cop.

"Yesssh, ssshombody stol my car!" Edward replies.

The cop asks, "Okay, where was your car the last time you saw it?". "It was at the end of this key", Edward replies.

 At this point the cop looks down to see that Edwards penis is hanging out of his trousers. The cop asks Edward , "Hey buddy, are you aware that you're exposing yourself?   Edward looks down sadly and moans, "OHHH GOD...they got Julie too!!! "

Employee Lay Off Decision

One day Mr. Smith, the president of a large corporation, called his vice-president, Dave, into his office and said, "We're making some cutbacks, so either Jack or Barbara will have to be laid off." Dave looked at Mr. Smith and said, "Barbara is my best worker, but Jack has a wife and three kids. I don't know whom to fire."

The next morning Dave waited for his employees to arrive. Barbara was the first to come in, so Dave said, "Barbara, I've got a problem. You see, I've got to lay you or Jack off and I don't know what to do?" Barbara replied, "You'd better jack off. I've got a headache."

Firming Up

One morning while making breakfast, a man walked up to his wife and pinched her on her butt and said, "You know if you firmed this up we could get rid of your girdle." While this was on the edge of intolerable, she thought herself better and replied with silence.

The next morning the man woke his wife with a pinch on the breast and said, "You know if you firmed these up we could get rid of your bra." This was beyond a silent response, so she rolled over and grabbed him by the penis. With a death grip in place she said, "You know if you firmed this up we could get rid of the postman, the gardener, the pool man and your brother."

High Tech Sex

Two friends meet in the office of one of them, a notorious techno-geek.

"Hey, bud, how are ya?"

"I'm good. Congratulations, that new secretary of yours is beautiful!"

"Well, I'm glad you like her. Believe it or not, she's a robot!"

"No way, how could that be?"

"Way! She's the latest model from Japan. Lemme tell you how she works. If you squeeze her left tit, she takes dictation. If you squeeze her right tit, she types a letter. And that's not all, she can have sex, too!"

"Holy shit! You're kidding, right?"

"No, she's something, huh? Tell you what, you can even borrow her."

So, his friend takes her into the restroom and is in there with her for a while. Suddenly, he hears him screaming "Eeeeyaaaaa! Heeelp" Ooooooh! Aaaaaaah! eeeeeeeeeaaargghhhh!"

The guy says, "Shit! I forgot to tell him her ass is a pencil sharpener!"

It Was the Year 2222

The year is 2222 and Mike and Maureen land on Mars after accumulating enough frequent flier miles. They meet a Martian couple and are talking about all sorts of things. Mike asks if Mars has a stock market, if they have laptop computers, how they make money, etc.

Finally, Maureen brought up the subject of sex. "Just how do you guys do it?" asks Maureen. "Pretty much the way you do," responds the Martian.

Discussion ensues and finally the couples decide to swap partners for the night and experience one another. Maureen and the male Martian go off to a bedroom where the Martian strips. He's got only a teeny, weeny member - about half an inch long and just a quarter inch thick.

"I don't think this is going to work," says Maureen.

"Why?" he asks, "What's the matter?"

"Well," she replies, "It's just not long enough to reach me!"

"No problem," he says, and proceeds to slap his forehead with his palm. With each slap of his forehead, his member grows until it's quite impressively long.

"Well," she says, "That's quite impressive, but it's still pretty narrow...."

"No problem," he says, and starts pulling his ears. With each pull, his member grows wider and wider until the entire measurement is extremely exciting to the woman.

"Wow!" she exclaims, as they fell into bed and made mad, passionate love.

The next day the couples rejoin their normal partners and go their separate ways. As they walk along, Mike asks "Well, was it any good?" "I hate to say it," says Maureen, "but it was pretty wonderful. How about you?" "It was horrible," he replies, All I got was a headache. All she kept doing the whole time was slapping my forehead and pulling my ears."

Jack Went to the Doctor

Jack went to the doctor and said, "Doc, I'm having trouble getting my penis erect. Can you help me?"

After a complete examination the doctor told Jack, "Well, the problem with you is that the muscles around the base of your penis are damaged. There's really nothing I can do for you except if you're willing to try an experimental treatment."

Jack asked sadly, "What is this treatment?"

"Well," the doctor explained, "what we would do is take the muscles from the trunk of a baby elephant and implant them in your penis."

Jack thought about it silently, and then said, "Well, the thought of going through life without ever having sex again is too much. Let's go for it."

A few weeks after the operation, Jack was given the green light to use his improved equipment. He planned a romantic evening for his girlfriend and took her to one of the nicest restaurants in the city. In the middle of dinner he felt a stirring between his legs that continued to the point of being painful. To release the pressure Jack unzipped his fly. His penis immediately sprung from his pants, went to the top of the table, grabbed a bun and then returned to his pants.

His girlfriend was stunned at first, but then said with a sly smile, "That was incredible! Can you do it again?"

Jack replied with his eyes watering, "Well, I guess so, but I don't think I can fit another bun in my ass."

Job For Mama

Maria had just got married and being a traditional Italian, she was still a virgin. So, on her wedding night, staying at her mother's house, she was nervous. But her mother reassured her. "Don't worry, Maria. Tony's a good man. Go upstairs and he'll take care of you."

So up she went. When she got upstairs, Tony took off his shirt and exposed his hairy chest. Maria ran downstairs to her mother and says, "Mama, Mama, Tony's got a big hairy chest." "Don't worry, Maria," says the mother," all good men have hairy chests. Go upstairs. He'll take good care of you."

So, up she went again. When she got up in the bedroom, Tony took off his pants exposing his hairy legs. Again, Maria ran downstairs to her mother. "Mama, Mama, Tony took off his pants and he's got hairy legs!"

"Don't worry. All good men have hairy legs. Tony's a good man. Go upstairs and he'll take good care of you." So up she went again. When she got up there, Tony took off his socks and on his left foot he was missing three toes. When Maria saw this, she ran downstairs. "Mama, Mama, Tony's got a foot and a half!"

"Stay here and stir the pasta," says the mother. "This is a job for Mama."

Lifesaver

Two girls were discussing their heavy smoking habits. "I get such a yen for a cigarette," said one, "that the only effective countermeasure is to pop a Life Saver into my mouth and suck hard." "That's fine for you," huffed her friend, "but I don't happen to live in a house that's right on the beach!"

Man Asking the Frog to Marry Him

There is this guy who has a 25 inch dick. He goes to a witch in the woods and asks her if she can make his dick smaller because he just can't please the ladies because it is just too big, he hasn't found a lady yet who likes it and he can't get any pleasure.

She tells him to go into the woods and he will find a frog when he finds the frog he is to ask it to marry him. If the frog says no, his cock will shrink 5 inches.

He goes into the woods and finds this frog. He asks "frog, will you marry me?" The frog says "no" And his prick shrinks five inches. The guys thinks to himself, "Wow, that was pretty cool. But, it's still too big." So he goes back to the frog and again asks the frog: "Frog, will you marry me?" Frog: "No, I won't marry you."

The guy's dick shrinks another five inches. But that's still 15 inches and he thinks his chop is still just a little bit too big. But he thinks that 10 inches would be just great. He goes back to the frog and asks: "Frog, will you marry me?"

Frog: How many times do I have to tell you NO, NO, NO!!!

Man Meets a Leprechaun

A man walks into a public bathroom and begins using one of the urinals. He looks to his left and sees a very short man peeing also. Suddenly, the short man looks up at the taller man, and the taller man is completely embarrassed about staring at the smaller man's penis. "Sorry," says the taller man. "I'm not gay or anything, but you have the longest penis I've ever seen, especially on a man so small!"

"Well," says the Leprechaun, "That's because I'm a Leprechaun! ALL Leprechauns have penises this size!"

The taller man says, "Incredible! I'd give anything if mine were that long."

"Well, what with me being a Leprechaun and all, I can give you your wish! If you let me take you into that stall over there and screw you, I'll give you your wish!"

"Gee," says the man, "I don't know about that----aw hell with it, OK!" Soon, the Leprechaun is behind the taller man, just humping away. "Say," says the Leprechaun, "How old are you, son?" Finding it difficult to turn with the Leprechaun humping him so ferociously, the tall man says over his shoulder, "Uh-Uh, Thirty-two."   "Imaging that," says the little man, "Thirty-two and still believes in Leprechauns!"

Plastic Surgery on His Penis

A man went to have plastic surgery on his penis.
The surgeon examined him and asked, "What happened?"

"Well, doc, I live in a trailer camp," the man explained, "And from where I am I can see this lovely chick next door. She's blonde and built like a brick shithouse. She's so horny that every night I see her take a hot dog from the refrigerator and stick it in a hole in the floor of her trailer. Then she gets down and masturbates herself on the hot dog."

"And?" prompted the doctor.

"Well, I felt this was a lot of wasted pussy, so one day I got under the trailer and when she put the hot dog in the hole, I removed it and substituted my dick."

"It was a great idea and everything was going well. Then someone knocked at the door, she jumped off my hot dog and tried to kick it under the stove."

Please Let This Be a Teabag

Morris wakes up in the morning. He has a massive hangover and can't remember anything he did last night. He picks up his bath robe from the floor and puts it on. He notices there's something in one of the pockets and it turns out to be a bra. He thinks "bloody hell what happened last night?" He walks towards the bathroom and finds a pair of panties in the other pocket of his robe. Again he thinks "what happened last night, what have I done? Must have been a wild party." He opens the bathroom door, walks in and has a look in the mirror. He notices a little string hanging out of his mouth and his only thought is "Please, if there's a God, please let this be a teabag."

Severe Headache Remedy

A guy is suffering from severe headaches for years with no relief. After trying all the usual cures he's referred to a headache specialist by his family doctor. The doctor asks him what his symptoms are and he replies, "I get these blinding headaches; kind of like a knife across my scalp and..."

He is interrupted by the doctor. "And a heavy throbbing right behind the left ear?"

"Yes! Exactly! How did you know?"

"Well I am the world's greatest headache specialist, you know. But I myself suffered from that same type of headache for many years. It is caused by a tension in the scalp muscles. This is how I cured it: Every day I would give my wife oral sex. When she came she would squeeze her legs together with all her strength and the pressure would relieve the tension in my head. Try that every day for two weeks and come back and let me know how it goes".

Two weeks go by and the man is back. "Well, how do you feel?" the doctor asked.

"Doc, I'm a new man! I feel great! I haven't had a headache since I started this treatment! I can't thank you enough. And by the way, you have a lovely home."

Sex In The Movies

So my wife comes up to me with a dreamy look in her eye and asks, "Why don't we make love like they do in the movies?"

So I grabbed her, bent her over the kitchen table, slapped her around, stuck it in her ass and came on her face.

Turns out we don't watch the same movies.

Superman Having a Problem

One sunny Sunday, Superman was flying around with nothing to do, so he decided to drop in on Batman.

"Hi, Bat", said Superman, "let's go down the pub and have a beer." "Not today, Super. My Batmobile's broken down and I've got to fix it. Can't fight crime without it, you know."

Disappointed, Superman went over to Spiderman's place. "Let's go down the pub for a drink, Spider." "Sorry Super. I've got a problem with my web gun. Can't fight without it, you know."

Dejectedly, Superman took to the air again, and decided to drop by on Wonder Woman. There she was, lying on her back out on her balcony, stark naked and writhing around. Superman conceived a cunning idea. "Everyone says I'm faster than a speeding bullet, and I've always wondered what sort of screw she'd be'.
So he zoomed down, did her in a flash and zoomed off.

What the hell was that!," cried Wonder Woman.

"I don't know, but it hurt like hell!" said the Invisible Man.

The Crying Horse

One day a guy walks into a bar. The bartender says "if you can make that horse over there laugh you can have free drinks for the rest of the night".

So he says "ok" and walks over to the horse and whispers something in his ear and he starts laughing and the bartender gives him free drinks for the rest of the night.

The next night the same guy comes back in and the bartender says "if you can make that horse over there cry I will give you free drinks for the rest of the night.

So he walks over there and does something and the horse starts crying, and the bartender gives him free drinks. Then the bartender asks what the man did to make the horse laugh and what he did to make him cry.

The man says "To make him laugh I told him I had a bigger dick than he does and to make him cry I showed him".

The Night's Air

Two hookers were on a street corner. They started discussing business, and one of the hookers said, "Gonna be a good night, I smell cock in the air." The other hooker looked at her and said, "No, I just burped."

Three Skiers

Three guys go to a ski lodge, and there aren't enough rooms, so they have to share a bed. In the middle of the night, the guy on the right wakes up and says, "I had this wild, vivid dream of getting a hand job!" The guy on the left wakes up, and unbelievably, he's had the same dream, too. Then the guy in the middle wakes up and says, "That's funny, I dreamed I was skiing!"

Tit for That

A woman was standing in a crowded lift of the hotel she was staying in. When a man got in and accidentally elbowed her in the breast. The man said, "I'm sorry! But if your heart is as soft as your tit, you'll forgive me." so the woman replies, "If you dick is as hard as your elbow then I am staying in room 113."

To Stutter or Not to Stutter

A man with a stuttering problem tries everything he can to stop stuttering, but he can't. Finally, he goes to a world renowned doctor for help. The doctor examines him and says "I've found your problem. Your penis is 12 inches long. It weighs so much it is pulling on your lungs, causing you to stutter." So the man asks, "What's he cure, doctor?" To which the doctor replies, "We have to cut off 6 inches." The man thinks about it, and eager to cure his stuttering, agrees to the operation. The operation is a success, and he stops stuttering.

Two months later he calls the doctor and tells him that since he had the 6 inches cut off, all of his girlfriends have dumped him, and his love life has gone down the tubes. He wants the doctor to operate to put back the six inches. Not hearing anything on the line, he repeats himself, "Hey doc, didn't you hear me? I want my 6 inches back!" Finally, the doctor responds, "F-f-f-f-f-uck Y-y-you!

Two Aliens Landed in the West Texas Desert

Two aliens landed in the West Texas desert near an abandoned gas station. They approached one of the gas pumps, and one of the aliens addressed it, "Greetings, Earthling. We come in peace. Take us to your leader."

The gas pump, of course, didn't respond.

The alien repeated the greeting. There was no response. The alien, annoyed by what he perceived to be the gas pump's haughty attitude, drew his ray gun, and said impatiently, "Greetings, Earthling. We come in peace. How dare you ignore us in this way! Take us to your leader, or I'll fire!"

The other alien shouted to his comrade "No, you don't want to make him mad!" But before he finished his warning, the first alien fired. There was a huge explosion that blew both of them 200 meters into the desert, where t hey landed in a heap.

When they finally regained consciousness, the one who fired turned to the other one and said, "What a ferocious creature. It damn near killed us! How did you know it was so dangerous?" The other alien answered, "If there's one thing I've learned during my travels through the galaxy...any guy who can wrap his dick around himself twice and then stick it in his own ear, is someone you shouldn't mess with!"

Two Fleas go to California

One winter year, these two little fleas headed for the warm sunny beaches of California to escape the cold. The first flea got there and started rubbing suntan lotion on his little flea arms and his little flee legs. Just then, the second flea arrived just a shiverin' and a shakin'. The first flea asked, "What the hell happened to you?" To which the second flea replied "I just rode out here on a bikers mustache and I'm so very coldddd!" The first flea said, "Don't you know the special trick to gettin here, first you go to the airport, go straight to the ladies commode, wait for a pretty young stewardess to come along, and when she sits down you climb right up in there where its nice and warm". The second flea agreed that this was a grand idea.

The next winter comes along and it was time for the fleas to head for the sunny beaches again. The first flea arrived and began putting suntan lotion on his little flea arms and his little flea legs. About that time, the second flea arrived again just a shiverin', shakin', and mumbling about how cold he was. The first flea exclaimed "Didn't you learn anything that I taught you about getting here nice and warm?" To which the second flea replied, "I did just as you said; I went to the ladies commode and this pretty stewardess came in and sat down, I climbed right up in there and it was so very warm. Next thing I know we stop at a bar and I fell asleep. All of a sudden I woke and there I was, right back on that bikers mustache!

Two Guys in a Strip Joint

Two guys are in a strip joint, one is sitting in front of the other. A woman comes on stage and starts stripping. The guy in back, Paul, says, "Oh yeah, Oh yeah!"

Then the first guy turns around and says, " Hey Paul, shut up!"

Then two women come out and start stripping. Paul, once again, starts, "Yeah baby..mmmm....yeah!"

Once again the guy in front turns around and tells Paul to be quiet. So three women come out and start stripping. Paul is silent.

The guy in front says, "Hey Paul, where's all your excitement now?"

Paul says, "All over your back!"

Two Lips and Seven Kisses

There was this old woman who heard a song called "Two Lips and Seven Kisses." She called up information after hearing the song on the radio to get the name of the record company. In dialing, she erroneously called up a gas station, and she asks, "Do you have "Two Lips and Seven Kisses?"

The gas station attendant who answered the phone said, "No, but I have two nuts and seven inches!"

So the woman asked, "Is this a record?"

To which the man replied, "No, its average!"

Two Whales

A male whale and a female whale were swimming off the coast of Japan when they noticed a whaling ship. The male whale recognized it as the same ship that had harpooned his father many years earlier. He said to the female whale, "Lets both swim under the ship and blow out of our air holes at the same time and it should cause the ship to turn over and sink. They tried it and sure enough, the ship turned over and quickly sank. Soon however, the whales realized the sailors had jumped overboard and were swimming to the safety of shore. The male was enraged that they were going to get away and told the female "lets swim after them and gobble them up before they reach the shore." At this point, he realized the female was becoming reluctant to follow him. "Look", she said, "I went along with the blow job, but I absolutely refuse to swallow the seamen."

Water For Sex

There are these three guys in a desert dying of dehydration. Off in the horizon they see a house and finally manage to struggle to it. The first guy goes up to the door to ask for water. The door is opened by this really old, wart-covered, puss covered, scaly, toothless old woman.

"C-c-c-can I h-h-h-have some w-w-w-water for me and m-my friends?" he asks.

She replied, "I will... if you have sex with me."

The guy pukes all over the woman and runs back to his friends.

"You guys would not believe who answered the door. Some really gross old lady!" he tells them. "She said we could have water if I had sex with her."

"Why didn't you then?" asks he second guy.

"Because she was so ugly, I was sick and couldn't do it!"

"Oh, you are such a wuss. I'll go up to the door," the second guy says.

He goes up to the door and rings the bell. The old hag answers.

"W-w-w-w-w-w-waaaaaa......" He uses all of his will power to not hurl.

"Water? Yes, I have water," she says knowingly. "But you have to have sex with me."

"AAAAAUUUUUUUGGGGGGGGGHHHHHHHHH!!"

He runs back to his friends and before he could say a word, the third guy goes to the door and rings the bell.

"What do you want for some water?"

"You have to have sex with me."

Knowing that if he doesn't do something, he and his friends will all die. So he follows the lady into her kitchen.

"Do me here," she told him.

He sees 3 ears of corn on the counter and gets an idea.

"Lay back and close your eyes. And keep them closed!"

The witch lays back and spreads her legs. The guy nearly pukes after seeing this. He picks up an ear of corn and screws her with it. Finally she is finished. He throws the corn out the window.

"Oh, God. That was the best orgasm of my life. If you do that again I will give you a million dollars."

"Then lay back and close your eyes again."

This she does and he does her with the second ear of corn until she is satisfied. Then he throws it out the window. This time she doesn't even open her eyes.

"If you do that again, I will give you a Jeep so you can get out of the desert."

"Eyes closed," he says.

Then he does her with the last piece of corn. He brings her to multiple orgasms.

"Ohhhhhhhhhh........ The water, money and Jeep are outside," she says as she squirms in ecstasy.

So he runs like hell outside and grabs the water and money and jumps into the Jeep. He wonders where his friends are and drives around to find them. He finds them by the window.

One of the guys says to him, "Hey, man. I hope you had fun. We just ate the three best pieces of buttered corn you could have imagined!"

Waxin' His Boat

Mike walks into a bar and sees Pat sitting at the end of the bar with a great big smile on his face. Mike says, "Pat, what are you so happy for?"

"Well Mike, I gotta tell ya... Yesterday I was out waxin' my boat, just waxin' my boat, and a redhead came up to me.. tits out to here, Mike. Tits out to here! She says, 'Can I have a ride in your boat?'

I said 'Sure you can have a ride in my boat.' So I took her way out, Mike. I turned off the key and I said 'It's either screw or swim!' She couldn't swim, Mike. She couldn't swim!"

The next day Mike walks into a bar and sees Pat sitting at the end of the bar with a even bigger smile on his face. Mike says, "What are you happy about today Pat?"

"Well Mike.... I gotta tell ya... Yesterday I was out waxin' my boat, just waxin' my boat and a BEAUTIFUL blond came up to me...tits out to here, Mike. Tits out to here! She said 'Can I have a ride in your boat?'

I told her 'Sure you can have a ride in my boat.' So I took her way out, Mike. Way out much further than the last one. I turned off the key and I said, 'It's either screw or swim!' She couldn't swim, Mike! She couldn't swim!"

A couple days pass and Mike walks into a bar and sees Pat down there cryin' over a beer. Mike says, "Pat, what are you so sad for?"

"Well Mike, I gotta tell ya.... Yesterday I was out waxin' my boat, just waxin' my boat, and the most desirable brunette came up to me... tits WAY out to here, Mike. Tits WAY out to here. She says, 'Can I have a ride in your boat?'

So I said, 'Sure you can have a ride in my boat.' So I took her way out, Mike, way WAY out... much further than the last two.

I turned off the key, and looked at her tits and said 'It's either screw or swim!'

She pulled down her pants and.....She had a pecker, Mike! She had this great BIG pecker! ... and I can't swim Mike! I can't swim!"

Animal

3 Dogs at the Pound

There are 3 dogs in a veterinarian clinic: a Poodle, a Chihuahua, and a Great Dane.

The poodle asks the Chihuahua," What are you in here for?" The Chihuahua says," Well usually I'm a good dog...but I have a huge problem with my mail man. I don't know why, I just always have to bite him, and I gave him a serious injury. So... they're going to put me to sleep today. What are you here for?" he asks the poodle.

The poodle says, "Well usually I'm a pretty good dog, but my owners son always sticks his finger in my food while I'm eating. And when he does that...I just got to bite him I don't know why. And I really hurt him. So there going to put me to sleep today."

The two dogs look at the Great Dane, and the Great Dane is like 20 times bigger than them. And they ask," DAMN MAN!!! What are you in here for? You never see Great Danes in the pound." And the Great Dane says," Awwww, you guys wouldn't believe me if I told you." And they said, "JUST TELL US!"

So the Great Dane says, "Well usually I'm a pretty good dog, but you see I have like the hottest owner in the world. She's a beautiful woman with a HOT RACK and SEXY ASS. One day when she got out of the shower, she bent over to get a towel. When she did, I totally lost all self-control. So I mounted her and started GOING AT IT!!!"

The two dogs say, "DAMN MAN!!! So they're going to put you to sleep too huh???" And the Great Dane replies, "HELL NO, I'M JUST HERE TO GET MY NAILS TRIMMED!"

A Bird in the Hand……..

A carpet installer decides to take a cigarette break after completing the installation in the first of several rooms he has to do. Finding them missing from his pocket he begins searching, only to notice a small lump in his recently completed carpet-installation. Not wanting to rip up all that work for a lousy pack of cigarettes he simply walks over and pounds the lump flat. He decides to forgo the break continues on to the other rooms to be carpeted.

At the end of the day he's completed his work and loading his tools into his trucks when two events occur almost simultaneously: he spies his pack of cigarettes on the dashboard of the truck, and the lady of the house calls out "Have you seen my parakeet?"

A Drinking Koala

A koala walks into a bar one night, slams his paw down on the table, and orders a drink. When he's done, slam goes his paw again for more. This goes on for about half an hour, and just when he was going to do it again, the barkeep told him if he was looking for a good time, there was some one in the back room who could help him, the koala decides why not and goes into the back room. There he meets a prostitute who is waiting for him. That night he has the best sex he has ever had. After the prostitute turns to the koala and says, "How about my money," the koala looked confused and the prostitute brought out a dictionary and it said...PROSTITUTE: Has sex for money.

So in response the koala turn to the definition for the koala and it says. KOALA: Eats bush and leaves.

A Lesson to be Learned

A guy is walking down the street with some chicken wire under his arm. His neighbor sees him and asks what he has. The guy replies, "Its chicken wire and I'm going to catch some chickens." His neighbor says, "You fool, you can't catch chickens with chicken wire." Later that night, he sees the guy walking down the street dragging 12 chickens.

The next day he sees him walking down the street with some duct tape under his arm. Once again he asks what the guy is up to. The guy says he has some duct tape and he is going to catch some ducks. He replies, "You fool, you can't catch ducks with duct tape." Sure enough later that night, he sees the guy walking down the street dragging 12 ducks behind him.

The next day, he sees the guy walking with something else under his arm. He asks what it is. The guy replies, "Its pussy willow." He says, "Hold on, let me get my hat."

American in Mexico

There was this American tourist in Mexico, and he was getting tired of walking around, so he went up to a donkey rental place and said, "Can I rent a donkey?'

The guy said, "We don't call them donkeys here, we call them asses. This is the only ass I have left, and you have to scratch him when you want to make him stop."

The guy rides his ass for a while, sees a hotdog stand, and asks for a hotdog. The vendor replies, "We don't call them hotdogs here we call the wieners."

Meanwhile his donkey is wandering away, so he goes up to another tourist and says "Will you hold my wiener while I scratch my ass?"

An Old Tired Mule

An old prospector shuffled into town leading an old tired mule. The old man headed straight for the only saloon to clear his parched throat. He walked up and tied his old mule to the hitch rail. As he stood there, brushing some of the dust from his face and clothes, a young gunslinger stepped out of the saloon with a gun in one hand

and a bottle of whiskey in the other.

The young gunslinger looked at the old man and laughed, saying, "Hey old man, have you ever danced?"

The old man looked up at the gunslinger and said, "No, I never did dance... never really wanted to." A crowd had gathered as the gunslinger grinned and said, "Well, you old fool, you're gonna dance now," and started shooting at the old man's feet.

The old prospector - not wanting to get a toe blown off - started hopping around like a flea on a hot skillet. Everybody was laughing, fit to be tied.

When his last bullet had been fired, the young gunslinger, still laughing, holstered his gun and turned around to go back into the saloon.

The old man turned to his pack mule, pulled out a double-barreled shotgun, and cocked both hammers. The loud clicks carried clearly through the desert air. The crowd stopped laughing immediately. The young gunslinger heard the sounds too, and he turned around very slowly. The silence was almost deafening. The crowd watched as the young gunman stared at the old timer and the large gaping holes of those twin barrels.

The barrels of the shotgun never wavered in the old man's hands, as he quietly said, "Son, have you ever kissed a mule's ass?" The gunslinger swallowed hard and said, "No sir, but I've always wanted to."

There are a few lessons for us all here:

Never be arrogant.

Don't waste ammunition.

Whiskey makes you think you're smarter than you are.

Always, always make sure you know who has the power

Don't mess with old men, they didn't get old by being stupid.

Bear Hunters

Two men went bear hunting. While one stayed in the cabin, the other went out looking for a bear. He soon found a huge bear, shot at it but only wounded it. The enraged bear charged toward him, he dropped his rifle and started running for the cabin as fast as he could.

He ran pretty fast but the bear was just a little faster and gained on him with every step. Just as he reached the open cabin door, he tripped and fell flat. Too close behind to stop, the bear tripped over him and went rolling into the cabin.

The man jumped up, closed the cabin door and yelled to his friend inside, "You skin this one while I go and get another one!"

Bear Joke

A bear walks into a bar and says to the bar tender, "I would like a bourbon and...... a coke." The bar tender says "What's up with the big pause?" The bear said "I've had them all my life"

Bus Incident

A woman got on a bus holding a baby. The bus driver looked at the child and blurted out, "That's the ugliest baby I've ever seen!"

Infuriated, the woman slammed her fare into the fare box and took an aisle seat near the rear of the bus. The man seated next to her sensed that she was agitated and asked her what was wrong.

"The bus driver insulted me," she fumed.

The man sympathized and said, "Why, he shouldn't say things to insult passengers. He could be fired for that."

"You're right," she said. "I think I'll go back up there and give him a piece of my mind!"

"That's a good idea," the man said. "Here, let me hold your monkey."

Chihuahua

A woman walks into a bar with her 5 pound Chihuahua and sits down next to this guy, whom she notices is feeling a little bit queasy.

A few minutes go by and the guy looks at her and throws up. He looks down and sees the little dog struggling in a pool of his vomit and says, "Whoa, I don't remember eating that!"

Cue Ball

A guy walks into a bar with his pet monkey. He orders a drink and while he's drinking, the monkey starts jumping all over the place. The monkey grabs some olives off the bar and eats them, then grabs some sliced limes and eats them, then jumps up on the pool table, grabs the cue ball, sticks it in his mouth and swallows it whole.

The bartender screams at the guy, "Did you see what your monkey just did?" The guy says, "No, what?" "He just ate the cue ball off my pool table - whole!" says the bartender. "Yeah, that doesn't surprise me," replies the patron. "He eats everything in sight, the little twerp. I'll pay for the cue ball and stuff." He finishes his drink, pays his bill, and leaves. Two weeks later he's in the bar again, and he has his monkey with him. He orders a drink and the monkey starts running around the bar again.

While the man is drinking, the monkey finds a maraschino cherry on the bar. He grabs it, sticks it up his butt, pulls it out, and eats it. The bartender is disgusted. "Did you see what your monkey did now?" "Now what?" asks the patron. "Well, he stuck a maraschino cherry up his butt, then pulled it out and ate it!" says the barkeeper.

"Yeah, that doesn't surprise me," replies the patron. "He still eats everything in sight, but ever since he ate that damn cue ball he measures everything first!"

Doggone Brilliant Joke

A wealthy man decided to go on a safari in Africa. He took his faithful pet dachshund along for company. One day, the dachshund starts chasing butterflies and before long the dachshund discovers that he is lost.

So, wandering about, he notices a leopard heading rapidly in his direction with the obvious intention of having him for lunch. The dachshund thinks, "OK, I'm in deep trouble now!" Then he noticed some bones on the ground close by, and immediately settles down to chew on the bones with his back to the approaching cat. Just as the leopard is about to leap, the dachshund exclaims loudly, "Boy, that was one delicious leopard. I wonder if there are any more around here." Hearing this, the leopard halts his attack in mid-stride, as a look of terror comes over him, and slinks away into the trees. "Whew," says the leopard. "That was close. That dachshund nearly had me." Meanwhile, a monkey, who had been watching the whole scene from a nearby tree, figures he can put this knowledge to good use and trade it for protection from the leopard. So, off he goes.

But the dachshund saw him heading after the leopard with great speed, and figured that something must be up.

The monkey soon catches up with the leopard, spills the beans and strikes a deal for himself with the leopard. The leopard is furious at being made a fool of and says, "Here monkey, hop on my back and see what's going to happen to that conniving canine." Now the dachshund sees the leopard coming with the monkey on his back, and thinks, "What am I going to do now?" But instead of running, the dog sits down with his back to his attackers, pretending he hasn't seen them yet ... and, just when they get close enough to hear, the dachshund says.................

"Where's that darn monkey? Sent him off half an hour ago to bring me another leopard."

Driving With Penguins

A man was driving down the road with twenty penguins in the back seat. The police stop him and say that he can't drive around with the penguins in the car and should take them to the zoo. The man agrees and drives off.

The next day the same man is driving down the road with twenty penguins in the back and again. He is stopped by the same police officer who says, "Hey! I though I told you to take those to the zoo."

The man replies "I did. Today I'm taking them to the movies."

Frog's Legs

A customer asks a waitress "Do you have frogs legs?" She replies "No, it's rheumatism that makes me walk this way."

Goldfish

Little Tim was in the garden filling in a hole when his neighbor peered over the fence. Interested in what the cheeky-faced youngster was up to, he politely asked, "What are you up to there, Tim?"

"My goldfish died," replied Tim tearfully, without looking up, "and I've just buried him."

The neighbor was concerned, "That's an awfully big hole for a goldfish, isn't it?"

Tim patted down the last heap of earth then replied, "That's because he's inside your stupid cat."

I Gotta Do The Cat

Three very macho mice are standing around trying to outdo each other. The first mouse says, "You know those little pellets they put out around the house trying to poison us? I love those things. I eat 'em like candy."

The second mouse, not to be outdone says, "Oh yeah? Well, you know those mousetraps they put out to try to catch us? What I do is get on the trap, grab the cheese, and then flip over onto my back, and when the steel bar comes swinging down I grab it and do bench presses with it."

The third mouse says, "You guys are really a couple of tough mice, and I'd love to keep hangin' out with you here, but I gotta go fuck the cat."

King of the Jungle?

A lion woke up one morning feeling really rowdy and mean. He went out and cornered a small monkey and roared, "Who is mightiest of all jungle animals?"

The trembling monkey says, "You are, mighty lion!

Later, the lion confronts an ox and fiercely bellows, "Who is the mightiest of all jungle animals?"

The terrified ox stammers, "Oh great lion, you are the mightiest animal in the jungle!"

On a roll now, the lion swaggers up to an elephant and roars, "Who is mightiest of all jungle animals?"

Fast as lightning, the elephant snatches up the lion with his trunk, slams him against a tree half a dozen times leaving the lion feeling like it'd been run over by a safari wagon. The elephant then stomps on the lion till it looks like a corn tortilla and ambles away.

The lion lets out a moan of pain, lifts his head weakly and hollers after the elephant, "Just because you don't know the answer, you don't have to get so upset about it!"

Mean Pit Bull

A woman was leaving a 7-11 with her morning coffee when she noticed a most unusual funeral procession approaching the nearby cemetery. A long black hearse was followed by a second long black hearse about 50 feet behind.

Behind the second hearse was a solitary woman walking a pit bull on a leash.

Behind her were 200 women walking single file.

The woman couldn't stand her curiosity. She respectfully approached the woman walking the dog and said "I am so sorry for your loss and I know now is a bad time to disturb you, but I've never seen a funeral like this.

Whose funeral is it?"

The woman replied "Well, that first hearse is for my husband."

"What happened to him?"

The woman replied "My dog attacked and killed him."

She inquired further, "Well, who is in the second hearse?"

The woman answered, "My mother-in-law. She was trying to help my husband when the dog turned on her."

A poignant and thoughtful moment of silence passes between the two women.

"Could I borrow that dog?"

"Get in line."

Penguin and The Mechanic

Once there was a penguin whose car broke down. He took it in to get it serviced, and while it was being worked on, he went shopping.

He returned later that day to see what had happened to his car, and the mechanic told hlm, "It looks like you've blown a seal."

The penguin, chuckling, and wiping his beak replied, "No, I've just eaten some ice-cream."

Police Dog Applies for a Job

A police dog responds to an ad for work with the FBI. "Well," says the personnel director, "You'll have to meet some strict requirements. First, you must type at least 60 words per minute."

Sitting down at the computer, the dog types out 80 words per minute.

"Also," says the director, "You must pass a physical and complete the obstacle course."

This perfect canine specimen finishes the course in record time.

"There's one last requirement," the director continues; "you must be bilingual."

With confidence, the dog looks up at him and says, "Meow!"

Praise the Lord

This preacher had a horse that a man wanted to buy, and the preacher says: "Ok, I'll sell him to you." So the man bought him, and the preacher told him: "Now, when you get ready for him to go say 'praise the lord', then when you want to stop say 'amen'."

The man says: "Ok, I got it". So he gets on him and said "praise the lord" and the horse took off. He repeated "praise the lord" faster and faster and the horse responded. Then the man noticed a deep canyon in front of him and hollered "amen" and the horse stopped just before they went over the edge, and the man looked up and said: "Praise the lord."

Snake Bite

"I hope I'm not poisonous," said the first snake.

"Why?" asked the second.

"Because I just bit my lip."

Stuttering Animals

Little Johnny is sitting in a biology class, and the teacher says that an interesting phenomenon of nature is that only humans stutter, no other animal in the world does this.

Johnny's hand shoots up. "Not correct, Miss!" he says.

"Please explain, Johnny," replies the teacher.

"Well, Miss, the other day I was playing with my cat on the verandah. The neighbors' Great Dane came around the corner, and my cat went "fffffffffff! fffffffffffff! ffffffffffff!", and before he could say "FUCK OFF!", the dog ate him!"

Taco Bell Chihuahua Wins

The Taco Bell Chihuahua, a Doberman and a Bulldog are in a bar having a drink when a great-looking female Collie comes up to them and says, "Whoever can say liver and cheese in a sentence can have me." So the Doberman says, "I love liver and cheese." The Collie replies, "That's not good enough." The Bulldog says, "I hate liver and cheese." She says, "That's not creative enough." Finally, the Chihuahua says, "Liver alone . . . cheese mine."

Talking Pig

One day the first grade teacher was reading the story of the Three Little Pigs to her class. She came to the part of the story where the first pig was trying to accumulate the building materials for his home.

She read, "...and so the pig went up to the man with the wheel barrow full of straw and said, "Pardon me sir, but may I have some of that straw to build my house?" The teacher paused then asked the class, "And what do you think that man said?"

One little boy raised his hand and said, "I think he said 'Holy Shit! A talking pig!'"

The teacher was unable to teach for the next 10 minutes.

The Four Cats

Four men were bragging about how smart their cats were.
The first man was an Engineer, the second man was an Accountant, the third man was a Chemist, and the fourth man was a Government Employee.

To show off, the Engineer called his cat, "T-square, do your stuff." T-square pranced over to the desk, took out some paper and pen and promptly drew a circle, a square, and a triangle.

Everyone agreed that was pretty smart.

But the Accountant said his cat could do better. He called his cat and said, "Spreadsheet, do your stuff." Spreadsheet went out to the kitchen and returned with a dozen cookies. He divided them into 4 equal piles of 3 cookies.

Everyone agreed that was good.

But the Chemist said his cat could do better. He called his cat and said, "Measure, do your stuff." Measure got up, walked to the fridge, took out a quart of milk, got a 10 ounce glass from the cupboard and poured exactly 8 ounces without spilling a drop into the glass.

Everyone agreed that was pretty good.

Then the three men turned to the Government Employee and said, "What can your cat do?" The Government Employee called his cat and said, "CoffeeBreak, do your stuff."

CoffeeBreak jumped to his feet, ate the cookies, drank the milk, sh*t on the paper, screwed the other three cats. claimed he injured his back while doing so, filed a grievance report for unsafe working conditions, put in for Workers Compensation...............and went home for the rest of the day on sick leave...........

AND THAT, MY FRIEND, IS WHY EVERYONE WANTS TO WORK FOR THE GOVERNMENT!!

Two Guys Walking Their Dogs

Two guys were walking their dogs------one had a German Shepherd and the other had a Chihuahua. The man with the shepherd suggested going into a bar for a drink. The other man says, "They're not going to let dogs into the bar." And the first guy says, "No? Watch this." He puts on some dark glasses, acts like the German shepherd is a Seeing Eye dog, walks into the bar, and orders a drink. And no one says anything.

So the second guy takes out some dark glasses, slips them on, and walks his Chihuahua into the bar. The bartender says, "Sorry---we don't allow dogs in here." And the man says, "It's okay---it's my Seeing Eye dog." The bartender laughs and says, "This Chihuahua is your Seeing Eye dog?" And the guy says, "They gave me a Chihuahua?"

Two Whales

A male whale and a female whale were swimming off the coast of Japan when they noticed a whaling ship. The male whale recognized it as the same ship that had harpooned his father many years earlier. He said to the female whale, "Lets both swim under the ship and blow out of our air holes at the same time and it should cause the ship to turn over and sink. They tried it and sure enough, the ship turned over and quickly sank.

Soon however, the whales realized the sailors had jumped overboard and were swimming to the safety of shore. The male was enraged that they were going to get away and told the female "lets swim after them and gobble them up before they reach the shore." At this point, he realized the female was becoming reluctant to follow him. "Look", she said, "I went along with the blow job, but I absolutely refuse to swallow the seamen."

Visiting the Zoo

Three mischievous boys skipped school one day and instead went to the zoo one day for an outing.

They decided to visit the elephant cage first, but soon enough, they were picked up by a zoo security officer for causing a commotion.

The officer hauled them off to the Security Office for questioning.

The supervisor in charge asked each of them to give their names and tell what they were doing at the elephant cage.

The first boy innocently said, "Okay, my name is Gary, and I was just throwing peanuts into the elephant cage."

The second added, "My name is Larry, and all I was doing was throwing peanuts into the elephant cage."

The third boy was a little more shaken up than his buddies and said,

"Well, my name is Peter, but my friends call me Peanuts."

Where Did You Get That Pig?

A drunk guy walks into a bar and looks up to see a lady with a French poodle. The drunk slurs, "Where did you get that pig?"

The lady, with a look of surprise, snaps back, "I'll have you know that it is a Frrrench poodle."

The drunk looks at her and says, "I was talking to the French poodle."

Bar

A Looser

There was this guy at a bar, just looking at his drink. He stays like that for half of an hour.

Then, this big trouble-making truck driver steps next to him, takes the drink from the guy, and just drinks it all down. The poor man starts crying. The truck driver says, "Come on man, I was just joking. Here, I'll buy you another drink. I just can't stand to see a man cry."

"No, it's not that. This day is the worst of my life. First, I fall asleep, and I go late to my office. My boss was outrageous and fires me. When I leave the building and I go to my car, I found out it was stolen. The police said that they can do nothing. I get a cab to return home, and when I leave it, I remember I left my wallet and credit cards there. The cab driver just drives away."

"I go home, and when I get there, I find my wife in bed with the gardener. I leave home, and come to this bar. And just when I was thinking about putting an end to my life, you show up and drink my poison."

A Strong Drunk

Two old drunks in a bar. The first one says, "Ya know, when I was 30 and got a hard-on, I couldn't bend it with either of my hands. By the time I was 40, I could bend it about 10 degrees if I tried really hard. "By the time I was 50, I could bend it about 20 degrees, no problem. I'm gonna be 60 next week, and now I can almost bend it in half with just one hand"

"So," says the second drunk, "what's your point?"

"Well," says the first, "I'm just wondering how much stronger I'm gonna get!"

A Tight Squeeze

A drunk gets up from the bar and heads for the bathroom. A few minutes later, a loud, blood curdling scream is heard from the bathroom. A few minutes after that, another loud scream reverberates through the bar.

The bartender goes into the bathroom to investigate why the drunk is screaming. "What's all the screaming about in there? You're scaring the customers!"

"I'm just sitting here on the toilet and every time I try to flush, something comes up and squeezes the hell out of my testicles."

With that, the bartender opens the door, looks in and says..."You idiot! You're sitting on the mop bucket!"

Alcohol Warnings

Due to increasing products liability litigation, beer manufacturers have accepted the FDA's suggestion that the following warning labels be placed immediately on all beer containers:

WARNING: Consumption of alcohol may make you think you are whispering when you are not.

WARNING: Consumption of alcohol is a major factor in dancing like an asshole.

WARNING: Consumption of alcohol may cause you to tell the same boring story over and over again until your friends want to SMASH YOUR HEAD IN.

WARNING: Consumption of alcohol may make you think you can logically converse with other members of the opposite sex without spitting.

WARNING: Consumption of alcohol may make you think you have mystical Kung Fu powers.

WARNING: Consumption of alcohol may cause you to roll over in the morning and see something really scary (whose species and or name you can't remember).

WARNING: Consumption of alcohol may lead you to believe you are invisible.

WARNING: Consumption of alcohol may actually CAUSE pregnancy.

An Inch or Two

A man is in a bar and has one too many drinks. This beautiful lady sits down next to him. He turns to her and says "Hey how bout it. You and me, getting' it on. I've got a couple dollars and it looks like you could use a little money." She stands up and says, "What makes you think I charge by the inch."

Being Cut Back

There's a few guys who always get together on Fridays after work for a drink...

One Friday, Jeff showed up late, sat down at the bar, and kicked back his entire first beer in one gulp... Then he turned to Bob and said, "Times are getting tough my friend, I mean, just today my wife told me that she's going to cut me back to only two times a week... I can't believe it"...

At which point Bob put his hand on Jeff's shoulder and said reassuringly, "You think you've got it bad, she's cut some guys out all together"

Cowboys and Indians

Jack and Tom, are having a beer in a saloon when a cowboy walks in with an Indian's head under his arm. He hands it to the bartender, and the bartender hands him money. The bartender turns to them and says, "I hate Indians. Last week they burnt my barn to the ground and killed my wife and three kids. Anybody brings me the head of an Indian, I'll give them a thousand bucks."

Jack and Tom guzzle their beers and leave to go hunt Indians. After a while, they finally spot one. Jack throws a rock, it hits him on the head, the Indian falls off his horse, and rolls seventy feet down a ravine. The two cowboys make their way down the ravine and Tom pulls out his knife to claim their trophy.

Jack says, "Tom, take a look at this." Tom says, "Not now, I'm busy."

Jack says, "I really think you should have a look." Tom says,

"Asshole, can't you see I'm busy? I've got a thousand dollars in my hand."

Jack says, "Please, Tom, take a look."

Tom looks up at the top of the ravine, and there's five thousand Indians standing there. Tom says, "Fuck! We're gonna be millionaires!"

Darts Master

A very drunk man goes into a bar and orders a drink. The bartender serves him and asks him if he would like to try the bar game of darts. Three darts in the bulls eye and win a prize. Only a dollar for three darts.

The drunk agrees and throws the first dart. A bulls eye!! He downs another drink, takes aim on wobbly feet, lets go...Two bulls eyes!!!! Two more quick drinks go down. Barely able to stand, he lets go of the last dart.

Three bulls eyes!!!

All are astounded. No one has ever won before. The bartender searches for a prize... grabs a turtle from the bar's terrarium and presents it to the drunk as his prize.

Three weeks pass... The drunk returns and orders more drinks, then announces he would like to try the dart game again. To the total amazement and wonderment of all the local drunks, he scores three more bulls eyes and demands his prize.

The bartender, being a sort of drunk himself, and a bit short of memory, doesn't know what to give, so he asks the drunk, "Say, what did you win the last time?"

And the drunk responds, "A roast beef sandwich on a hard roll!"

Drunk Staggers Out of a Bar

A drunk staggers out of a bar and into a nearby cathedral. He eventually stumbles his way down the aisle and into a confessional. After a lengthy silence, the priest asks, "May I help you, my son?"

"I dunno," comes the drunk's voice from behind the partition. "You got any toilet paper on your side?"

Fastest Thing in The World

There were 4 guys sitting in a bar. One of them decided to play a little game about what each of them thought was the fastest thing in the world.

Well the first guy says, "I think a Concord Jet is the fastest thing in the world, because it can go faster than the speed of sound."

Well the second guy says, "Well I think I got you beat on that one! I think lightning is the fastest thing in the world, because it can go faster than the speed of light and sound."

Well the third guy says, "Well I believe I have both of you beat. The brain is the fastest thing in the world, because whenever you need something, it is right there for you."

Well the fourth guys clearly states, "Well I have got you all beat! I think the anal sphincter muscle is the fastest thing in the world."

The other three guys say really? Why's that?

And the fourth guys says, "Well I was on a Concord Jet, it got struck by lightning, and I didn't know what to do ... so I shit my pants!"

Free Beer

A new guy in town walks into a bar and reads a sign that hangs over the bar... FREE BEER! FREE BEER FOR THE PERSON WHO CAN PASS THE TEST! So the guy asks the bartender what the test is.

Bartender replies "Well, first you have to drink that whole gallon of pepper tequila, the WHOLE thing at once and you can't make a face while doing it. Second, there's a 'gator out back with a sore tooth...you have to remove it with your bare hands. Third, there's a woman up-stairs who's never had an orgasm. You gotta make things right for her." The guy says, "Well, as much as I would love free beer, I won't do it. You have to be nuts to drink a gallon of pepper tequila and then get crazier from there.

Well, as time goes on and the man drinks a few, he asks, "Wherez zat teeqeelah?"

He grabs the gallon of tequila with both hands, and downs it with a big slurp and tears streaming down his face. Next, he staggers out back and soon all the people inside hear the most frightening roaring and thumping, then silence. The man staggers back into the bar, his shirt ripped and big scratches all over his body.

"Now" he says "Where's that woman with the sore tooth?"

Going to Heaven

A preacher goes into a bar and says "Anybody who wants to go to heaven, stand up." Everybody stands up except for a drunk in the corner. The preacher says "My son, don't you want to go to heaven when you die?" The drunk says "When I die? Sure. I thought you were taking a load up now."

Golden Saloon

A guy comes home completely drunk one night. He lurches through the door and is met by his scowling wife, who is most definitely not happy. "Where in tarnation have you been all night?" she demands.

"At this fantastic new bar," he says. "The Golden Saloon. Everything there is golden. It's got huge golden doors, a golden floor, the works - heck, even the urinal's gold!"

The wife still doesn't believe his story, and the next day checks the phone book, finding a place across town called the Golden Saloon. She calls up the place to check her husband's story.

"Is this the Golden Saloon?" she asks when the bartender answers the phone.

"Yes it is," bartender answers.

"Do you have huge golden doors?"

"Sure do." "Do you have golden floors?"

"Most certainly do."

"What about golden urinals?"

There's a long pause, then the woman hears the bartender yelling, "Hey, Duke, I think I got a lead on the guy that peed in your saxophone last night!"

Having A Bad Day

A guy walks into a bar and orders 6 shooters. The bartender says, "Looks like you are having a bad day."

The guy says, "Am I ever! To start, I woke up late for work. On my way to work I got in an accident. When I got to work I was four hours late, so the boss fired me. Then to top everything off I came home to my wife screwing my best friend."

The bartender says, "What did you say to your wife?"

The guy says, "I told her to get out, and I never want to see her again."

The bartender says, "What did you say to your best friend?"

The guy says, "I said BAD DOG!"

Superman

A guy is sitting at a bar in a skyscraper restaurant high above the city. He's slamming tequila left and right. he grabs one, drinks it, goes over to a window and jumps out.

The guy who was sitting next to him couldn't believe that the guy had just done that. He was more surprised when, ten minutes later, the same guy, unscathed, comes walking back into the bar and sits back down next to him.

The astonished guy asks," How did you do that???? I just saw you jump out that window and we're hundreds of feet above the ground!!!" The jumper responds by slurring, "Well, I don't get it either. I slam a shot of tequila and when I jump out the window, the tequila makes me slow down right before I hit the ground. Watch."

He takes a shot, slams it down, goes tot the window and jumps out. The other guy runs to the window and watches as the guy falls until right before the ground, slows down and lands softly on his feet. A few minutes later, the guy walks back into the bar.

The other guy has to try it too, so he orders a shot of tequila. He drinks it and goes to the window and jumps. As he reaches the bottom, he doesn't slow down at all....SPLAT!!!!!!

The first guy orders another shot of tequila and the bartender says to him," You're really a jerk when you're drunk, Superman."

The Best Bar

A Scotsman, American, and an Irishman are in a bar.
They are having a good time and all agree that the bar is a nice place.

Then the Scotsman says, "Aye, this is a nice bar, but where I come from, back in Glasgow, there's a better one. At MacDougal's, you buy a drink, you buy another drink, and MacDougal himself will buy your third drink!"

The others agree that sounds like a good place.

Then the American says, "Yeah, that's a nice bar, but where I come from, there's a better one. Over in Brooklyn, there's this place, Vinny's. At Vinny's, you buy a drink, Vinny buys you a drink. You buy another drink, Vinny buys you another drink."

Everyone agrees that sounds like a great bar.

Then the Irishman says, "You think that's great? Where I come from in Dublin, there's this place called Murphy's. At Murphy's, they buy you your first drink, they buy you your second drink, they buy you your third drink, and then, they take you in the back and get you laid!"

"Wow!" say the other two. "That's fantastic! Did that actually happen to you?"

"No," replies the Irish guy, "but it happened to me sister!"

Tits Wrong

"My god! What happened to you?" the bartender asked Kelly as he hobbled in on a crutch, one arm in a cast.

"I got in a tiff with Riley."

"Riley? He's just a wee fellow," the barkeep said surprised.

"He must have had something in his hand."

"That he did," Kelly said. "A shovel it was."

"Dear Lord. Didn't you have anything in your hand?"

"Aye, that I did -- Mrs. Riley's left tit." Kelly said. "And a beautiful thing it was, but not much use in a fight!"

Toilet Paper

This bartender is in a bar, when this really hot chick walks up and says in a sexy seductive voice, "May I please speak to your manager?"

He says, "Not right now, is there anything I can help you with?"

She replies, "I don't know if you're the man to talk to...its kind of personal..."

Thinking he might get lucky, he goes, "I'm pretty sure I can handle your problem, miss."

She then looks at him with a smile, and puts two of her fingers in his mouth...and he begins sucking them, thinking "I'm in!!!"

She goes, "Can you give the manager something for me?" The bartender nods...yes. "Tell him there's no toilet paper in the ladies restroom."

True Love

Three men were drinking at a bar -- a doctor, an attorney and a biker.

As the doctor was drinking his white wine he said, "For her birthday, I'm going to buy my wife a fur coat and a diamond ring. This way, if she doesn't like the fur coat she will still love me because she got a diamond ring."

As the attorney was drinking his martini he said, "For my wife's birthday, I'm going to buy her a designer dress and a gold bracelet. This way, if she doesn't like the dress she will still love me because she got the gold bracelet."

As the biker was drinking his shots of whiskey he said, "I'm going to buy my wife a T-shirt and a vibrator. This way, if she doesn't like the T-shirt she can go fuck herself!"

Two Career Drunks buy Sausage

Two career drunks were extremely thirsty one Saturday night and decided to go to the store to get some cheap booze. In the store, the first drunk says, "All right, I have 87 cents; how much do you have?" His friend replies, "I have a dollar. What can we get for $1.87?" The first spots a big Italian sausage on the rack for only $1.80 and has a great idea. "Hey, here's what we can do" he says. "We'll buy that sausage there and put it in my pants. We'll go into a bar and order drinks. After the drinks are gone, I'll pull out the sausage and you start sucking on it. They'll kick us out of the bar and we won't have to pay!"

The second drunk agrees and they head off to the bar. They walk in and order two beers and drink them down. When the beer is gone, the first drunk whips the sausage out and the second starts sucking on it. "What the hell are you doing?

Get out of my bar!" says the bartender, and the two run out laughing. "That was great, and it didn't cost us a cent" says the second drunk. "Let's do it again!"

So off they run to another bar for a repeat performance. This continues through the night. At the end of the night, after about the 20th bar, the second drunk says "Man what a great night. All this drinking is making me hungry. Hey, pull out that sausage and let's eat it."

"Sausage?" says the first. "I ate the sausage about eight bars ago!"

Two Drunks

Two drunks had just gotten thrown out of the bar and are walking down the street when they come across this dog, sitting on the curb, licking his balls. They stand there watching and after a while one of them says, "I sure wish I could do that!"

The other one looks at him and says, "Well, I think I'd pet him first".

Worst Way

A guy goes into a bar and says to the bartender, "Man, I'm dying to have sex in the worst way. So the bartender says, "Well, the worst way I know of is standing up in a hammock."

Wrong Door

One night a man was getting very drunk in a pub. He staggered back to take a piss, whipping his prick out as he went in the door. However, he had wandered into the ladies room by mistake, surprising a woman sitting on the can, "This is for ladies!" she screamed. The drunk waved his dick at her and said "So is this!"

Blonde Jokes

A $99 Cruise

A blonde walks by a travel agency and notices a sign in the window, "Cruise Special -- $99!". She goes inside, lays her money on the counter and says, "I'd like the $99 cruise special, please." The agent grabs her, drags her into the back room, ties her to a large inner tube, then drags her out the back door and downhill to the river, where he pushes her in and sends her floating. A second blonde comes by a few minutes later, sees the sign, goes inside, lays her money on the counter, and asks for the $99 special. She too is tied to an inner tube and sent floating down the river. Drifting into stronger current, she eventually catches up with the first blonde. They float side by side for a while before the first blonde asks, "Do they serve refreshments on this cruise? The second blonde replies, "They didn't last year."

A Blonde, a Brunette, and a Redhead

A Blonde, a Brunette, and a Redhead all work at the same office for a female boss who always goes home early.

"Hay, girls," says the Brunette, "Let's go home early tomorrow. She'll never know."

So the next day, they all leave right after the boss does. The Brunette gets some extra gardening done, the Redhead goes to a bar, and the Blonde goes home. She goes up stairs and finds her boss having sex with her husband! The Blonde quietly closes the bedroom door, sneaks out of the house and returns to work.

"That was fun," says the Brunette the next day at work. "We should do it again sometime."

"No way," says the Blonde, "I almost got caught."

A Blonde in Church

An Alabama preacher said to his congregation, 'Someone in this congregation has spread a rumor that I belong to the Ku Klux Klan. 'This is a horrible lie and one which a Christian community cannot tolerate I am embarrassed and do not intend to accept this. Now, I want the party who did this to stand and ask forgiveness from God and this Christian Family.'

No one moved.

The preacher continued, 'Do you have the nerve to face me and admit this is a falsehood? Remember, you will be forgiven and in your heart, you will feel glory. Now stand and confess your transgression.'

Again, all was quiet.

Then slowly, a drop-dead gorgeous blonde with a body that would stop traffic rose from the third pew. Her head was bowed and her voice quivered as she spoke, 'Reverend there has been a terrible misunderstanding. I never said you were a member of the Ku Klux Klan. I simply told a couple of my friends that you were a wizard under the sheets.'

The preacher fell to his knees, his wife fainted, and the Congregation roared.

A Blonde Wanted to Sell Her Car...

A blonde wanted to sell her car, but couldn't find any buyers. She called her friend for advice, and her friend asked her how many miles she had on her car. She said it had 235,000 miles.

Her friend told her that was the problem. But the blonde's friend told her that her brother is a mechanic and could put the odometer back to whatever miles she wanted. So the blonde went to the mechanic and told him to put the miles at 40,000.

Two days later the blonde's friend asked her if she sold the car since her brother dropped the miles. The blonde told her, "Why would I sell the car? There are only 40,000 miles on it!"

A Blonde's New Tattoo

A blonde is showing off her new tattoo of a giant seashell on her inner thigh.

Her friends ask her why she would get such a tattoo and in that location.

She responds, "It's really cool. If you put pour left ear up against it, You can smell the ocean."

A Guy in a Bar with a Crocodile

A guy walks into a bar with a crocodile on a leash and puts it up on the bar. He turns to the amazed drinkers, "Here's the deal. I'll open this crocodile's mouth and place my genitals inside. Then the croc will close his mouth for one minute. He'll then open his mouth and I'll remove my wedding tackle unscathed. In return for witnessing this spectacle, each of you will buy me a drink." After a few moments' silence, the crowd murmurs approval.

The man stands up on the bar, drops his trousers, and places his privates in the crocodile's mouth. The croc closes his mouth as the crowd gasps. After a minute, the man grabs a beer bottle and raps the crocodile hard on the top of its head. The croc opens his mouth and the man removes his genitals – unscathed as promised. The crowd cheers and the first of his free drinks is delivered.

The man calls for silence and makes another offer. "I'll pay anyone $1,000 who's willing to give it a try." A hush falls over the crowd. After a while, a hand goes up at the back. It's a Blonde. "I'll try," she says, "But only if you promise not to hit me on the head with the beer bottle."

A Tennis Ball

One day while jogging, a middle-aged man noticed a tennis ball lying by the side of the walk.

Being fairly new and in good condition, he picked the ball up, put it in his pocket and proceeded on his way.

Waiting at the cross street for the light to change, he noticed a beautiful blonde standing next to him smiling.

"What do you have in your pocket?" she asked.

"Tennis ball?" the man said smiling back.

"Wow," said the blonde looking upset. "That must hurt. I once had tennis elbow and the pain was unbearable!"

Blonde and Cop

A highway patrolman pulled alongside a speeding car on the freeway. Glancing at the car, he was astounded to see that the blonde behind the wheel was knitting!

Realizing that she was oblivious to his flashing lights and siren, the trooper cranked down his window, turned on his bullhorn and yelled, "PULL OVER!"

"NO," the blonde yelled back, "IT'S A SCARF!"

Blonde and the Sheep Farmer

A dumb blonde was really tired of being made fun of, so she decided to have her hair died so she would look like a brunette. When she had brown hair, she decided to take a drive in the country.

After she had been driving for a while, she saw a farmer and a flock of sheep and thought, "Oh! Those sheep are so adorable!" She got out and walked over to the farmer and said, "If I can guess how many sheep you have, can I take one home?"

The farmer, being a bit of a gambler himself, said she could have a try.

The blonde looked at the flock and guessed, "157."

The farmer was amazed - she was right! So the blonde, (who looked like a brunette), picked one out and got back into her car.

Before she left, farmer walked up to her and said. "If I can guess the real color of your hair, can I have my dog back?"

Blonde Buys A New Car

A blonde bought a brand new car and decided to drive down from some place far off, to meet this friend. She reached there in a few hours. After spending a few days there, she decided to return, and called up her mother to expect her in the evening. But she didn't reach home in the evening and not the next day either. When she finally reached home on the third day, her distraught mother ran and asked her what happened? She got out, obviously very tired from a long journey, and said, "These car designers are crazy! They have four gears for going forward, but only one for going back!"

Blonde City Girl

A blonde city girl marries a Colorado rancher.

One morning, on his way out to check on the cows, the rancher says to Amy, 'The insemination man is coming over to impregnate one of our cows today. I drove a nail into the 2 by 4 just above the cow's stall in the barn. You show him where the cow is when he gets here, OK?'

The rancher leaves for the fields.

After a while, the artificial insemination man arrives and knocks on the front door. Amy takes him down to the barn. They walk along the row of cows and when she sees the nail, she tells him, 'This is the one right here.'
The man, assuming he is dealing with an airhead blonde, asks, 'Tell me lady, 'cause I'm dying to know; how would YOU know this is the cow to be bred?'

'That's simple. By the nail over its stall,' Amy explains very confidently.

Laughing rudely at her, the man says, 'And what, pray tell, is the nail for?'

The blonde turns to walk away and says sweetly over her shoulder, 'I guess it's to hang your pants on.'

Blonde in a Boat

There was a blonde driving down the road one day. She glanced to her right and noticed another blonde sitting in a nearby field, rowing a boat with no water in sight.

The blonde angrily pulled her car over and yelled at the rowing blonde, "What do you think you're doing? It's things like this that give us blondes a bad name. If I could swim, I'd come out there and kick your butt!"

Blonde in Pain

A blonde told her doctor that she was really worried because every part of her body hurt.

The doctor looked concerned and said, "Show me where."

The blonde touched her own arm and screamed, "Ouch!"

Then she touched her leg and screamed, "Ouch!"

She touched her nose and cried, "Ouch!"

She looked at her doctor and said, "See? It hurts everywhere!"

The doctor laughed and said, "Don't worry; it's not serious. You"ve just got a broken index finger."

Blonde Observations:

1. Took a new scarf back to store because it was too tight.
2. Fired from pharmacy job for failing to print labels....."duh"....bottles won't fit in typewriter!!!!
3. Got excited....finished jigsaw puzzle in 6 months....box said "2-4 years"!!!
4. Trapped on escalator for hours....power went out!!!!
5. Tried to made Kool-Aid...8 cups of water won't fit into those little packets!!!!
6. Tried to go water skiing....couldn't find a lake with a slope.
7. Lost breast stroke swimming competition....learned later other swimmers cheated, they used their arms!!!!
8. Got locked out of car in rain storm....car swamped, because top was down.
9. The capital of California is "C"....isn't it?
10. Hate M & M's....they are so hard to peel.
11. Baked turkey for 41/2 days....instructions said 1 hour per pound and I weigh 108!!!!

12.   Couldn't call 911…."duh"….there's no "eleven" button on the phone!!!!

Blonde on a River

A blonde was walking along the river bank when she noticed another blonde walking along the river on the other side. She called out to the other blonde and asked, "How do you get to the other side of the river?"

The blonde on the other side yelled back, "You ARE on the other side!"

Blonde Puzzle

One morning this blonde calls her friend and says "Please come over and help me. I have this killer jigsaw puzzle, and I can't figure out how to start it."

Her friend asks, "What is it a puzzle of?"

The blonde says, "From the picture on the box, it's a tiger."

The blonde's friend figures that he's pretty good at puzzles, so he heads over to her place. She lets him in the door and shows him to where she has the puzzle spread all over the table. He studies the pieces for a moment, then studies the box.

He then turns to her and says: "First, no matter what I do, I'm not going to be able to show you how to assemble these to look like the picture of that tiger." "Second, I'd advise you to relax, have a cup of coffee, and put all these Frosted Flakes back in the box.

Blonde Truck Driver

A Roadway driver is driving east on Route 66 he sees a truck driving west and the CB crackles to life. "Hey Roadway driver, who are the two biggest fags in America?" comes from the CB. The blonde Roadway driver replies, "I don't know." The other trucker says "You and your brother." Well the blonde Roadway driver gets annoyed but the other driver tells him "It's just a joke - tell it to the next truck you see."

Well the blonde Roadway driver drives for about an hour and finally sees another truck. He gets on the CB and says "Hey other truck, do you know who the two biggest fags in the world are?" The other trucker says, "I don't know, who?" The blonde Roadway driver replies "Me and my brother."

Blonde's Mother Dies

A blonde goes into work one morning crying her eyes out. Her boss, concerned about his employee's well being, asks sympathetically, "What's the matter?"

The blonde replies, "Early this morning I got a phone call saying that my mother had passed away."

"I'm terribly sorry to hear that. Why don't you go home for the day... we aren't terribly busy. Just take the day off to relax and rest."

The blonde very calmly explains, "No, I'd be better off here. I need to keep my mind off it and I have the best chance of doing that here."

The boss agrees and allows the blonde to work as usual. "If you need anything, just let me know," he says. A few hours pass and the boss decides to check on the blonde. He looks out over his office and sees the blonde crying hysterically. He rushes out to her, and asks, "Are you going to be okay? Is there anything I can do to help?"

"No," replies the blonde, "I just got a call from my sister, and she said that HER mom died too!"

Cheerio's

A blonde wakes up in the morning to a huge rumble in her tummy. She walks down stairs into the pantry. She has a choice of Trix, Lucky Charms, Raisin Bran, or Cheerio's. So she takes out the Cheerio's and pours out a bowl of them. She says "OH Wow! doughnut seeds!"

Christmas Tree Cutting

Two blondes decided that they were going to cut down their own Christmas tree. They went into the woods on this cold winter day and searched for hours for a tree. Finally one blonde said to the other, "I give up. I am going to cut down the very next tree; I don't care if it isn't decorated!"

Drunken Man and Blonde

After a really good party a man walks into a bar and orders a drink. Already drunk and delirious, the man turns to the person sitting next to him and says, "You wanna hear a blonde joke?"

The person replies, "I am 240 pounds, world kickboxing champion and a natural blonde. My friend is 190 pounds, world judo champion and is a natural blonde. And my other friend is 200 pounds, world arm wrestling champion and is also a natural blonde. Do you still want to tell me that blonde joke?"

The man thinks for a while and replies, "Not if I have to explain it three times."

Eleven Blondes and one Brunette

Eleven Blondes and one Brunette are handing on a rope. If one of them does not let go of the rope, it will break and they will all die.

The Brunette says she will sacrifice herself and let go because the Blondes are such good friends that they would all grieve too much if one of them was to die and wreck their lives.

She finishes her speech and the Blondes are so touched by her generosity that they all begin to clap.

Milk Bath

A blonde heard that milk baths make you beautiful, so she left a note for her milkman to leave her 15 gallons of milk.

When the milkman read the note, he felt there must be a mistake. He thought she probably meant 1.5 gallons, so he knocked on the door to clarify her request.

The blonde came to the door and the milkman said: "I found your note to leave 15 gallons of milk. Did you mean 15 gallons or 1.5 gallons?"

The blonde said, "I want 15 gallons. I'm going to fill my bathtub with milk and take a milk bath."

The milkman asked, "You want it pasteurized?"

OK, are you ready for this?

The blonde said, "No, just up to my nipples."

Misunderstood

A young ventriloquist is touring the clubs and one night he's doing a show in a small club in a small town in Arkansas. With his dummy on his knee, he's going through his usual dumb blonde jokes when a blonde woman in the fourth row stands on her chair and starts shouting: "I've heard enough of your stupid blonde jokes. What makes you think you can stereotype women that way? What does the color of a person's hair have to do with her worth as a human being? It's guys like you who keep women like me from being respected at work and in the community and from reaching our full potential as a person, because you and your kind continue to perpetuate discrimination against, not only blondes, but women in general...and all in the name of humor!"

The ventriloquist is embarrassed and begins to apologize, when the blonde yells, "You stay out of this, mister! I'm talking to that little idiot on your knee!"

NEW ORLEANS CRABS

A man boarded an airplane in New Orleans with a box of frozen crabs and asked a blonde, female crew member to take care of the box for him. She took the box and promised to put it in the crew's refrigerator.

He pointedly advised her that he was holding her personally responsible for the crabs staying frozen, mentioned that he was a lawyer, and proceeded to rant at her about what would happen if she let them thaw out.

Needless to say, she was annoyed by his behavior.

Shortly before landing in New York, she used the intercom to announce to the entire cabin, "Would the gentleman who gave me the crabs in New Orleans, please raise your hand?"

Not one hand went up ... So she took them home and ate them.

> Two lessons here:
> 1. Men never learn.
> 2. Blondes aren't as dumb as most men think.

Pregnant Turkey Story

One year at Thanksgiving, my mom went to my sister's house for the traditional feast.

Knowing how gullible my sister is, my mom decided to play a trick. She told my sister that she needed something from the store.

When my sister left, my mom took the turkey out of the oven, removed the stuffing, stuffed a Cornish hen, and inserted it into t he turkey, and re-stuffed the turkey.

She then placed the bird(s) back in the oven

When it was time for dinner, my sister pulled the turkey out of the oven and proceeded to remove the stuffing. When her serving spoon hit something, she reached in and pulled out the little bird.

With a look of total shock on her face, my mother exclaimed, "Patricia, you've cooked a pregnant bird!" At the reality of this horrifying news, my sister started to cry.

It took the family two hours to convince her that turkeys lay eggs!

Yep..................SHE'S BLONDE!

Quick Blonde Jokes

Q: Why did the blonde keep putting quarters in the soda vending machine?

A: Because she thought she was winning.

Q: Why did the blonde take 16 friends to the movies?

A: Under 17 not admitted!

Q: Why did the blonde bake a chicken for 3 and a half days?

A: It said cook it for half an hour per pound, and she weighed 125.

She was so Blonde that:

1. She sent me a fax with a stamp on it
2. She tried to put M&M's in alphabetical order
3. She thought a quarterback was a refund
4. If you gave her a penny for her thought, you'd get change back
5. She tripped over a cordless phone
6. She took a ruler to bed to see how long she slept
7. At the bottom of the application where it says, "sign here" she put "Sagittarius"
8. If she spoke her mind, she'd probably be speechless
9. She studied for a blood test – and failed
10. It takes her two hours to watch 60 minutes
11. She sold the car for petrol money
12. When she took you to the airport and saw the sign that said, "Airport Left" she turned around and went home

Silver Dildo

A blonde a brunette and a redhead walk into an adult store. The redhead asks: "How much for the black dildo?" "50 bucks", says the clerk. The brunette asks: "How much for the white dildo?" "50 bucks", says the clerk. The blonde picks up a big silver one and says: "How much for this one?" "Oh, I have to get 100 dollars for that one."

They all three make their purchases. The clerk is chuckling as the women leave and his partner asked why he was laughing. "Well", he says, "I sold the black and the white dildos for 50 bucks apiece. Oh, and by the way, I sold your thermos for 100 dollars."

The Execution of Three Women

Three women are about to be executed. One's a brunette, one's a redhead and one's a blonde.

The guard brings the brunette forward and the executioner asks if she has any last requests. She says no and the executioner shouts, "Ready! Aim!" Suddenly the brunette yells, "EARTHQUAKE!!!" Everyone is startled and throws themselves on the ground while she escapes.

The guard brings the redhead forward and the executioner asks if she has any last requests. She say no and the executioner shouts, "Ready! Aim!" Suddenly the redhead yells, "TORNADO!!!" Everyone is startled and looks around for cover while she escapes.

By now the blonde has it all figured out. The guard brings her forward and the executioner asks if she has any last requests. She says no and the executioner shouts, Ready! Aim!" and the blonde yells, "FIRE!!!"'

Two Blondes Talking

The two blondes were talking and one asked the other, "Which is further away – the moon or Florida? The other replied, "Helloooo, can you see Florida?"

Educational

Dumb Jocks

Two football players were taking an important final exam. If they failed, they would be on academic probation and not allowed to play in the big game the following week. The exam was fill-in-the-blank.

The last question read, "Old MacDonald had a _____."

Bubba was stumped. He had no idea what to answer. But he knew he needed to get this one right to be sure he passed.

Making sure the professor wasn't watching, he tapped Tiny on the shoulder. "Pssst. Tiny. What's the answer to the last question?" Tiny laughed. He looked around to make sure the professor hadn't noticed then he turned to Bubba.

"Bubba, you're so stupid. Everyone knows Old MacDonald had a FARM."

"Oh yeah," said Bubba. "I remember now." He picked up his No. 2 pencil and started to write the answer in the blank. He stopped. Tapping Tiny's shoulder again, he whispered, "Tiny, how do you spell farm?"

"You are really dumb, Bubba. That's so easy. Farm is spelled E-I-E-I-O."

Great Truths

GREAT TRUTHS THAT LITTLE CHILDREN HAVE LEARNED:
1) No matter how hard you try, you can't baptize cats.
2) When your Mum is mad at your Dad, don't let her brush your hair.
3) If your sister hits you, don't hit her back. They always catch the second person.
4) Never ask your 3-year old brother to hold a tomato.
5) You can't trust dogs to watch your food.
6) Don't sneeze when someone is cutting your hair.

7) Never hold a Dust-Buster and a cat at the same time.
8) You can't hide a piece of broccoli in a glass of milk.
9) Don't wear polka-dot underwear under white shorts.
10) The best place to be when you're sad is Grandpa's lap.

GREAT TRUTHS THAT ADULTS HAVE LEARNED:
1) Raising teenagers is like nailing jelly to a tree.
2) Wrinkles don't hurt.
3) Families are like fudge...mostly sweet, with a few nuts.
4) Today's mighty oak is just yesterday's nut that held its ground.
5) Laughing is good exercise. It's like jogging on the inside.
6) Middle age is when you choose your cereal for the fiber, not the toy.
7) Do not store your clothes in a closet because they shrink when you go to put them on after a few months.

GREAT TRUTHS ABOUT GROWING OLD:
1) Growing old is mandatory; growing up is optional.
2) Forget the health food. I need all the preservatives I can get.
3) When you fall down, you wonder what else you can do while you're down there.
4) You're getting old when you get the same sensation from a rocking chair that you once got from a roller coaster.
5) It's frustrating when you know all the answers but nobody bothers to ask you the questions.
6) Time may be a great healer, but it's a lousy beautician.
7) Wisdom comes with age, but sometimes age comes alone.

THE FOUR STAGES OF LIFE:
1) You believe in Santa Claus.
2) You don't believe in Santa Claus.
3) You are Santa Claus.
4) You look like Santa Claus.

SUCCESS:
At age 4 success is . . . not piddling in your pants.
At age 12 success is . . . having friends.
At age 17 success is . . . having a drivers license.
At age 35 success is . . . having money.
At age 50 success is . . . having money.

At age 70 success is . . . having a drivers license.
At age 75 success is . . . having friends.
At age 80 success is . . . not piddling in your pants.

Pass this on to someone who could use a laugh.
Always remember to forget the troubles that pass your way; BUT
NEVER Forget the blessings that come each day.
Have a wonderful day with many *smiles*
Take the time to live!!!
Life is too short. Dance naked

3 Minute Management Course

Lesson 1
A man is getting into the shower just as his wife is finishing up her shower, when the doorbell rings. The quickly wraps herself in a towel and runs downstairs. When she opens the door, there stands Bob, the next-door neighbor. Before she says a word, Bob says, "I'll give you $800 to drop that towel." After thinking for a moment, the woman drops her towel and stands naked in front of Bob. After a few seconds, Bob hands her $800 and leaves. The woman wraps back up in the towel and goes back upstairs. When she gets to the bathroom, her husband asks, "Who was that?" "It was Bob the next door neighbor," she replies. "Great!" the husband says, "did he say anything about the $800 he owes me?"

Moral of the story:
If you share critical information pertaining to credit and risk with your shareholders in time, you may be in a position to prevent avoidable exposure.

Lesson 2
A priest offered a Nun a lift. She got in and crossed her legs, forcing her gown to reveal a leg. The priest nearly had an accident. After controlling the car, he stealthily slid his hand up her leg. The nun said, "Father, remember Psalm 129?" The priest removed his hand. But, changing gears, he let his hand slide up her leg again. The nun once again said, "Father, remember Psalm 129?" The priest

apologized "Sorry sister but the flesh is weak." Arriving at the convent, the nun went on her way. On his arrival at the church, the priest rushed to look up Psalm 129. It said, "Go forth and seek, further up, you will find glory."

Moral of the story:
If you are not well informed in your job, you might miss a great opportunity.

Lesson 3
A sales rep, an administration clerk, and the manager are walking to lunch when they find an antique oil lamp. They rub it and a Genie comes out. The Genie says, "I'll give each of you just one wish.

" Me first! Me first!" says the admin clerk. "I want to be in the Bahamas, driving a speedboat, without a care in the world." Puff! She's gone.

"Me next! Me next!" says the sales rep. "I want to be in Hawaii, relaxing on the beach with my personal masseuse, an endless supply of Pena Coladas and the love of my life." Puff! He's gone.

"OK, you're up," the Genie says to the manager. The manager says, "I want those two back in the office after lunch."

Moral of the story:
Always let your boss have the first say.

Lesson 4
An eagle was sitting on a tree resting, doing nothing. A small rabbit saw the eagle and asked him, "Can I also sit like you and do nothing?" The eagle answered: "Sure, why not." So, the rabbit sat on the ground below the eagle and rested. All of a sudden, a fox appeared, jumped on the rabbit and ate it.

Moral of the story:
To be sitting and doing nothing, you must be sitting very, very high up.

Lesson 5
A turkey was chatting with a bull. "I would love to be able to get to the top of that tree," sighed the turkey, "but I haven't got the energy." "Well, why don't you nibble on some of my droppings?" replied the bull. They're packed with nutrients." The turkey pecked at a lump of dung, and found it actually gave him enough strength to reach the lowest branch of the tree. The next day, after eating some more dung, he reached the second branch. Finally after a fourth night, the turkey was proudly perched at the top of the tree. He was promptly spotted by a farmer, who shot him out of the tree.

Moral of the story:
Bull Shit might get you to the top, but it won't keep you there.

Lesson 6
A little bird was flying south for the winter. It was so cold the bird froze and fell to the ground into a large field. While he was lying there, a cow came by and dropped some dung on him. As the frozen bird lay there in the pile of cow dung, he began to realize how warm he was. The dung was actually thawing him out! He lay there all warm and happy, and soon began to sing for joy. A passing cat heard the bird singing and came to investigate. Following the sound, the cat discovered the bird under the pile of cow dung, and promptly dug him out and ate him.

Morals of the story:
(1) Not everyone who shits on you is your enemy
(2) Not everyone who gets you out of shit is your friend
(3) And when you're in deep shit, it's best to keep your mouth shut!

This ends the 3-minute management course.

Never Underestimate Illiterates.!!!!

A big city lawyer went duck hunting in rural North Wairarapa . He shot and dropped a bird, but it fell into a farmer's field on the other side of a fence. As the lawyer climbed over the fence, an elderly farmer drove up on his tractor and asked him what he was doing. The litigator responded, "I shot a duck and it fell in this field, and now I'm going to retrieve it."

The old farmer replied, "This is my property, and you are not coming over here."

The indignant lawyer said, "I am one of the best trial attorneys in New Zealand and, if you don't let me get that duck, I'll sue you and take everything you own."

The old farmer smiled and said, "Apparently, you don't know how we settle disputes in North Wairarapa. We settle small disagreements like this with the 'Three Kick Rule.'"

The lawyer asked, "What is the 'Three Kick Rule'?"

The Farmer replied, "Well, because the dispute occurs on my land, I get to go first. I kick you three times and then you kick me three times and so on back and forth until someone gives up."

The attorney quickly thought about the proposed contest and decided that he could easily take the old codger. He agreed to abide by the local custom.

The old farmer slowly climbed down from the tractor and walked up to the attorney. His first kick planted the toe of his heavy steel toed work boot into the lawyer's groin and dropped him to his knees! His second kick to the midriff sent the lawyer's last meal gushing from his mouth. The lawyer was on all fours when the farmer's third kick to his rear end, sent him face-first into a fresh cow pie.

The lawyer summoned every bit of his will and remaining strength and very slowly managed to get to his feet. Wiping his face with the arm of his jacket, he said, "Okay, you old fart. Now it's my turn."

The old farmer smiled and said, "Nah, I give up. You can have the duck."

This Equation Should Be Taught in All Schools

What Makes 100%? What does it mean to give **MORE than 100%?** Ever wonder about those people who say they are giving more than 100%? We have all been to those meetings where someone wants you to give over 100%. How about achieving 103%? What makes up 100% in life?

Here's a little mathematical formula that might help you answer these questions:

If:
A B C D E F G H I J K L M N O P Q R S T U V W X Y Z
is represented as:
1 2 3 4 5 6 7 8 9 10 11 12 13 14 15 16 17 18 19 20 21 22 23 24 25 26.

Then:

H-A-R-D-W-O-R-K
8+1+18+4+23+15+18+11 = **98%**

And

K-N-O-W-L-E-D-G-E
11+14+15+23+12+5+4+7+5 = **96%**

But,

A-T-T-I-T-U-D-E
1+20+20+9+20+21+4+5 = **100%**

And,

B-U-L-L-S-H-I-T
2+21+12+12+19+8+9+20 = **103%**

AND, look how far ass kissing will take you.

A-S-S-K-I-S-S-I-N-G
1+19+19+11+9+19+19+9+14+7 = 127%

So, one can conclude with mathematical certainty that While Hard Work and Knowledge will get you close, and Attitude will get you there, it's the Bullshit and Ass kissing that will put you over the top!

If I may add one more equation:

W-H-O Y-O-U K-N-O-W
23+8+15+25+15+21+11+14+15+23 = **170%**

What is your percentage of effort?

Train Ride

One morning three Alabama good old boys and three Yankees were in a ticket line at the Birmingham train station heading to Atlanta for a big football game.

The three Northerners each bought a ticket and watched as the three Southerners bought just one ticket between them.

"How are the three of you going to travel on only one ticket?" asked one of the Yankees.

"Watch and learn," answered one of the boys from the South.

When the six travelers boarded the train, the three Yankees sat down, but the three Southerners crammed into a bathroom together and closed the door.

Shortly after the train departed, the conductor came around to collect tickets.

He knocked on the bathroom door and said, "Ticket, please." The door opened just a crack and a single arm emerged with a ticket in hand. The conductor took it and moved on.

The Yankees saw this happen and agreed it was quite a clever idea. Indeed, so clever that they decided to do the same thing on the return trip and save some money.

That evening after the game when they got to the Atlanta train station, they bought a single ticket for the return trip while to their astonishment the three Southerners didn't buy even one ticket.

"How are you going to travel without a ticket?" asked one of the perplexed Yankees.

"Watch and learn," answered one of the Southern boys.

When they boarded the train, the three Northerners crammed themselves into a bathroom and the three Southerners crammed themselves into the other bathroom across from it.

Shortly after the train began to move, one of the Southerners left their bathroom and walked quietly over to the Yankees' bathroom. He knocked on the door and said, "Ticket, please."

There's just no way on God's green earth to explain how the Yankees won the war.

Employment

Advertising for a Gynecologist's Assistant

A young man goes into the Job Centre in Jacksonville, Florida , and sees a card advertising for a Gynecologist's Assistant. Interested he goes to learn more - 'Can you give me some more details about this?' he asks the guy behind the desk.

The Job Centre man sorts through his files & replies - 'Oh yes here it is: The job entails you getting the lady patients ready for the gynecologist. You have to help them out of their underwear, lie them down and carefully wash their genital regions. You then apply shaving foam and gently shave off all their pubic hair then rub in soothing oils so that they're ready for the gynecologist's examination. There's an annual salary of $45,000, but you're going to have to go to Oxford, Mississippi. That's about 620 miles from here.'

'Oh why, is that where the job's is located?'

'No sir - that's where the end of the applicant's line is!'

Job Candidate

Reaching the end of a job interview, the Human Resources Person asked a young Engineer fresh out of MIT, "And what starting salary were you looking for?"

The Engineer replied, "In the neighborhood of $125,000 a year, depending on the benefits package."

The interviewer said, "Well, what would you say to a package of 5-weeks vacation, 14 paid holidays, full medical and dental, company matching retirement fund to 50% of salary, and a company car leased every 2 years - say, a red Corvette?"

The Engineer sat up straight and said, "Wow! Are you kidding?"

And the interviewer replied, "Yes, but you started it."

Last Name

The manager of a large office noticed a new man one day and told him to come into his office. "What is your name?" was the first thing the manager asked him.

"John," the new guy replied.

The manager scowled, "Look, I don't know what kind of a namby-pamby place you worked at before, but I don't call anyone by their first name. It breeds familiarity and that leads to a breakdown in authority. I refer to my employees by their last name only -- Smith, Jones, Baker -- that's all. I am to be referred to only as Mr. Robertson. Now that we got that straight, what is your last name?"

The new guy sighed and said, "Darling. My name is John Darling."

"Okay, John, the next thing I want to tell you is..."

Sleep Cure

Tom had this problem of getting up late in the morning and was always late for work. His boss was mad at him and threatened to fire him if he didn't do something about it. So Tom went to his doctor who gave him a pill and told him to take it before he went to bed. Tom slept well, and in fact, beat the alarm in the morning. He had a leisurely breakfast and drove cheerfully to work.

"Boss", he said, "The pill actually worked!"

"That's all fine" said the boss, "But where were you yesterday?"

Three Envelopes

A new manager spends a week at his new office with the manager he is replacing. On the last day the departing manager tells him, "I have left three numbered envelopes in the desk drawer. Open an envelope if you encounter a crisis you can't solve."

Three months down the track there is a major drama, everything goes wrong - the usual stuff - and the manager feels very threatened by it all. He remembers the parting words of his predecessor and opens the first envelope. The message inside says "Blame your predecessor!" He does this and gets off the hook.

About half a year later, the company is experiencing a dip in sales, combined with serious product problems. The manager quickly opens the second envelope. The message read, "Reorganize!" This he does, and the company quickly rebounds.

Three months later, at his next crisis, he opens the third envelope. The message inside says "Prepare three envelopes".

Ethnic

An Old Italian

An old Italian Mafia Don is dying and he called his grandson to his bed, "Grandson I wanta you to listen to me. I wanta you to take mya 45 automatic pistol, so you will always remember me." "But grandpa I really don't like guns, how about you leaving me your Rolex watch instead."

"You lisina to me, some day you goin a be runna da bussiness, you goina have a beautiful wife, lotsa money, a biga home and maybe a couple od bambino, some day you goina come hom and maybe finda you wife in be with another man. Whata you gonna do then? Pointa to you watch and say, TIMES UP?"

(This is very funny if you tell it with an Italian accent)

Ancient Chinese Torture

A young man was lost wandering in a forest, when he came upon a small house. He knocked on the door and was greeted by an ancient Chinese man with a long, grey beard "I'm lost," said the man. "Can you put me up for the night?"

"Certainly," the Chinese man said, "but on one condition. If you so much as lay a finger on my daughter, I will inflict upon you the three worst Chinese tortures known to man."

"Ok," said the man, thinking that the daughter must be pretty old as well, and entered the house.

Before dinner, the daughter came down the stairs. She was young, beautiful, and had a fantastic figure. She was obviously attracted to the young man since she couldn't keep her eyes off him during the meal. Remembering the old man's warning, he ignored her and went up to bed alone. But during the night, he could bear it no longer, and sneaked into her room for a night of passion. He was careful to keep everything quiet so the old man wouldn't hear. Near dawn he crept back to his room, exhausted, but happy.

He woke to feel a pressure on his chest. Opening his eyes he saw a large rock on his chest with a note on it that read, "Chinese Torture 1: Large rock on chest." "Well, that's pretty crappy," he thought. "If that's the best the old man can do then I don't have much to worry about." He picked the boulder up, walked over to the window and threw the boulder out. As he did so he noticed another note on it that read: "Chinese Torture 2: Rock tied to left testicle." In a panic he glanced down and saw the rope that was already getting close to the end. Figuring that a few broken bones was better than castration, he jumped out of the window after the boulder. As he plummeted downward he saw a large sign on the ground that read, "Chinese Torture 3: Right testicle tied to bedpost."

Confucius Say:

Man who run in front of car get tired.

Man who run behind car get exhausted.

Man who scratch butt should not bite fingernails.

Man who eat many prunes get good run for money.

War does not determine who is right, war determine who is left.

Wife who put husband in doghouse soon find him in cathouse.

Man who drive like hell, bound to get there.

Man who live in glass house should change clothes in basement.

Man who fish in other man's well often catch crabs.

Crowded elevator smell different to midget.

Passionate kiss like spider's web, soon lead to undoing of fly.

Virginity like bubble, one prick all gone.

Foolish man give wife grand piano, wise man give wife upright organ.

Man who walk thru airport turnstile sideways going to Bangkok.

Baseball is wrong, man with four balls cannot walk.

Panties not best thing on earth but next to best thing on earth.

Man who fight with wife all day get no piece at night.

It take many nails to build crib but one screw to fill it.

Man who stand on toilet is high on pot.

Man who farts in church sits in own pew.

Man who drops watch in toilet bound to have crappy time.

Elevator and an Amish Father and Son

An Amish boy and his father were in a mall. They were amazed by almost everything they saw, but especially by two shiny, silver walls that could move apart and then slide back together again.

The boy asked, "What is this, Father?" The father (never having seen an elevator) responded, "Son, I have never seen anything like this in my life, I don't know what it is."

While the boy and his father were watching with amazement, a fat old lady in a wheel chair moved up to the moving walls and pressed a button. The walls opened, and the lady rolled between them into a small room. The walls closed, and the boy and his father watched the small numbers above the walls light up sequentially. They continued to watch until it reached the last number, and then the numbers began to light in the reverse order. Finally the walls opened up again and a gorgeous 24-year-old blond stepped out. The father, not taking his eyes off the young woman, said quietly to his son . . "Get Your Mother!"

Eyo Toct

A short Polish immigrant went to the DVLA to apply for a driver's license. First, of course, he had to take an eye sight test. The optician showed him a card with the letters. On the bottom row were these letters:

'C Z W I N O S T A C Z.'

'Can you read this?' the optician asked.

'Read it?' the Polish guy replied - 'I know the fellow.'

Polish Sausage

A man goes into a store and tells the clerk, "I'd like some Polish sausage."

The clerk looks at him and says, "Are you Polish?"

The guy, clearly offended, says, "Well, yes I am. But let me ask you something. If I had asked for Italian sausage would you ask me if I was Italian?

Or if I had asked for German bratwurst, would you ask me if I was German?

Or if I asked for kosher hot dog would you ask me if I was Jewish?

Or if I had asked for a taco would you ask if I was Mexican? Would ya, huh? Would ya?"

The clerk says, "Well, no."

"And if I asked for some Irish whiskey, would you ask if I was Irish?"

"Well, I probably wouldn't."

With deep self-righteous indignation, the guy says, "Well, all right then, why did you ask me if I'm Polish just because I ask for Polish sausage?"

The clerk replies, "Because you're at Home Depot."

Steering Wheel

An Irish man walks into a bar. The bartender looks at him and notices he has a steering wheel stuck down the front of his pants. "Hey," he says, "What's with the steering wheel down your pants?" "Ach," says the Irish man, "it's drivin' me nuts!"

The Canadians

The Canadian government is going to help America with the war on terrorism. They have pledged 2 of their biggest battle ships, 6000 ground troops and 6 fighter jets.

Unfortunately, after the exchange rate conversion, we ended up with 2 canoes, 1 Mountie, and some flying squirrels.

Two Arabs and an Israeli Traveling

Two Arabs boarded a shuttle out of Washington for New York. One sat in the window seat, the other in the middle seat.

Just before takeoff a fat, little Israeli guy got on and took the aisle seat next to the Arabs. He kicked off his shoes, wiggled his toes and was settling in when the Arab in the window seat said, "I think I'll go up and get a coke."

"No problem," said the Israeli. "I'll get it for you."

While he was gone, the Arab picked up the Israelis shoe and spit in it.

When the Israeli returned with the coke, the other Arab said, "That looks good. I think I'll have one too."

Again, the Israeli obligingly went to fetch it, and while he is gone the other Arab picked up the other shoe and spit in it.

The Israeli returned with the coke, and they all sat back and enjoyed the short flight to New York. As the plane was landing the Israeli slipped his feet into his shoes and knew immediately what had happened. "How long must this go on?" he asked. "This enmity between our peoples..... this hatred... this animosity... this spitting in shoes and peeing in cokes?"

Two Dwarfs

Two dwarfs decide to treat themselves to a vacation in Las Vegas. At the hotel bar, they're dazzled by two women, and wind up taking them to their separate rooms.

The first dwarf is disappointed, however, as he's unable to reach a certain physical state that would enable him to join with his date. His depression is enhanced by the fact that, from the next room, he hears cries of ONE, TWO, THREE...HUH! all night long.

In the morning, the second dwarf asks the first, How did it go? The first whispers back: It was so embarrassing. I simply couldn't get an erection. The second dwarf shook his head. You think that's embarrassing? I couldn't even get on the bed!

What a Scotsman Wears Under His Kilt

A kilted Scotsman was walking down a country path after finishing off a large amount of whisky at a local pub. He felt quite sleepy and decided to nap against a tree.

As he slept, two female tourists heard his loud snoring. When they found him, one said, "I've always wondered what a Scotsman wears under his kilt."

She boldly walked over to the sleeper, raised his kilt, and saw that he wore nothing at all. Her friend said, "Well, the mystery is solved! Let's thank him for sharing!"

She took off her pretty blue hair ribbon and gently tied it around the Scotsman's endowment. A while later, the Scotsman was awakened by the call of nature. He raised his kilt and was bewildered at the sight of the neatly tied blue ribbon. He stared for a minute, then said, "I don't know where y'been laddie... but it's nice ta see you won firrrst prrrize!"

Flying

Aerial Photos

A photographer for a national magazine was assigned to take pictures of a great forest fire. He was advised that a small plane would be waiting to fly him over the fire.

The photographer arrived at the airstrip just an hour before sundown. Sure enough, a small Cessna airplane was waiting. He jumped in with his equipment and shouted, "Let's go!" The tense man sitting in the pilot's seat swung the plane into the wind and soon they were in the air, though flying erratically.

"Fly over the north side of the fire," said the photographer, "and make several low-level passes." "Why?" asked the nervous pilot. "Because I'm going to take pictures!" yelled the photographer. "I'm a photographer, and photographers take pictures."

The pilot replied, "You mean you're not the flight instructor?"

Area 51

You've heard of the Air Force's ultra-high-security, super-secret base in Nevada, known simply as "Area 51?"

Well, late one afternoon, the Air Force folks out at Area 51 were surprised to see a Cessna landing at their "secret" base. They immediately impounded the aircraft and hauled the pilot into an interrogation room.

The pilot's story was that he took off from Vegas, got lost, and spotted the Base just as he was about to run out of fuel. The Air Force started a full FBI background check on the pilot and held him overnight during the investigation.

By the next day, they were finally convinced that the pilot really was lost and wasn't a spy. They gassed up his airplane, gave him a terrifying "you-did-not-see-a-base" briefing, complete with threats of spending the rest of his life in prison, told him Vegas was that-a-way on such-and-such a heading, and sent him on his way.

The next day, to the total disbelief of the Air Force, the same Cessna showed up again. Once again, the MP's surrounded the plane... only this time there were two people in the plane.

The same pilot jumped out and said, "Do anything you want to me, but my wife is in the plane and you have to tell her where I was last night!"

Flying Forever

An airplane was flying from LA to New York. About an hour into the flight, the pilot announced, "We have lost an engine, but don't worry, there are three left. However, instead of 5 hours it will take 7 hours to get to New York."

A little later, the pilot announced, "A second engine failed, but we still have two left. However, it will take 10 hours to get to New York."

Somewhat later, the pilot again came on the intercom and announced, "A third engine had died. Never fear, because the plane can fly on a single engine. However, it will now take 18 hours to get to New York."

At this point, a blonde passenger said, "Gee, I hope we don't lose that last engine, or we'll be up here forever!"

Little Guy on a Plane

A little guy gets on a plane and sits next to the window.

A few minutes later, a big, heavy, strong, mean-looking, hulking guy plops down in the seat next to him and immediately falls asleep.

The little guy starts to feel a little airsick, but he's afraid to wake the big guy up to ask if he can move aside to let him go to the bathroom. He knows he can't climb over him, and so the little guy is sitting there, looking at the big guy, trying to decide what to do. Suddenly, the plane hits an air pocket and an uncontrollable wave of nausea passes through the little guy. He can't hold it in any longer and hurls all over the big guy's chest.

About five minutes later the big guy wakes up, looks down, and sees the vomit all over him

"So," says the little guy, "are you feeling any better now?"

On A Passenger Flight

On a passenger flight, the pilot comes over the public address system as usual and to greet the passengers. He tells them at what altitude they'll be flying, the expected arrival time, and a bit about the weather, and advises them to relax and have a good flight.

Then, forgetting to turn off the microphone, he says to his co-pilot, "What would relax me right now is a cup of coffee and a blowjob." All the passengers hear it. As a stewardess immediately begins to run toward the cockpit to tell the pilot of his slip-up, one of the passengers stops her and says "Don't forget the coffee!"

Oneliners

"Though I Fly Through the Valley of Death ... I Shall Fear No Evil. For I am at 80,000 Feet and Climbing."
-- *At the entrance to the old SR-71 operating base Kadena, Japan*

"The only time you have too much fuel is when you're on fire."

"Blue water Navy truism: There are more planes in the ocean than submarines in the sky."
-- *From an old carrier sailor*

"When one engine fails on a twin-engine airplane you always have enough power left to get you to the scene of the crash."

"What is the similarity between air traffic controllers and pilots? If a pilot screws up, the pilot dies; If ATC screws up, the pilot dies."

"Never trade luck for skill."

"Weather forecasts are horoscopes with numbers."

"Airspeed, altitude and brains. Two are always needed to successfully complete the flight."

"Flashlights are tubular metal containers kept in a flight bag for the purpose of storing dead batteries."

"When a flight is proceeding incredibly well, something was forgotten."

"There is no reason to fly through a thunderstorm in peacetime."
-- *Sign over squadron ops desk at Davis-Monthan AFB, AZ, 1970*

"If something hasn't broken on your helicopter, it's about to."

"You know that your landing gear is up and locked when it takes full power to taxi to the terminal."

Pilot's Out Cry

A plane was taking off from Kennedy. After it reached a comfortable cruising altitude, the captain made an announcement over the intercom, "Ladies and Gentlemen, this is your captain speaking. Welcome to Flight number 293, non-stop from New York to Los Angeles. The weather ahead is good and therefore we should have a smooth flight, Now, sit back and relax. - OH MY GOD!"

Silence Then, the captain came back on the intercom and said: "Ladies and Gentlemen, I an so sorry if I scared you earlier, but while

I was talking the flight attendant brought me a cup of coffee and spilled the hot coffee in my lap. You should see the front of my pants!"

A passenger in Coach said: "That's nothing. He should see the back of mine!"

Smart Ass Pilot

A young and foolish pilot wanted to sound cool on the aviation frequencies. This was his first time approaching a field during the nighttime, and instead of making any official requests to the tower, he said, "Guess who?" The controller switched the field lights off and replied, "Guess where!"

Gay

Ordaining Twelve Monks

Twelve monks were about to be ordained. The final test was for them to line up, nude, in a garden while a nude model danced before them. Each monk had a small bell attached to his privates, and they were told that anyone whose bell rang would not be ordained because he had not reached a state of spiritual purity.

The model danced before the first monk candidate, with no reaction. She proceeded down the line with the same response until she got to the final monk. As she danced, his bell rang so loudly it fell off and clattered to the ground. Embarrassed, he bent down to pick up the bell, and eleven other bells began to ring......

Queen Trumps Princess

I once was on a plane where I was served by an obviously homosexual male flight attendant. At one point, he bounced over to where I was sitting and announced "The Captain has asked me to announce that he will be landing the big scary plane shortly, so if you could just put up your trays, that would be great." I did as he had instructed but the woman sitting next to me did not.

A few moments later, our flight attendant came back and said to her: "Ma'am, perhaps you couldn't hear me over the big scary engine, but I asked you to please put up your tray so that the captain can land the plane." She still wouldn't comply. Now he was getting angry and asked her again to put up the tray.

She then calmly turned to him and said: "In my country, I am called a Princess. I take orders from no one." The flight attendant replied, "Oh yeah? Well in MY country, I'm called a Queen and I outrank you, Bitch, so put the tray up!"

Quick Gay Jokes

Q. Did you hear about the gay guy that's on the patch?
A. He's down to four butts a day.

Q. Did you hear that the new and politically correct name for "lesbian".
A. It has been changed to "vagitarian".

Q. What's the definition of "Tender Love?"
A. Two gays with hemorrhoids.

Q. Did you hear about the two poofters who went to London?
A. They were REALLY pissed off when they found out Big Ben was a clock.

Q. What does a poof and an ambulance have in common?
A. They both get loaded from the rear and go whoo-whoo!

Q. How can you tell if you are in a gay amusement park?
A. They issue gerbils at the tunnel of love.

Q. Did you know 70% of the gay population were born that way?
A. The other 30% were sucked into it.

Q. Hear about the new gay sitcom?
A. "Leave it, it's Beaver."

Q. Did you hear about the gay rabbit?
A. He found a hare up his ass.

Q. How can you tell if a novel is homosexual?
A. The hero always gets his man in the end.

Q. How can you tell if a Western is homosexual?
A. All the good guys are hung.

Q. Why can't scientists find a cure for AIDS?
A. They can't get the laboratory mice to arse fuck.

Q. Why did the gay man take two aspirin with his Viagra?
A. So sex wouldn't be such a pain in the arse.

Q. Did you hear about the two gay judges?
A. They tried each other.

Q. What's the biggest crime committed by transvestites?
A. Male fraud.

Q. Did you hear Richard Simmons had plastic surgery to get his love handles removed?
A. Yeah...now he has no ears.

Q. Why is it difficult to find men who are sensitive, caring, and good looking?
A. They already have boyfriends.

Q. How can you tell a tough lesbian bar?
A. Even the pool table has no balls.

Q. What do you call a lesbian with fat fingers?
A. Well hung.

Q. What do you call three lesbians in bed together?
A. Ménage à twat.

Q. What do gay kids get for Christmas?
A. Erection Sets.

Q. Where do fags park?
A. In the rear.

Q. What's the difference between a lesbian and a Ritz cracker?
A. Ones a snack cracker, and the others a crack snacker!

Q: What do you call a lesbian dinosaur?
A: Lickalotopuss.

Q. What did one gay sperm say to the other gay sperm?
A. I can't see a thing with all this shit in here!

Q. Did you hear about the two gay guys that had an argument in the bar?
A. They went outside to exchange blows.

Q. Why did the gay guy think his lover was cheating on him?
A. He came home shit faced.

General Humor

0 to 200 in 6 Seconds

Bob was in trouble. He forgot his wedding anniversary. His wife was really pissed.

She told him "Tomorrow morning, I expect to find a gift in the driveway that goes from 0 to 200 in 6 seconds AND IT BETTER BE THERE !!"

The next morning he got up early and left for work. When his wife woke up, she looked out the window and sure enough there was a box gift-wrapped in the middle of the driveway.

Confused, the wife put on her robe and ran out to the driveway, brought the box back in the house. She opened it and found a brand new bathroom scale.

Bob has been missing since Friday.

2010 Darwin Awards

Yes, it's again that magical time of the year when the Darwin Awards are bestowed, honoring the least evolved among us.

Here is the glorious Winner:

1. When his 38-caliber revolver failed to fire at his intended victim during a hold-up in Long Beach, California, would-be robber James Elliot did something that can only inspire wonder. He peered down the barrel and tried the trigger again. This time it worked.

And Now, the Honorable Mentions:

2. The chef at a hotel in Switzerland lost a finger in a meat-cutting machine and submitted a claim to his insurance company. The

company expecting negligence sent out one of its men to have a look for himself. He tried the machine and he also lost a finger. The chef's claim was approved.

3. A man who shoveled snow for an hour to clear a space for his car during a blizzard in Chicago returned with his vehicle to find a woman had taken the space. Understandably, he shot her.

4. After stopping for drinks at an illegal bar, a Zimbabwean bus driver found that the 20 mental patients he was supposed to be transporting from Harare to Bulawayo had escaped. Not wanting to admit his incompetence, the driver went to a nearby bus stop and offered everyone waiting there a free ride. He then delivered the passengers to the mental hospital, telling the staff that the patients were very excitable and prone to bizarre fantasies. The deception wasn't discovered for 3 days.

5. An American teenager was in the hospital recovering from serious head wounds received from an oncoming train. When asked how he received the injuries, the lad told police that he was simply trying to see how close he could get his head to a moving train before he was hit.

6. A man walked into a Louisiana Circle-K, put a $20 bill on the counter, and asked for change. When the clerk opened the cash drawer, the man pulled a gun and asked for all the cash in the register, which the clerk promptly provided. The man took the cash from the clerk and fled, leaving the $20 bill on the counter. The total amount of cash he got from the drawer: $15. (If someone points a gun at you and gives you money, is a crime committed?)

7. Seems an Arkansas guy wanted some beer pretty badly. He decided that he'd just throw a cinderblock through a liquor store window, grab some booze, and run. So he lifted the cinderblock and heaved it over his head at the window. The cinderblock bounced back and hit the would-be thief on the head, knocking him unconscious. The liquor store window was made of Plexiglas. The whole event was caught on videotape.

8. As a female shopper exited a New York convenience store, a man grabbed her purse and ran. The clerk called 911 immediately, and the woman was able to give them a detailed description of the snatcher. Within minutes, the police apprehended the snatcher. They put him in the car and drove back to the store. The thief was then taken out of the car and told to stand there for a positive ID. To which he replied, "Yes, officer, that's her. That's the lady I stole the purse from."

9. The Ann Arbor News crime column reported that a man walked into a Burger King in Ypsilanti, Michigan, at 5 a.m., flashed a gun, and demanded cash. The clerk turned him down because he said he couldn't open the cash register without a food order. When the man ordered onion rings, the clerk said they weren't available for breakfast. The man, frustrated, walked away.

******A 5-STAR STUPIDITY AWARD WINNER*****

10. When a man attempted to siphon gasoline from a motor home parked on a Seattle street, he got much more than he bargained for. Police arrived at the scene to find a very sick man curled up next to a motor home near spilled sewage. A police spokesman said that the man admitted to trying to steal gasoline and plugged his siphon hose into the motor home's sewage tank by mistake. The owner of the vehicle declined to press charges, saying that it was the best laugh he'd ever had.

A Case of the Bitter Being Bit

This is something to think about when negative people are doing their best to rain on your parade. So remember this story the next time someone who knows nothing and cares less tries to make your life miserable.

A woman was at her hairdresser's getting her hair styled for a trip to Rome with her husband.. She mentioned the trip to the hairdresser, who responded:

"Rome ? Why would anyone want to go there? It's crowded and dirty. You're crazy to go to Rome. So, how are you getting there?"

"We're taking Continental," was the reply. "We got a great rate!"

"Continental?" exclaimed the hairdresser. "That's a terrible airline. Their planes are old, their flight attendants are ugly, and they're always late. So, where are you staying in Rome?"

"We'll be at this exclusive little place over on Rome's Tiber River called Teste."

"Don't go any further. I know that place. Everybody thinks its gonna be something special and exclusive, but it's really a dump."

"We're going to go to see the Vatican and maybe get to see the Pope."

"That's rich," laughed the hairdresser. You and a million other people trying to see him. He'll look the size of an ant.

Boy, good luck on this lousy trip of yours. You're going to need it."

A month later, the woman again came in for a hairdo. The hairdresser asked her about her trip to Rome.

"It was wonderful," explained the woman, "not only were we on time in one of Continental's brand new planes, but it was overbooked, and they bumped us up to first class. The food and wine were wonderful, and I had a handsome 28-year-old steward who waited on me hand and foot.

And the hotel was great! They'd just finished a $5 million remodeling job, and now it's a jewel, the finest hotel in the city. They, too, were overbooked, so they apologized and gave us their owner's suite at no extra charge!"

"Well," muttered the hairdresser, "that's all well and good, but I know you didn't get to see the Pope."

"Actually, we were quite lucky, because as we toured the Vatican, a Swiss Guard tapped me on the shoulder, and explained that the Pope likes to meet some of the visitors, and if I'd be so kind as to step into his private room and wait, the Pope would personally greet me. Sure enough, five minutes later, the Pope walked through the door and shook my hand! I knelt down and he spoke a few words to me."

"Oh, really! What'd he say?"

He said: "Who fucked up your hair?"

A Case Where The Biter Got Bit

While enjoying a drink with a buddy one night, this guy decides to try his luck with an attractive young girl sitting alone by the bar. To his surprise, she asks him to join her for a drink and eventually asks him if he'd like to come back to her place. The pair jump into a taxi and go back to her place.

Later, the young man pulls out a cigarette from his jeans and searches for his lighter. Unable to find it, he asks the girl if she has one at hand. "There might be some matches in the top drawer," she replies. Opening the drawer of the bedside table, he finds a box of matches sitting neatly on top of a framed picture of another man. Naturally, the guy begins to worry.

"Is this your husband?" he inquires nervously. "No, silly," she replies, snuggling up to him. "Your boyfriend then?" "No, don't be silly," she says, nibbling away at his ear. "Well, who is he then?" demands the bewildered fellow. Calmly, the girl takes a match, strikes it across the side of her face and replies, "That's me before the operation."

A Cowboy Rides Into Town

A cowboy rode into town and stopped at the saloon for a drink. Unfortunately, the locals always had a habit of picking on newcomers. When he finished, he found his horse had been stolen.

He comes back into the bar, handily flips his gun into the air, catches it above his head without even looking and fires a shot into the ceiling. "Who stole my horse?" he yelled with surprising forcefulness.

No one answered.

"I'm gonna have another beer and if my horse ain't back outside by the time I'm finished, I'm gonna do what I dun back in Texas and I don't want to have to do what I dun back in Texas!"

Some of the locals shifted restlessly.

He had another beer, walked outside, and his horse was back! He saddled up and started to ride out of town.

The bartender wandered out of the bar and asked, "Say partner, what happened in Texas?"

The cowboy turned back and said, "I had to walk home!"

A Little Girl Asked Her Mother...

A little girl asked her mother, "How did the human race appear?" The mother answered, "God made Adam and Eve and they had children, and so was all mankind made.."

Two days later the girl asked her father the same question.. The father answered, "Many years ago there were monkeys from which the human race evolved."

The confused girl returned to her mother and said, "Mom, how is it possible that you told me the human race was created by God, and Dad said they developed from monkeys?"

The mother answered, "Well, dear, it is very simple. I told you about my side of the family and your father told you about his."

A Man Went Into a Grocery Store

A man went into a grocery store, got 3 cans of dog food, and walked up to the checkout counter. The cashier asks the man, "Sir, do you own a dog?"

The man replies, "Yes I do."

The cashier then asks, "Do you have the dog with you?"

The man replies, "No, I left it at home."

The cashier then says, "I'm sorry, but I can't sell you this dog food unless I see your dog."

A few days later the man walks into the same store, gets 3 cans of cat food, and walks up to the checkout counter. The same cashier asks, "Sir, do you own a cat?"

The man replies, "Yes I do."

The cashier then asks, "Do you have your cat with you?"

And the man replies, "No, I left it at home."

Then the cashier says, "I'm sorry, but I can't sell you this cat food unless I see your cat."

A few days later the man walks into the store, this time carrying a paper bag. He walks up to the same cashier, and asks him to put his hand into the bag. The cashier says, "It feels warm, soft, and gooey." The man then says, "Now, can I go back and get 3 rolls of toilet paper?"

A Successful Knight

A Knight and his men return to their castle after a long hard day of fighting. "How are we faring?" asks the King.

"Sire," replies the Knight, "I have been robbing and pillaging on your behalf all day, burning the towns of your enemies in the West."

"What?" shrieks the King. "I don't have any enemies to the West."

"Oh?," says the Knight. "Well, you do now."

A Tiny Person

A teacher took a class of first-grade students to a racetrack on a field trip. Seeing one tiny person squirming, she led him into the bathroom and started to help unzip his pants.

Astonished at what she saw when the job was done, she asked, "Are you in the first?"

The tiny person answered, "No, I'm riding Black Bart in the fifth!"

A Young Ventriloquist is Touring the Outback

A young ventriloquist is touring the outback and stops to entertain at a bar at the back of beyond. He's going through his usual country bumpkin jokes, when a big, burly guy in the audience stands up and says, "I've heard just about enough of your smart ass jokes. We ain't all stupid here, you know."

Flustered, the ventriloquist begins to apologize.

But the big guy cuts him off, "You just stay out of this mister, I'm talking to the little smart ass sitting on your knee!"

An Exhibitionist

There was an exhibitionist who was taking a trip on an airplane. At the top of the stairs there was a stewardess who was collecting tickets. So when the man got to the top of the stairs, he opened his coat and exposed himself. The stewardess said, "I'm sorry sir. You have to show your ticket here, not your stub."

An Old Man, A Boy & A Donkey

An old man, a boy & a donkey were going to town. The boy rode on the donkey & the old man walked. As they went along they passed some people who remarked it was a shame the old man was walking & the boy was riding.

The man & boy thought maybe the critics were right, so they changed positions.

Later, they passed some people that remarked, "What a shame, he makes that little boy walk."

They then decided they both would walk! Soon they passed some more people who thought they were stupid to walk when they had a decent donkey to ride. So, they both rode the donkey.

Now they passed some people that shamed them by saying how awful to put such a load on a poor donkey.

The boy & man said they were probably right, so they decide to carry the donkey. As they crossed the bridge, they lost their grip on the animal & he fell into the river and drowned.

The moral of the story?

If you try to please everyone, you might as well...
Kiss your ass good-bye.

An Old Man Dying

An old man was laying on his death bed. With only hours to live, he suddenly noticed the scent of chocolate chip cookies coming from the kitchen. With his last bit of energy, the old man pulled himself out from his bed, across the floor to the stairs, and down the stairs to the kitchen.

There, the old man's wife was baking chocolate chip cookies. With his last ounce of energy, the old man reached for a cookie. His wife, however, quickly smacked him across the back of his hand, and exclaimed, "Leave them alone, they're for the funeral!"

Asleep on Beach

This guy fell asleep on the beach one day and the wind came up and blew sand all over him until he was covered with only his big toe sticking out.

An old nympho was walking down the beach, saw the toe sticking up, pulled down her bikini bottom and squatted over the toe. She humped away till she was satisfied, pulled up her drawers and left.

The guy woke up, brushed the sand away and left, not knowing what happened. The next day his foot itched like hell, and had a sore on it. He went to the Dr. and after an exam the doc told him he had syphilis of the big toe.

"Syphilis of the big toe?", he inquired, "isn't that rare."

The doc said "You think that's rare, I had a woman in here this morning with athlete's pussy."

Aspirin Cure

A man goes in for an interview for a job as a TV news broadcaster. The interview went quite well but the trouble was he kept winking and stammering.

The interviewer said, "Although you have a lot of the qualities we're looking for, the fact that you keep winking and stammering disqualifies you."

"Oh, that's no problem," said the man. "If I take a couple of aspirin I stop winking and stammering for an hour."

"Show me," said the interviewer.

So the man reached into his pocket. Embarrassingly he pulled out loads of condoms of every variety - ribbed, flavored, colored and everything before he found the packet of aspirin. He took the aspirin and soon talked perfectly and stopped winking.

The interviewer said, "That's amazing, but I don't think we could employ someone who'd be womanizing all over the country."

"Excuse me!" exclaimed the man, "I'm a happily married man, not a womanizer!"

"Well how do you explain all the condoms, then?" asked the interviewer.

The man replied, "Have you ever gone into a pharmacy, stammering and winking, and asked for a packet of aspirin?"

Assumed Close

A while back, when I was considerably younger, I picked up my date at her parents' home. I'd scraped together enough money to take her to a very nice restaurant. She ordered the most expensive items on the menu: Shrimp cocktail, Lobster, Champagne.

I asked her, "Does your Mother feed you like that when you eat at home?"

"No," she replied, "but my Mother's not expecting sex tonight."

I said, "Enjoy"

At His Fingertips

A guy is tossing peanuts into the air and catching them in his mouth. In the middle of catching one, his wife asks him a question, and as he turns to answer, the peanut falls into his ear. He tries to dig it out, but that only pushes it in deeper, so he and his wife decide to go to the hospital.

As they're about to go out the door, their daughter comes in with her date. They explain, and the daughter's date says, "I can get the peanut out."

He tells the father to sit down, shoves two fingers into the father's nose, and tells him to blow hard. The father blows and the peanut flies out of his ear. The mother and daughter are all excited, but the daughter's date says, "Ah, it was nothing."

After her daughter takes her date to the kitchen for something to eat, the mother turns to the father and says, "Isn't he smart? I wonder what he plans to be."

The father says, "From the smell of his fingers, I'd say our son-in-law."

Bad Brakes

Jill's car was unreliable and she called John for a ride every time it broke down. One day John got yet another one of those calls.

"What happened this time?" he asked.

"My brakes went out," Jill said. "Can you come to get me?"

"Where are you?" John asked.

"I'm in the drugstore," Jill responded.

"And where's the car?" John asked.

Jill replied, "It's in here with me."

Birthday Sex

Did you hear about the fellow that was talking to his buddy, and he said, "I don't know what to get my wife for her birthday - she has everything, and besides, she can afford to buy anything she wants, so I'm stumped."

His buddy said, "I have an idea - why don't you make up a certificate saying she can have 60 minutes of great sex, any way she wants it - she'll probably be thrilled." So the fellow did.

The next day his buddy said, "Well? Did you take my suggestion?" "Yes, I did," said the fellow. "Did she like it?" His buddy asked. "Oh yes! she jumped up , thanked me, kissed me on the forehead and ran out the door, yelling "I'll be back in an hour!!"

Bobbitt Family Update

In a recent news broadcast, it was announced that Lorena Bobbitt's sister Louella was arrested for an alleged attempt to perform the same act on her husband as her famous sister had done several years ago. Sources reveal the sister was not as accurate as Lorena.

She allegedly missed the target and stabbed her husband in the upper thigh causing severe muscle and tendon damage.

The husband is reported to be in serious, but stable condition and Luella has been charged with...
?

?

A Misdewiener!

You know darn well you're going to send this on to somebody !!

Boyfriend's Request

This boy has just taken his girlfriend back to her home after being out together, and when they reach the front door he leans with one hand on the wall and says to her, "Sweetie, why don't you give me a blowjob.

"What? You're crazy!" she said.

"Look, don't worry," he said. "It will be quick, I promise you."

"Nooooooo! Someone may see us, a neighbor, anybody..."

"At this time of the night no one will show up. Come on, sweetie, I really need it."

"I've already said NO, and NO is final!"

"Honey, it'll just be a really small blowie... I know you like it too."

"NO!!! I've said NO!!!"

Desperately, he says, "My love, don't be like that. I promise you I love you and I really need this blowjob."

At this moment the younger sister shows up at the door in her nightgown and her hair totally in disorder. Rubbing her eyes she says: "Dad says, 'Damit, give him the blowjob or I'll have to blow him but for God's sake, tell your boyfriend to take his hand off the intercom button so the rest of the family can get some sleep.'"

Brain Exercise

Exercise of the brain is as important as exercise of the muscles. As we grow older, it's important that we keep mentally alert. The saying: "If you don't use it, you will lose it" also applies to the brain.

Below is a very private way to gauge your loss or non-loss of intelligence. So take the following test presented here and determine if you are losing it or are still a MENSA candidate. OK, relax, clear your mind and . . . begin.

1. What do you put in a toaster?

The answer is bread. If you said "toast", then give up now and go do something else. Try not to hurt yourself. If you said, "bread", go to question 2.

2. Say "silk" five times. Now spell "silk". What do cows drink?

Answer: Cows drink water. If you said "milk", please do not attempt the next question. Your brain is obviously overstressed and may even overheat. It may be that you need to content yourself with reading something more appropriate such as "Children's World". If you said, "water" then proceed to question three.

3. If a red house is made from red bricks and a blue house is made from blue bricks and a pink house is made from pink bricks and a black house is made from black bricks, what is a greenhouse made from?

Answer: Greenhouses are made from glass. If you said "green bricks", what the heck are you still doing here reading these questions? If you said "glass", then go on to question four.

4. Twenty years ago, a plane is flying at 20,000 feet over Germany. If you will recall, Germany at the time was politically divided into West Germany and East Germany. Anyway, during the flight, TWO of the engines fail. The pilot, realizing that the last remaining engine is also failing, decides on a crash landing procedure. Unfortunately the engine fails before he has time and the plane crashes smack in the middle of "no man's land" between East Germany and West Germany. Where would you bury the survivors - East Germany or West Germany or in "no man's land"?

Answer: You don't, of course, bury survivors. If you said ANYTHING else, you are a real dunce and you must NEVER try to rescue anyone from a plane crash. Your efforts would not be appreciated. If you said, "Don't bury the survivors" then proceed to the next question.

5. If the hour hand on a clock moves 1/60th of a degree every minute then how many degrees will the hour hand move in one hour?

Answer: One degree. If you said "360 degrees" or anything other than "one degree", you are to be congratulated on getting this far, but you are obviously out of your league. Turn your pencil in and exit the room. Everyone else proceed to the final question.

6. Without using a calculator - You are driving a bus from London to Milford Haven in Wales. In London, 17 people get on the bus. In Reading, six people get off the bus and nine people get on. In Swindon, two people get off and four get on. In Cardiff, 11 people get off and 16 people get on. In Swansea, three people get off and five people get on. In Carmathen, six people get off and three get on. You then arrive at Milford Haven. What was the name of the bus driver?

Answer: Oh, for goodness sake! It was YOU, Read the first line!!!

Brave Swimmer

Once there was a millionaire, who collected live alligators. He kept them in the pool in back of his mansion. The millionaire also had a beautiful daughter who was single.

One day, the millionaire decides to throw a huge party, and during the party he announces, "My dear guests, I have a proposition to every man here. I will give one million dollars, or my daughter, to the man who can swim across this pool full of alligators and emerge unharmed!" As soon as he finished his last word, there was the sound of a large splash in the pool. The guy in the pool was swimming with all his might, and the crowd began to cheer him on. Finally, he made it to the other side of the pool unharmed.

The millionaire was impressed. He said, "That was incredible! Fantastic! I didn't think it could be done! Well, I must keep my end of the bargain. Do you want my daughter or the one million dollars?" The guy catches his breath, then says, "Listen, I don't want your money! And I don't want your daughter! I want the asshole who pushed me in the pool!"

Bubba and Junior and a Flag Pole

Bubba and Junior were standing at the base of a flagpole, looking up.

A woman walked by and asked what they were doing. "We're supposed to find the height of the flagpole," said Bubba, "but we don't have a ladder."

The woman took a wrench from her purse, loosened a few bolts, and laid the pole down. Then she took a tape measure from her pocket, took a measurement and announced, "Eighteen feet, six inches," and walked away.

Junior shook his head and laughed. "Ain't that just like a dumb blonde! We ask for the height, and she gives us the length!"

Capital 4

Dwayne met Patricia Ann from Birmingham at a Tus-caloosa ballroom. They danced every dance together. When the evening was over, he asked if he could see her next time he was in town. "Yes," replied Patricia Ann shyly. The young man hurriedly took out his pad and pencil and asked, "What's your number?" "CApitol 4-6173." After a long embarrassed pause, Dwayne asked, "How do yew make a capital 4?"

Cletus' Order

Cletus walks into a building and goes up to a lady and says "Can I have a cheeseburger, fries and a shake?"

The lady looks at him dumbfounded and says, "Cletus, this is a library."

So Cletus moves closer and whispers, "Can I have a cheeseburger, fries and a shake?"

Clinic Check Up

Two children, Bill and Bob, were sitting outside a clinic. Bill happened to be crying very loudly.

"Why are you crying?" Bob asked.

"I came here for a blood test," sobbed Bill.

"So? Are you afraid?"

"No. For the blood test, they cut my finger.

As Bob heard this, he immediately began crying profusely.

Astonished, Bill stopped his tears and asked Bob, "Why are you crying now?"

To which Bob replied, "I came for a urine test!"

Cold Water

A boy went to his grandfather's house for a week. On the first night at dinner he found a thick, slimy goo on his plate, so he said to his grandfather "Grandpa is this plate clean?"

"As clean as cold water can get them." his grandfather answered.

This went on for the rest of the week. On the last day when the boy was leaving the dog wouldn't let him through. So he said "Grandpa your dog won't let me through."

His grandfather replied "Cold Water go lie down"

Computer Generated

Daddy, how was I born? 'Well, son, Your Mom and I first got together in a chat room on Yahoo. Then I set up a date via e-mail with your

Mom and we met at a cyber-cafe. We sneaked into secluded room, and googled each other. There your mother agreed to a download from my hard drive. As soon as I was ready to upload, we discovered that neither one of us had used a firewall, and since it was too late to hit the delete button, nine months later a little Pop-Up appeared that said: 'You got Male!'

Cooking Woes

Becky prepared a pasta dish for a dinner party she was having. In her haste, however, she forgot to refrigerate the spaghetti sauce, and it sat on the counter all day. She was worried about spoilage, but it was too late to cook up another batch.

She called the local Poison Control Center and voiced her concern. They advised Becky to boil the sauce again.

That night, the phone rang during dinner, and one of the guests volunteered to answer it. Becky's face dropped as the guest called out, "It's the Poison Control Center. They want to know how the spaghetti sauce turned out."

Cough Syrup

The owner of a drug store walks in to find a guy leaning heavily against a wall   The owner asks the clerk, "What's with that guy over there by the wall?"

The clerk says, "Well, he came in here this morning to get something for his cough. I couldn't find the cough syrup, so I gave him an entire bottle of laxative."

The owner says, "You idiot! You can't treat a cough with laxatives!"

The clerk says, "Oh yeah? Look at him, he's afraid to cough!"

Cranky Druggist

Upon arriving home in eager anticipation of a leisurely evening, the husband was met at the door by his sobbing wife. Tearfully she explained, "It's the druggist! He insulted me terribly this morning on the phone."

Immediately the husband drove downtown to accost the druggist and demand an apology. Before he could say more than a word or two, the druggist told him, "Now, just a minute, listen to my side of it. This morning the alarm failed to go off, so I was late getting up. I went without breakfast and hurried out to the car, but I'll be darned if I didn't lock the house with both house and car keys inside. I had to break a window to get my keys.

"Driving a little too fast, I got a speeding ticket. Then, about three blocks from the store, I had a flat tire.

"When I finally got to the store there was a bunch of people waiting for me to open up. I got the store opened and started waiting on these people, and all the time the darn phone was ringing its head off.

"Then I had to break a roll of nickels against the cash register drawer to make change, and they spilled all over the floor. I got down on my hands and knees to pick up the nickels - the phone is still ringing - when I came up I cracked my head on the open cash drawer, which made me stagger back against a showcase with a bunch of perfume bottles on it, and half of them hit the floor and broke.

"The phone is still ringing with no let up, and I finally got back to answer it. It was your wife -- she wanted to know how to use a rectal thermometer. "Well, Mister, I told her!"

Dead and Dying

An English guy was very ill and his son went to visit him in the hospital. Suddenly, the father began to breathe heavily and grabbed the pen and pad by the bed. With his last ounce of strength he wrote a note, dropped it, and died. The son was so overcome with grief that he didn't remember slipping the note into his pocket. At the funeral, he reached into the pocket of his coat and immediately felt the note. He excitedly read it thinking it might be something he could recite during the service. It said: YOU WANKER -- GET OFF MY OXYGEN TUBE!!!

Dead Last

Last year I entered the New York City Marathon. The race started and immediately I was the last of the runners. It was embarrassing.

The guy who was in front of me, second to last, was making fun of me. He said, "Hey buddy, how does it feel to be last?"

I replied: "You really want to know?"

Then I dropped out of the race.

Definitely

A kindergarten teacher one day is trying to explain to her class the definition of the word "definitely" to them. To make sure the students have a good understanding of the word, she asks them to use it in a sentence. The first student raised his hand and said "The sky is definitely blue". The teacher said, "Well, that isn't entirely correct, because sometimes it's gray and cloudy".

Another student says, "Grass is definitely green." The teacher again replies "If grass doesn't get enough water it turns brown, so that isn't really correct either."

Another student raises his hand and asks the teacher "Do farts have lumps?" The teacher looked at him and said "No...But that isn't really a question you want to ask in class discussion." So the student replies, "Then I definitely shit my pants."

Directions

A little boy was waiting for his mother to come out of the grocery store. As he waited, he was approached by a man who asked, "Son, can you tell me where the Post Office is?" The little boy replied, "Sure! Just go straight down this street a cupla blocks and turn to your right."

The man thanked the boy kindly and said, "I'm the new pastor in town. I'd like for you to come to church on Sunday. I'll show you how to get to Heaven." The little boy replied with a chuckle. "Awww, come on... You don't even know the way to the Post Office."

Do You Like Pussycats?

A recently widowed Jewish lady was sitting on a beach towel at Cocoa Beach, Florida. She looked up and noticed that a man her age had walked up, placed his blanket on the sand nearby and began reading a book.

Smiling, she attempted to strike up a conversation with him. "Hello, sir, how are you?"

"Fine, thank you," he responded, and turned back to his book.

"I love the beach. Do you come here often?" she asked.

"First time since my wife passed away last year," he replied, and again turned back to his book.

"Do you live around here?" she asked.

"Yes, I live over in Suntree," he answered, and then resumed reading.

Trying to find a topic of common interest, Sarah persisted. "Do you like pussycats?"

With that, the man threw his book down, jumped off his blanket onto hers, tore off both their swimsuits and gave her the most passionate ride of her life!

As the cloud of sand began to settle, Sarah gasped and asked the man, "How did you know that was what I wanted?"

The man replied, "How did you know my name was Katz?"

Door Signs

A person checks into a hotel for the first time in his life, and goes up to his room. Five minutes later he calls the desk and say, "You've given me a room with no exit. How do I leave?"

The desk clerk says, "Sir, that's absurd. Have you looked for the door?"

The person says, "Well, there's one door that leads to the bathroom. There's a second door that goes into the closet. And there's a door I haven't tried, but it has a 'do not disturb' sign on it."

Dumb Daddy

Two parents take their son on vacation and go to a nude beach. The father goes for a walk on the beach and the son goes to play in the water. Shortly thereafter, the boy runs to his mother and says, "Mommy, I saw some ladies with boobies a lot bigger than yours!"

The mother cleverly replies, "The bigger they are, the dumber they are!"

With that, the little boy runs back into the water and continues to play. Several minutes later, though, the little boy runs back to his mother and says, "Mommy, I saw some men with dongs a lot bigger than Daddy's!"

"The bigger they are, the dumber they are!" she replies.

With that, the little boy runs back into the water and continues to play. Several minutes later, though, the little boy runs back to his mother and says, "Mommy, I just saw Daddy talking to the dumbest lady I ever saw and the more he talked, the dumber he got!"

Embarrassing Day

It was many years ago since the embarrassing day when a young woman, with a baby in her arms, entered his butcher shop and confronted him with the news that the baby was his and asked what was he going to do about it?

Finally he offered to provide her with free meat until the boy was 16. She agreed.

He had been counting the years off on his calendar, and one day the teenager who had been collecting the meat each week, came into the shop and said, "I'll be 16 tomorrow."

"I know," said the butcher with a smile, "I've been counting too, tell your mother, when you take this parcel of meat home, that it is the last free meat she'll get, and watch the expression on her face."

When the boy arrived home he told his mother. The woman nodded and said,

"Son, go back to the butcher and tell him I have also had free bread, free milk, and free groceries for the last 16 years and watch the expression on HIS face!"

Excellent Skydiving Advice

Recently, I got to thinking about my first skydiving instructor. During class he would always take the time to answer any of our stupid first-timer questions.

One guy asked, "If our chute doesn't open, and the reserve doesn't open, how long do we have until we hit the ground?"

Our jumpmaster looked at him and in perfect deadpan and answered, "The rest of your life."

Eyes On You

A man is dining in a fancy restaurant and there is a gorgeous redhead sitting at the next table. He has been checking her out since he sat down, but lacks the nerve to talk with her.

Suddenly she sneezes, and her glass eye comes flying out of its socket toward the man. He reflexively reaches out, grabs it out of the air, and hands it back.

'Oh my, I am so sorry,' the woman says as she pops her eye back in place. 'Let me buy your dinner to make it up to you,' she says.

They enjoy a wonderful dinner together, and afterwards they go to the theatre followed by drinks. They talk, they laugh, she shares her deepest dreams and he shares his. She listens.

After paying for everything, she asks him if he would like to come to her place for a nightcap and stay for breakfast. They had a wonderful, wonderful time. The next morning, she cooks a gourmet meal with all the trimmings. The guy is amazed. Everything had been SO incredible!

'You know,' he said, 'you are the perfect woman. Are you this nice to every guy you meet?'

'No,' she replies. . .   Wait for it. . .   It's coming. . .

The suspense is killing you, isn't it?

She says:

'You just happened to catch my eye.'

Farmer and His Cow

A farmer was milking his cow. He was just starting to get a good rhythm going when a bug flew into the barn and started circling his head.

Suddenly, the bug flew into the cow's ear.

The farmer didn't think much about it, until the bug squirted out into his bucket.

It went in one ear and out the udder.

First Date

A guy has been asking the prettiest girl in town for a date and finally she agrees to go out with him. He takes her to a nice restaurant and buys her a fancy dinner with expensive wine. On the way home, he pulls over to the side of the road in a secluded spot. They start necking and he's getting pretty excited. He starts to reach under her skirt and she stops him, saying she's a virgin and wants to stay that way.

"Well, okay," he says, "how about a blow job?" "Yuck!" she screams. "I'm not putting that thing in my mouth!"

He says, "Well, then, how about a hand job?" "I've never done that," she says. "What do I have to do?"

"Well," he answers, "remember when you were a kid and you used to shake up a Coke bottle and spray your brother with it?" She nods. "Well, it's just like that."

So, he pulls it out and she grabs hold of it and starts shaking it. A few seconds later, his head flops back on the headrest, his eyes close, snot starts to run out of his nose, wax blows out of his ear and he screams out in pain.

"What's wrong?!" she cries out.

"Take your thumb off the end!!"

First Grader Test

A first-grade teacher, Ms Brooks, was having trouble with one of her students. The teacher asked, 'Harry, what's your problem?'

Harry answered, 'I'm too smart for the 1st grade. My sister is in the 3rd grade and I'm smarter than she is! I think I should be in the 3rd grade too!'

Ms. Brooks had had enough. She took Harry to the principal's office.

While Harry waited in the outer office, the teacher explained to the principal what the situation was. The principal told Ms. Brooks he would give the boy a test. If he failed to answer any of his questions he was to go back to the 1st grade and behave. She agreed.

Harry was brought in and the conditions were explained to him and he agreed to take the test.

Principal: 'What is 3 x 3?'

Harry: '9.'

Principal: 'What is 6 x 6?'

Harry: '36.'

And so it went with every question the principal thought a 3rd grader should know.

The principal looks at Ms. Brooks and tells her, 'I think Harry can go to the 3rd grade'

Ms. Brooks says to the principal, 'Let me ask him some questions.'

The principal and Harry both agreed.

Ms. Brooks: 'What does a cow have four of that I have only two of?'

Harry: after a moment: 'Legs.'

Ms. Brooks: 'What is in your pants that you have but I do not have?'

The principal wondered why would she ask such a question!

Harry: 'Pockets.'

Ms. Brooks: 'What does a dog do that a man steps into?'

Harry· 'Pants '

The principal sat forward with his mouth hanging open.

Ms. Brooks: 'What goes in hard and pink then comes out soft and sticky?'

The principal's eyes opened really wide and before he could stop the answer.

Harry: 'Bubble gum.'

Ms. Brooks: 'What does a man do standing up, a woman does sitting down and a dog does on three legs?'

Harry: 'Shake hands.'

The principal was trembling.

Ms. Brooks: 'What word starts with an 'F' and ends in 'K' that means a lot of heat and excitement?'

Harry: 'Firetruck.'

The principal breathed a sigh of relief and told the
teacher, 'Put Harry in the fifth-grade, I got the last seven questions wrong.

First Time Sex

A girl asks her boyfriend to come over Friday night to meet, and have a dinner with her parents.

Since this is such a big event, the girl announces to her boyfriend that after dinner, she would like to go out and make love for the first time.

The boy is ecstatic, but he has never had sex before, so he takes a trip to the pharmacist to get some condoms. He tells the pharmacist it's his first time and the pharmacist helps the boy for about an hour. He tells the boy everything there is to know about condoms and sex.

At the register, the pharmacist asks the boy how many condoms he'd like to buy, a 3-pack, 10-pack, or family pack. The boy insists on the family pack because he thinks he will be rather busy, it being his first time and all. That night, the boy shows up at the girl's parent's house and meets his girlfriend at the door.

"Oh, I'm so excited for you to meet my parents, come on in!"

The boy goes inside and is taken to the dinner table where the girl's parents are seated. The boy quickly offers to say grace and bows his head. A minute passes, and the boy is still deep in prayer, with his head down. 10 minutes pass, and still no movement from the boy. Finally, after 20 minutes with his head down, the girlfriend leans over and whispers to the boyfriend, 'I had no idea you were this religious.'

The boy turns, and whispers back,
'I had no idea your father was a pharmacist.'

Friend or Foe

I shall take you to bed and have my way with you.
I will make you ache, shake and sweat until you moan and groan.
I will make you beg for mercy, beg for me to stop.
I will exhaust you to the point that you will be relieved when I'm finished with you.

And, when I am finished, you will be weak for days.

All my love,
The Flu

(Now, get your mind out of the gutter and go get your flu shot.)

Friends

Four men got together at a reunion. Three of them had sons and they started bragging about them, while the fourth guy went to the can to take a shit. The first man said his son was doing so well, he now owned a factory, manufacturing furniture. Why, just the other day he gave his best friend a whole house full of brand new furniture.

The second man said his son was doing just as well. He was a manager at a car sales firm. Why, just the other day he gave his best friend a Ferrari. The third man said his was doing well too. He was a manager at a bank. Why, just the other day he gave his best friend the money to buy a house.

The fourth man came back, and the other three told him they were just talking about how successful their sons are. He just shook his head and said his son was gay and hadn't amounted to much. But he must be doing something right because, just the other day he was given a house, furniture and a Ferrari by his friends!

Frisky Love

A young couple is out for a romantic walk along a country lane. They walk hand in hand and as they stroll the guy's lustful desire rises to a peak. He is just about to get frisky when she says, "I hope you don't mind but I really do need to pee."

Slightly taken aback by this vulgarity he replies, "OK. Why don't you go behind this hedge."

She nods agreement and disappears behind the hedge. As he waits he can hear the sound of nylon panties rolling down her voluptuous legs and imagines what is being exposed. Unable to contain his animal thoughts a moment longer, he reaches a hand through the hedge and touches her leg. He quickly brings his hand further up her thigh until suddenly and with great astonishment finds himself gripping a long, thick appendage hanging between her legs.

He shouts in horror, "My God Mary ... have you changed your sex?"

"No," she replies. "I've changed my mind, I'm having a shit instead."

Frog Noise, Please

A sister and brother are talking to each other when the little boy gets up and goes over to his Grandpa and says, "Grandpa, please make a frog noise."

The Grandpa says, "No."

The little boys goes on, "Please….Please make a frog noise."

The Grandpa says, "No, now go play."

The little boy then says to his sister, "Go tell Grandpa to make a frog noise."

The little girl says, "Please….Please make a frog noise."

The Grandpa says, "Why do you want me to make a frog noise?"

The little girl replied, "Because mommy said when you croak we can go to Disney World."

Gas Power

A man was driving down the road and ran out of gas. Just at that moment, a bee flew in his window.

The bee said, 'What seems to be the problem?'
'I'm out of gas,' the man replied.

The bee told the man to wait right there and flew away. Minutes later, the man watched as an entire swarm of bees flew to his car and into his gas tank. After a few minutes, the bees flew out.

'Try it now,' said one bee.

The man turned the ignition key and the car started right up. 'Wow!' the man exclaimed, 'what did you put in my gas tank'?
The bee answered, "BP"

Geek Goes To Jail

A computer geek goes to prison for fraud, they put him in a cell with a 300LB guy, Having heard what happens to geeks in prison and being nervous he figures he had better introduce himself, He extends his hand and says with a quivering voice, Hi my name is John Smith.

The big guy who actually is a nice guy extends his and says my name is Turner Brown. The geek passes out.

The big guy fans him and brings him too. Why did you pass out he asked?

The geek replies, what did you say your name was?

"Turner Brown," he replies.

"Oh God," the geek says, "I thought you said 'TURN AROUND'."

Glasses?

A policeman stops a lady and asks for her license. He says "Lady, it says here that you should be wearing glasses."

The woman answered "Well, I have contacts."

The policeman replied "I don't care who you know! You're getting a ticket!"

GOTTA PEE

Two women friends had gone for a girl's night out. Both were very faithful and loving wives, however they had gotten over-enthusiastic on the Bacardi Breezers.

Incredibly drunk and walking home they needed to pee, so they stopped near the cemetery.

One of them had nothing to dry with so she thought she would take off her panties and use them.

Her friend, however, was wearing a rather expensive pair of panties and did not want to ruin them.

She was lucky enough to squat down next to a grave that had a wreath with a ribbon on it, so she proceeded to dry with that.

After the girls did their business they proceeded to go home.

The next day one of the woman's husband was concerned that his normally sweet and innocent wife was still in bed hung over, so he phoned the other husband and said: 'These girl nights out have got to stop! I'm starting to suspect the worst. .. my wife came home with no panties!!'

'That's nothing' said the other husband, 'Mine came back with a card stuck to her ass that read... ..

**'From all of us at the Fire Station.
We'll never forget you."**

Grandpa on the Porch

A boy was walking down the street when he noticed his grandpa sitting on the porch, in the rocking chair, with nothing on from the waist down. "Grandpa what are you doing?" he exclaimed. The old man looked off in the distance and did not answer him. "Grandpa, what are you doing sitting out here with nothing on below the waist?" he asked again. The old man slowly looked at him and said, "Well, last week I sat out here with no shirt on, and I got a stiff neck. This is your Grandma's idea."

Guy falls asleep on the beach

A guy falls asleep on the beach for several hours and gets a horrible sunburn. He goes to the hospital, and is promptly admitted after being diagnosed with second-degree burns. With his skin already starting to blister, and the severe pain he was in, the doctor prescribes continuous intravenous feeding with saline, electrolytes, a sedative, and a Viagra pill every four hours.

The nurse, who is rather astounded, says, "What good will Viagra do for him, Doctor?

The doctor replied, "It will keep the sheets off his legs."

Hair Color

There was a blonde, brunette and green haired lady. They were all talking about each others hair. The blonde said: "Oh, I poured bleach on mine." The brunette said: "Oh, I dyed mine." The green haired lady sneezed into her hair and said: "It's natural."

Hammer Fall

Little Johnny came downstairs bellowing lustily. His mother asked, "What's the matter now?"

"Dad was hanging pictures, and just hit his thumb with a hammer," said Johnny through his tears.

"That's not so serious," soothed his mother. "I know you're upset, but a big boy like you shouldn't cry at something like that. Why didn't you just laugh?"

"I did!" sobbed Johnny

Hot Things Hot and Cold Things Cold

One day Mike was sitting in his apartment when his doorbell unexpectedly rang. He answered the door and found a salesman standing on his porch with a strange object. "What is that?" Mike asked.

"It's a thermos," the salesman replied.

"What does it do?" asked Mike.

"This baby," the salesman said, "keeps hot things hot and cold things cold."

After some deliberation Mike bought one, deciding it would really help his lunch situation. The next day he arrived at the plant where he works. Sure enough, all the other employees were curious about his new object.

"What is it?" they asked.

"It's a thermos," Mike replied.

"What does it do?" they asked.

"Well," Mike says in a bragging manner, "It keeps hot things hot and cold things cold."

"What do ya got in it?"

To which Mike says, "Three cups of coffee and a popsicle."

I Was Afraid it Was Going to Bark

A young lady in the maternity ward just prior to labor is asked by the midwife if she would like her husband to be present at the birth. "I'm afraid I don't have a husband" she replies

"O.K. do you have a boyfriend?" asks the Midwife "No, no boyfriend either."

"Do you have a partner then?" "No, I'm unattached, I'll be having my baby on my own."

After the birth the midwife again speaks to the young woman. "You have a healthy bouncing baby girl, but I must warn you before you see her that the baby is black"

"Well," replies the girl. "I was very down on my luck, with no money and nowhere to live, and so I accepted a job in a Porno movie. The lead man was black."

"Oh, I'm very sorry," says the midwife, "that's really none of my business and I'm sorry that I have to ask you these awkward questions but I must also tell you that the baby has blonde hair."

"Well yes," the girl again replies, "you see I desperately needed the money and there was this Swedish guy also involved in the movie, what else could I do?"

"Oh, I'm sorry," the midwife repeats, "that's really none of my business and I hate to pry further but your baby has slanted eyes."

"Well yes," continues the girl, "I was incredibly hard up and there was a little Chinese man also in the movie, I really had no choice."

At this the midwife again apologizes collects the baby and presents her to the girl, who immediately proceeds to give baby a slap on the bum. The baby starts crying and the mother exclaims, "Well thank the fuck for that!"

"What do you mean?" says the midwife, shocked.

"Well," says the girl extremely relieved, "I had this horrible feeling that the little bastard was going to bark!"

I Was Afraid You Were About to Blow!

A large, powerfully-built guy meets a woman at a bar. After a number of drinks, they agree to go back to his place. As they are making out in the bedroom, he stands up and starts to undress. After he takes his shirt off, he flexes his muscular arms and says, "See that, baby? That's 1000 pounds of dynamite!"

She begins to drool.

The man drops his pants, strikes a body builder's pose, and says, referring to his bulging thighs, "See those, baby? That's 1000 pounds of dynamite!"

She is aching for action at this point.

Finally, he drops his underpants, and after a quick glance, she grabs her purse and runs screaming to the front door. He catches her before she is able to leave and asks, "Why are you in such a hurry to go?" She replies, "With 2000 pounds of dynamite and such a short fuse, I was afraid you were about to blow!"

Idiot Joke

Two men were digging a ditch on a very hot day. One said to the other, "Why are we down in this hole digging a ditch when our boss is standing up there in the shade of a tree?"

"I don't know," responded the other. "I'll ask him." So he climbed out of the hole and went to his boss. "Why are we digging in the hot sun and you're standing in the shade?"

"Intelligence," the boss said.

"What do you mean, intelligence'?"

The boss said, "Well, I'll show you. I'll put my hand on this tree and I want you to hit it with your fist as hard as you can."

The ditch digger took a mighty swing and tried to hit the boss' hand. The boss removed his hand and the ditch digger hit the tree. The boss said, "That's intelligence!"

The ditch digger went back to his hole. His friend asked, "What did he say?"

"He said we are down here because of intelligence."

"What's intelligence?" said the friend.

The ditch digger put his hand on his face and said, "Take your shovel and hit my hand."

I'm The Boss

The company boss was complaining in a staff meeting that he wasn't getting any respect. Later that morning he went to a local sign shop and bought a small sign that read: "I'm the Boss!"

He then taped it to his office door.

Later that day when he returned from lunch, he found that someone had taped a note to the sign that said:

"Your wife called, she wants her sign back!"

Important Rules For Men

1.   It's important to have a woman who helps at home, who cooks from time to time, cleans up and has a job.

2. It's important to have a woman who can make you laugh.

3. It's important to have a woman who you can trust and who doesn't lie to you.

4. It's important to have a woman who is good in bed and who likes to be with you.

5. It's very, very important that these four women don't know each other.

In The Groove

A hippy walks into a Bar and Grill. The waiter comes up to him and asks him if he wants anything.

So the Hippy says 'Yeah a cheeseburger. Not too well done, not to rare, but right in the groove.'

So the waiter brings his burger and asks if he wants anything to drink.

He says 'A cup of tea. Not too hot, not too cold, but right in the Groove.'

The waiter's kinda getting pissed now, but he brings the tea and kinda slams it on the table. Little while later the waiter comes back and asks the Hippy if he wants any dessert.

He says 'Yeah some ice cream. Not too chocolate, not too vanilla, but right in the Groove.'

So the waiter says 'Why don't you kiss my ass. Not the right cheek, not the left cheek, but right in the Groove!'

Iron Supplements

A ranch woman takes her three sons to the doctor for physicals for the first time in their lives.

The doctor examines the boys and tells the woman that they are healthy but she needs to give them iron supplements. She goes home and wonders exactly what iron supplements are. Finally, she goes to the hardware store and buys iron ball bearings (BB's) and mixes them into their food.

Several days later the youngest son comes to her and tells her that he is pissing BB's. She tells him that it is normal because she had put them in his food. Later the middle son comes to her and says that he is crapping BB's. Again, she says that it is ok.

That evening the eldest son comes in very upset. He says "Ma, you won't believe what happened". She says "I know, you're passing BB's". "No", he says. "I was out behind the barn jacking off and I shot the dog".

It's Contagious

"Doc, I think my son has gonorrhea," a patient told his urologist on the phone. "The only woman he's screwed is our maid."

"Ok, don't be hard on him. He's just a kid," the medic soothed. "Get him in here right away and I'll take care of him."

"But, Doc. I've been screwing the maid too and I've got the same symptoms he has."

"Then you come in with him and I'll fix you both up." Replied the doctor. "Well," the man admitted, " I think my wife now has it too."

"Son of a bitch!" the physician roared. "That means we've all got it!"

It's Precious

Miss Annabell had just returned from her big trip to New York City and was having refreshments on the front porch of her daddy's mansion with her southern belle friends. She tells them the stories of her trip as they stare spellbound. "You just wouldn't believe what they have there in New York City," says Miss Annabell. "They have men there who kiss other men on the lips."

Miss Annabell's friends fan themselves and say, "Oh my! Oh my!"

"They call them homosexuals," proclaims Miss Annabell.

"Oh my! Oh my," proclaim the girls as they fan themselves.

"They also have women there in New York City who kiss other women on the lips!"

"Oh my! Oh my," exclaim the girls. "What do they call them?" they ask.

"They call them lesbians," says Miss Annabell.

"They also have men who kiss women between the legs, there in New York City," sighs Miss Annabell.

"Oh my! Oh my! Oh my," exclaim the girls as they sit on the edge of their chairs and fan themselves even faster. "What do they call them?" they ask in unison. Miss Annabell leans forward and says in a hush, "Why when I caught my breath, I called him Precious."

Know It All

Chaffee could talk on any subject whether he knew anything about it or not. Mostly he didn't. One day his neighbor Nibley could stand no more. "Do you realize," asked Nibley, "that you and I know all there is to be known?"

"Do you really think so?" said Chaffee. "How do you figure that?"

"Easy," answered Nibley. "You know everything except that you're a damn idiot. And I know that!"

Lemons

A woman went to a Florida lemon grove to apply for a job, but the foreman thought she seemed way too qualified for the position. "Do you even have any actual experience picking lemons?" he asked.

"Well, I think I do." she replied. "I've been divorced three times."

Let's Talk

A guy was seated next to a 10-year-old girl on an airplane. Being bored, he turned to the girl and said, "Let's talk. I've heard that flights go quicker if you strike up a conversation with your fellow passenger."

The girl, who was reading a book, closed it slowly and said to the guy, "What would you like to talk about?"

Oh, I don't know," said the guy. "How about nuclear power?"

"OK," she said. "That could be an interesting topic. But let me ask you a question first. A horse, a cow and a deer all eat the same stuff... grass. Yet a deer excretes little pellets, while a cow turns out a flat patty, and a horse produces clumps of dried grass. Why do you suppose that is?"

The guy thought about it and said, "Hmmm, I have no idea."

To which the girl replied, "Do you really feel qualified to discuss nuclear power when you don't know shit?"

Like The Way You Think

Teacher - "Right, there are five birds sitting on a telephone line. A farmer comes along with his gun and shoots one of them. How many are left?"

Little Johnny - "None Miss".

Teacher - "Could you tell me why?"

Little Johnny - "Well Miss, when the farmer shot the bird, the sound of the gun would have frightened the other birds away".

Teacher - "Well, the answer I was looking for was four. But I like your thinking."

Little Johnny - "Miss, while we're asking questions, could I ask you one?"

Teacher - "Its a bit irregular, but go on then"

Little Johnny - "There are three women sitting on a bench in the park, eating ice lollies. One of them is licking the lolly; one is biting it; and one is putting it in and out of her mouth. Which one is married?"

Teacher (rather embarrassed) - "Err... I suppose it was the last one."

Little Johnny - "Well I'd have said the one with the wedding ring. But I like your thinking."

Mad at His Stubborn Girlfriend

A young guy was complaining to his Boss about the problems he was having with his stubborn girlfriend. "She gets me so angry sometimes I could hit her," the young man exclaimed.

"Well, I'll tell you what I used to do with my wife" replied the Boss. "Whenever she got out of hand I'd take her pants down and spank her".

Shaking his head the young guy replied "I've tried that... it doesn't work for me. Once I get her pants down I'm not mad anymore."

Medical Distinction Between Guts and Balls

There is a medical distinction between Guts and Balls. We've all heard about people having Guts or Balls. But do you really know the difference between them? In an effort to keep you informed, here are the definitions:

GUTS - Is arriving home late after a night out with the boys, being met by your wife with a broom, and having the guts to ask: 'Are you still cleaning, or are you flying somewhere?'

BALLS - Is coming home late after a night out with the guys, smelling of perfume and lipstick on your collar, slapping your wife on the butt and having the balls to say: 'You're next, Chubby.'

I hope this clears up any confusion on the definitions. Medically, speaking there is no difference in the outcome...both result in death!

Microsoft Support

A Microsoft support man goes to a firing range. He shoots 10 bullets at the target 50m away.

Then the supervisors check the target and see that there's not even a single hit, and they shout to him that he missed completely.

So he tells them to recheck, and gets the same answer.

Then he put his finger at the top of the gun and shoots, blasting off his finger.

When he saw it he shouted back "I don't know, it's working perfectly here, the problem must yours..."

MISSISSIPPI

A bus stops and 2 men get on. They sit down and engage in an animated conversation.

The lady sitting next to them ignores them at first, but her attention is galvanized when she hears one of them say the following:

"Emma come first.
Den I come.
Den two asses come together.
I come once-a-more! .
Two asses, they come together again.
I come again and pee twice.
Then I come one lasta time."

The lady can't take this any more, "You foul-mouthed sex obsessed pig," she retorted indignantly. "In this country. we don't speak aloud in Public places about our sex lives."

"Hey, coola down lady," said the man.

"Who talkin'abouta sex? I'm a justa tellin' my frienda how to spell 'Mississippi'."

(I bet you're gonna read this joke again!)

Motorcycle Ride

There were two guys on a motorcycle driving down the road. The driver was wearing a leather jacket that didn't have a zipper or any buttons.

Finally he stopped the bike and told the other guy, "I can't drive anymore with the air hitting me in my chest."

After thinking for a while he decided to put the coat on backwards to block the air from hitting him. So they were driving down the road and they came around this curb and wrecked. The farmer that lived there called the police and told them what happened.

The police asked him, "Are either of them showing any life signs?"

The farmer then said, "Well, that first one was 'til I turned his head around the right way."

Multiple Meanings

There is a two-letter word that perhaps has more meanings than any other two-letter word, and that is "UP."

It's easy to understand UP, meaning toward the sky or at the top of the list, but when we awaken in the morning, why do we wake UP? At a meeting, why does a topic come UP? Why do we speak UP and why are the officers UP for election and why is it UP to the secretary to write UP a report? We call UP our friends. And we use it to brighten UP a room, polish UP! the silver, we warm UP the leftovers and clean UP the kitchen. We lock UP the house and some guys fix UP the old car. At other times the little word has real special meaning. People stir UP trouble, line UP for tickets, work UP an appetite, and think UP excuses. To be dressed is one thing but to be dressed UP is special.

And this UP is confusing: A drain must be opened UP because it is stopped UP. We open UP a store in the morning but we close it UP at night.

We seem to be pretty mixed UP about UP! To be knowledgeable about the proper uses of UP, look the word UP in the dictionary. In a desk-sized dictionary, it takes UP almost 1/4th of the page and can add UP to about thirty definitions. If you are UP to it, you might try building UP a list of the many ways UP is used. It will take UP a lot of your time, but if you don't give UP, you may wind UP with a hundred or more. When it threatens to rain, we say it is clouding UP. When the sun comes out we say it is clearing UP.

When it rains, it wets the earth and often messes things UP.

When it doesn't rain for awhile, things dry UP.

One could go on and on, but I'll! wrap it UP, for now my time is UP, so..........Time to shut UP!

Oh...one more thing:

What is the first thing you do in the morning and the last thing you do at night? U-P

My Magic Green Hat

The other day I needed to go to the emergency room.
Not wanting to sit there for 4 hours, I put on my MAGIC GREEN HAT.
When I went into the E.R., I noticed that 3/4 of the people got up and left.

I guess they decided that they weren't that sick after all.
Cut at least 3 hours off my waiting time.

Here's the hat.

It also works at DMV. It saved me 5 hours.

At the Laundromat, three minutes after entering, I had my choice of any machine, most still running.

But...don't try it at McDonald's. *The <u>whole crew</u> got up and left and I never got my order!*

NEW EMPLOYEE POLICY

As a result of the money budgeted for department areas, we are forced to cut down our number of personnel. Under this plan older employees will be asked to go on to early retirement, thus permitting the retention of younger employees who represent our future. Therefore, a program to phase out our older personnel by the end of the current fiscal year, via retirement, will be placed into effect immediately.

This program will be known as SLAP (Sever Late-Aged Personnel). Employees who are SLAPPED will be given the opportunity to look for jobs outside the company. SLAPPED employees can request a review of their employment records before actual retirement takes place. This phase of the program is called SCREW (Survey of Capabilities of Retiring Early Workers).

All employees who have been SLAPPED or SCREWED may file an appeal with upper management. This is called SHAFT (Study by Higher Authority Following Termination). Under the terms of the new policy, an employee may be SLAPPED once, SCREWED twice, but may be SHAFTED as many times as the company deems appropriate.

If an employee follows the above procedures, he or she will be entitled to get HERPES (Half Earnings for Retired Personnel's Early Severance) or CLAP (Combined Lump-sum Assistance Payment), unless he or she already has AIDS (Additional Income from Dependents or Spouse). As HERPES or CLAP are considered benefit plans, any employee who has received HERPES OR CLAP will no longer be SLAPPED or SCREWED by the company.

Management wishes to assure the younger employees who remain on board that the company will continue its policy of training employees through our Special High Intensity Training (SHIT). This company takes pride in the amount of SHIT our employees receive. We have given our employees more SHIT than any company in this area. If any employee feels they do not receive enough SHIT on the job, see your immediate supervisor.

Your supervisor is specially trained to make sure you receive all the SHIT that you can stand.

Newly Weds

A couple had only been married for two weeks. The husband, although very much in love, couldn't wait to go out on the town and party with his old buddies. So, he said to his new wife, "Honey, I'll be right back."

Where are you going, Coochy Coo?" asked the wife.

"I'm going to the bar, Pretty Face. I'm going to have a beer."

The wife said, "You want a beer, my love?" She opened the door to the refrigerator and showed him 25 different kinds of beer -- brands from 12 different countries including Germany, Holland, Japan, Czech Republic, etc.

The husband didn't know what to do, and the only thing that he could think of saying was, "Yes, Lollipop... but at the bar... You know... they have frozen glasses."

He didn't get to finish the sentence, because the wife interrupted him by saying, "You want a frozen glass, Puppy Face?" She took a huge beer mug out of the freezer, so frozen that chunks of ice were forming out of the air on it.

The husband, looking a bit pale, said, "Yes, Tootsie Roll, but at the bar they have those hors d'oeuvres. I won't be long. I'll be right back. I promise. OK?"

"You want hors d'oeuvres, Poochie Pooh?" She opened the oven and took out several kinds of hot, home-made hors d'oeuvres.

"But my sweet honey... at the bar.... you know there's swearing, dirty words and all that...."

"You want dirty words, Cutie Pie? Fine! Sit your ass down, shut the hell up, drink your beer in your frozen mug, and eat your hors d' oeuvres because your married ass isn't going to a damned bar! Got it, jackass?"

And they lived happily ever after. Isn't that a sweet story?

Nice Suit

A guy goes into a clothing store to buy a new suit, but he doesn't want to spend too much money. The tailor shows him a really nice suit for $400, but the guy says it's too much. He shows him another suit for $200, and the guy says it's still too much. After showing him several others, he finally shows him one for $10.

"That's more like it!", the guy says, and he goes to try it on. He comes back and looks in the mirror and one sleeve is about two inches shorter than the other.

"No problem," says the tailor, "Just hunch up your right shoulder."

So the guy hunches his right shoulder way up, and the sleeves look OK, but the lapels are crooked.

"No problem," says the tailor, "Just stick out your left arm and cock it like a bird's wing."

So the guy sticks out his left arm and the lapels look OK. But then he notices that one pant leg is shorter than the other.

"Well, just keep that leg stiff," says the tailor, "and no one will notice."

"I'll take it!" the guy says.

So the guy leaves the tailor shop wearing the suit, walking with his left leg stiffened, one arm stuck out like a bird's wing, and one shoulder hunched way up.

As he's walking down the street he passes two orthopedic surgeons. One of the doctors says to the other, "I have never seen anyone in such bad shape in my twenty-five years of practice!"

"Me neither," the other doctor says. "But he sure has a nice suit!"

No Ears

A man with no ears is trying to find a new reporter for their news show.

The first guy walks in and the boss says, "This job requires you noticing a lot of details. What is one thing you notice about me?" And the guy says, "Well shit! You got no ears man!" So the boss yells "Get out!".

So the next guy comes in and the boss says to him, "This job requires you noticing a lot of details. What is something you notice about me?" And the guy says, "That's easy. You got no ears!" So the boss says, to him, "Get out!"

As the second guy leaves he sees the third guy about to go in and says to him, "The boss has no ears so don't say anything about them, he is really sensitive about it." So the guy goes in and the boss says, "This job requires you to notice a lot of details. What is one that you notice about me?" So the guy says, "Your wearing contacts!" And the boss says, "Yeah, how did you know?" So the guy replies, "Well shit, you can't wear glasses 'cause you ain't got no ears."

No Hangover from Jet Fuel

A couple of drinkin' buddies, who are airplane mechanics, are in the hangar at Logan; it's fogged in and they have nothing to do. One of them says to the other, "Man, have you got anything to drink?"

The other one says, "Nah, but I hear you can drink jet fuel, and that it will kinda give you a buzz."

So they drink it, get smashed and have a great time; like only drinkin' buddies can do. The following morning, one of them gets up and is surprised he feels good, in fact, he feels great - NO hangover! The phone rings, it's his buddy.

The buddy says, "Hey, how do you feel?"

He said, "I feel great!!", and the buddy says, "I feel great too!! You don't have a hangover?" and he says, "No -that jet fuel is great stuff - no hangover - we ought to do this more often."

"Yeah, we could, but there's just one thing....."

"What's that?"

"Did you fart yet?"

"No"

"Well, DON'T, 'cause I'm in Phoenix!"

Nymphomania Convention

A man boarded an airplane and took his seat. As he settled in, he glanced up & saw the most beautiful woman boarding the plane.

He soon realized she was heading straight towards his seat. As fate would have it, she took the seat right beside his.

Eager to strike up a conversation he blurted out, "Business trip or pleasure?"

She turned, smiled and said, "Business. I'm going to the Annual Nymphomaniacs of America Convention in Boston."

He swallowed hard. Here was the most gorgeous woman he had ever seen sitting next to him and she was going to a meeting of nymphomaniacs. Struggling to maintain his composure, he calmly asked, "What's your business role at this convention?"

"Lecturer," she responded. "I use information that I have learned from my personal experiences to debunk some of the popular myths about sexuality."

"Really?" he said. "And what kind of myths are there?"

"Well," she explained,   one popular myth is that African-American men are the most well-endowed of all men, when in fact it is the Native American Indian who is most likely to possess that trait.

Another popular myth is that Frenchmen are the best lovers when actually it is men of Jewish descent who are the best. I have also discovered that the lover with absolutely the best stamina is the Southern Redneck."

Suddenly the woman became a little uncomfortable and blushed. "I'm sorry," she said, "I shouldn't really be discussing all of this with you. I don't even know your name."

"Tonto," the man said, "Tonto Goldstein, but my friends call me Bubba."

Once Upon a Time There Lived a King

Once upon a time there lived a King.
The king had a beautiful daughter, the PRINCESS.

But there was a problem. Everything the Princess touched would melt.

No matter what; metal, wood, stone,

Anything she touched would melt.

Because of this, men were afraid of her. Nobody would dare marry her.

The King despaired. What could he do to help his daughter?

He consulted his wizards and magicians. One wizard told the King, 'If your daughter touches one thing that does not melt in her hands, she will be cured.'

The King was overjoyed and came up with a plan next day, he held a competition. Any man that could bring his daughter an object that would not melt would marry her and inherit the King's wealth.

THREE YOUNG PRINCES TOOK UP THE CHALLENGE.

The first brought a sword of the finest steel.

But alas, when the Princess touched it, it melted, and t he prince went away sadly.

The second Prince brought diamonds.

He thought diamonds are the hardest substance in the world and would not melt. But alas, once the Princess touched them, they melted. He too was sent away disappointed.

The third Prince approached. He told the Princess,

'Put your hand in my pocket and feel what is in there.'

The Princess did as she was told, though she turned red.

She felt something hard. She held it in her hand.

And it did not melt!!!

The King was overjoyed. Everybody in the kingdom was overjoyed. And the third Prince married the Princess and they both lived happily ever after.

Question: What was in the Prince's pants?

(Scroll down for the answer)

M&M's of course. They melt in your mouth, not in your hand.

What were you thinking??

Pancakes

Two brothers went downstairs for breakfast, where their mother was cooking.

"What do you want for breakfast?" asked the mother.

"Shit, I want some fucking pancakes," said the first brother.

The mother slapped him across the face.

"We don't talk like that in this house. Now, how about you, son? I hope you've learned a lesson from your brother. What do you want for breakfast?"

"I've sure learned my lesson! You can bet your ass I don't want any fucking pancakes!"

Party Entertainment...

A lady is throwing a party for her granddaughter, and had gone all out..... a caterer, band, and a hired clown. Just before the party started, two bums showed up looking for a handout. Feeling sorry for the bums, the woman told them that she would give them a meal if they would help chop some wood for her out back. Gratefully, they headed to the rear of the house.

The guests arrived, and all was going well with the children having a wonderful time. But the clown hadn't shown up. After a half an hour, the clown finally called to report that he was stuck in traffic, and would probably not make the party at all.

The woman was very disappointed and unsuccessfully tried to entertain the children herself. She happened to look out the window and saw one of the bums doing cartwheels across the lawn. She watched in awe as he swung from tree branches, did midair flips, and leaped high in the air.

She spoke to the other bum and said, "What your friend is doing is absolutely marvelous. I have never seen such a thing. Do you think your friend would consider repeating this performance for the children at the party? I would pay him $100!"

The other bum says, "Well, I dunno. Let me ask him. HEY WILLIE! FOR $100, WOULD YOU CHOP OFF ANOTHER TOE?"

Payback is Hell

Two high school sweethearts who went out together for four years in high school were both virgins; they enjoyed losing their virginity with each other in 10th grade. When they graduated, they wanted to both go to the same college but the girl was accepted to a college on the east coast, and the guy went to the west coast. They agreed to be faithful to each other and spend anytime they could together.

As time went on, the guy would call the girl and she would never be home, and when he wrote, she would take weeks to return the letters. Even when he emailed her, she took days to return his messages.

Finally, she confessed to him she wanted to date around. He didn't take this very well and increased his calls, letters, and emails trying to win back her love. Because she became annoyed, and now had a new boyfriend, she wanted to get him off her back.

So, what she did is this: she took a Polaroid picture of her having sex with her new boyfriend and sent it to her old boyfriend with a note reading, "I found a new boyfriend, leave me alone." Well, needless to say, this guy was heartbroken but, even more so, was pissed. So, what he did next was awesome.

He wrote on the back of the photo the following, "Dear Mom and Dad, having a great time at college, please send more money!" and mailed the picture to her parents.

PECANS IN THE CEMETERY

On the outskirts of a small town, there was a big, old pecan tree just inside the cemetery fence. One day, two boys filled up a bucketful of nuts and sat down by the tree, out of sight, and began dividing the nuts.

"One for you, one for me. One for you, one for me," said one boy. Several dropped and rolled down toward the fence.

Another boy came riding along the road on his bicycle. As he passed, he thought he heard voices from inside the cemetery. He slowed down to investigate. Sure enough, he heard, "One for you, one for me. One for you, one for me."

He just knew what it was. He jumped back on his bike and rode off. Just around the bend he met an old man with a cane, hobbling along.

"Come here quick," said the boy, "you won't believe what I heard! Satan and the Lord are down at the cemetery dividing up the souls."

The man said, "Beat it kid, can't you see it's hard for me to walk." When the boy insisted though, the man hobbled slowly to the cemetery.

Standing by the fence they heard, "One for you, one for me. One for you, one for me."

The old man whispered, "Boy, you've been tellin' me the truth. Let's see if we can see the Lord."

Shaking with fear, they peered through the fence, yet were still unable to see anything. The old man and the boy gripped the wrought iron bars of the fence tighter and tighter as they tried to get a glimpse of the Lord.

At last they heard, "One for you, one for me. That's all. Now let's go get those nuts by the fence and we'll be done."

They say the old man made it back to town a full 5 minutes ahead of the kid on the bike.

PEE or Not To PEE

A mother took her little boy to church. While in church the little boy said, "Mommy, I have to pee." The mother said to the little boy, "It's not appropriate to say the word 'pee' in church. So, from now on whenever you have to 'pee' just tell me that you have to 'whisper.'"

The following Sunday, the little boy went to church with his father and during the service said to his father, "Daddy, I have to whisper." The father looked at him and said, "Okay, why don't you whisper in my ear."

Peek-A-Boo

A guy walks into a psychiatrist's office covered only in Saran Wrap. He says to the doctor, "I've felt so weird lately, Doc, can you tell me what's wrong?"

The doctor replied, "Well, I can clearly see your nuts!"

Pepper

A man and a woman are sitting beside each other in the first class section of the plane. The woman sneezes, takes a tissue, gently wipes her nose, and shudders quite violently in her seat. The man isn't sure why she is shuddering and goes back to reading. A few minutes pass. The woman sneezes again. She takes a tissue, gently wipes her nose and shudders quite violently in her seat. The man is becoming more and more curious about the shuddering. A few more minutes pass. The woman sneezes yet again. She takes a tissue, gently wipes her nose and shudders violently again.

The man has finally had all he can handle. He turns to the woman and says, "Three times you've sneezed and three times you've taken a tissue and wiped your nose then shuddered violently! Are you sending me signals, or are you going crazy?"

The woman replies, "I'm sorry if I disturbed you. I have a rare condition and when I sneeze, I have an orgasm."

The man, now feeling a little embarrassed but even more curious says, "I've never heard of that before. What are you taking for it?"

The woman looks at him and says, "Pepper."

Preposition Ending

A gentleman wanders around the campus of a college looking for the library. He approaches a student and asked, "Excuse me young man. Would you be good enough and tell me where the library is at?"

The student, in a very arrogant and belittling tone, replied, "I'm sorry, sir, but at this school, we are taught never to end a sentence with a preposition!"

The gentleman smiled, and in a very apologetic tone replied, "I beg your pardon. Please allow me to rephrase my question. Would you be good enough to tell me where the library is at, dummy?"

Purina weight loss Diet

Yesterday I was buying a large bag of Purina dog chow for Blanche, our hunting dog, at Wal-Mart and was standing in line about to check out. A woman behind me asked if I had a dog. First thing I thought was 'where is your sign lady' but decided to go with it...

So.. on impulse, I told her that no, I didn't have a dog, and that I was starting the Purina weight loss diet again. I said I probably shouldn't because I had ended up in the hospital last time. That I'd lost 50 pounds before I awakened in an intensive care ward with tubes coming out of most of my orifices and IVs in both arms.

I told her that it was essentially a perfect diet and that the way that it works is, you load your pants pockets with Purina nuggets and simply eat one or two every time you feel hungry and that the food is nutritionally complete... so I was going to try it again. I have to mention here that practically everyone in the line was by now enthralled with my story to say the least.

Totally horrified, the lady asked if I ended up in intensive care because the dog food poisoned me. I told her no; I had stepped off a curb to sniff an Irish Setter's ass and a car hit both of us.

I thought the guy behind her was going to have a heart attack he was laughing so hard.

Wal-Mart asked me not to shop there anymore.

Read The Labels

As I was conditioning my hair in the shower this morning, I took time to read my shampoo bottle. I am in shock! The shampoo I use in the shower that runs down my entire body says "for extra volume and body"! Seriously, why have I not noticed this before? Now I understand why I am so "full-figured!" Tomorrow I am going to start using "Dawn" dish soap. It says right on the label "dissolves fat that is otherwise difficult to remove."

It pays to read the warning labels my friends!

Rodeo Style

These two boys were talking about their sex lives and different techniques to make it really good. One of the guys asked the other if he knew how to do it rodeo-style. The other guy said no and asked him to explain.

"That's where you start out doing it doggy-style, hold a breast in each hand, tell her that she feels SO much like your ex-girlfriend, then see if you can hold on for 8 seconds!'

Sad News...

Please join me in remembering a great icon of the entertainment industry. The Pillsbury Doughboy died yesterday of a yeast infection and trauma complications from repeated pokes in the belly. He was 71.

Doughboy was buried in a lightly greased coffin. Dozens of celebrities turned out to pay their respects, including Mrs.

Butterworth, Hungry Jack, the California Raisins, Betty Crocker, the Hostess Twinkies, and Captain Crunch. The grave site was piled high with flours. Aunt Jemima delivered the eulogy and lovingly described Doughboy as a man who never knew how much he was kneaded.

Doughboy rose quickly in show business, but his later life was filled with turnovers. He was not considered a very smart cookie, wasting much of his dough on half-baked schemes. Despite being a little flaky at times he still was a crusty old man and was considered a positive roll model for millions.

Doughboy is survived by his wife Play Dough, two children, John Dough and Jane Dough, plus they had one in the oven. He is also survived by his elderly father, PopTart. The funeral was held at 3:50 for about 20 minutes.

If this made you smile for even a brief second, please rise to the occasion and take time to pass it on and share a smile with someone else who may be having a crumby day and kneads it. Enjoy the sunrise and sunset today and always!

Salesman First Day on the Road

"So, how did you do?" the boss asked his new salesman after his first day on the road.

"All I got were two orders."

"What were they? Anything good?"

"Nope," the salesman replied. "They were 'Get out!' and 'Stay out!'"

Salesman Selling Toothbrushes

The top toothbrush salesman at the company was asked by his boss how he managed to sell so many brushes. He replied "It's easy" and he pulled out his card table, setting his display of brushes on top. He told his boss, I lay the brushes out like this, and then I put out some potato chips and dip to draw in the customers. He laid out his chips and dip.

His boss said, "That's a very innovative approach" and took one of the chips, dipped it, and stuck it in his mouth. "Yuck, this tastes terrible!" his boss yelled.

The salesman replied "IT IS! Want to buy a toothbrush?"

Scaffolding Accident

Steve, Bob, and Jeff were working on a very high scaffolding one day when suddenly, Steve falls off and is killed instantly. After the ambulance leaves with Steve's body, Bob and Jeff realize that one of them is going to have to tell Steve's wife.

Bob says he's good at this sort of sensitive stuff, so he volunteers to do the job. After two hours he returns, carrying a six-pack of beer.

"So did you tell her?" asks Jeff.

"Yep", replied Bob.

"Say, where did you get the six-pack?"

Bob informs Jeff. "She gave it to me!"

"What??" exclaims Jeff, "you just told her that her husband died and she gave you a six-pack??"

"Sure," Bob says.

"Why?" asks Jeff.

"Well," Bob continues, "when she answered the door, I asked her, 'are you Steve's widow?'

'Widow?' she said, 'no, no, you're mistaken, I'm not a widow!'

So I said: "I'll bet you a six-pack you ARE!"

Screw For The Hinge

Bubba was fixing a door and he found that he needed a new hinge, so he sent Mary Louise to the hardware store. At the hardware store Mary Louise saw a beautiful teapot on a top shelf while she was waiting for Joe Bob to finish waiting on a customer. When Joe Bob was finished, Mary Louise asked how much for the teapot? Joe Bob replied "That's silver and it costs $100!"

"My goodness, that sure is a lotta money!" Mary Louise exclaimed. She then proceeded to describe the hinge that Bubba had sent her to buy, and Jo Bob went to the backroom to find a hinge. From the backroom Joe Bob yelled "Mary Louise, you wanna screw for that hinge?' To which Mary Louise replied, "No, but I will for the teapot."

Shaky Arms Hotel

A man and his wife check into a hotel. The husband wants to have a drink at the bar, but his wife is extremely tired so she decides to go on up to their room to rest. She lies down on the bed... just then, and elevated train passes by very close to the window and shakes the room so hard she's thrown out of the bed. Thinking this must be a freak occurrence, she lies down once more. Again a train shakes the room so violently, she's pitched to the floor.

Exasperated, she calls the front desk, asks for the manager. The manager says he'll be right up. The manager is skeptical but the wife insists the story is true.

"Look... lie here, here on the bed -- you'll be thrown right to the floor!"

So he lies down next to the wife. Just then the husband walks in. "What," he says, "are you doing here?"

The manager calmly replies, "Would you believe I'm waiting for a train?"

Should be Hung

A man is lounging in his favorite chair, drinking a beer, while his wife is cutting the lawn.

A lady walking by sees this and yells at the man: "You should be hung!"

The man takes a drink of his beer, and says to the lady: "I am. That's why she's cutting the grass."

Six Foot Asshole

While she was 'flying' down the road yesterday, a woman passed over a bridge only to find a cop with a radar gun on the other side lying in wait.

The cop pulled her over, walked up to the car, with that classic patronizing smirk we all know and love, asked, 'What's your hurry?'

To which she replied, 'I'm late for work.'

'Oh yeah,' said the cop, 'what do you do?'

'I'm a rectum stretcher,' she responded.

The cop stammered, 'A what? A rectum stretcher?
And just what does a rectum stretcher do?'

'Well,' she said, 'I start by inserting one finger, then work my way up to two fingers, then three, then four, then with my whole hand in. I work from side to side until I can get both hands in, and then I slowly but surely stretch it, until it's about 6 feet wide.'

'And just what the heck do you do with a 6 foot butthole? ' he asked.

'You give him a radar gun and park him behind a bridge...'

Smart Pills

One day two boys were walking through the woods when they saw some rabbit turds. One of the boys said, "What is that?"

"They're smart pills," said the other boy. "Eat them and they'll make you smarter.

So he ate them and said, "These taste like shit."

"See," said the other boy, "you're getting smarter already."

Southern Skinny Dippin' . . .

An elderly man in North Carolina had owned a large farm for several years. He had a large pond in the back, fixed up really nice, along with some picnic tables, horseshoe courts, and some apple and peach trees. The pond was properly shaped and fixed up for swimming when it was built.

One evening the old farmer decided to go down to the pond, as he hadn't been there for a while, and look it over. He grabbed a five gallon bucket to bring back some fruit.

As he neared the pond, he heard voices shouting and laughing with glee. When he came closer, he realized it was a bunch of young women skinny-dipping in his pond. He made the women aware of his presence and they all went to the deep end to shield themselves.

One of the women shouted to him, "We're not coming out until you leave!"

The old man frowned and replied, "I didn't come down here to watch you ladies swim naked or make you get out of the pond naked." Holding the bucket up he said, "I'm here to feed the alligator."

Moral of the story: Old men may move slow but can still think fast.

Stroke of Bad Luck

A guy heard from his doctor that masturbating before sex could help him last longer. So he decided to try it. He spent the rest of the day thinking about where to do it. He couldn't do it in his office, so he thought about the restroom, but that was too open. He considered an alley, but figured he might get mugged.

Finally, he was inspired. On his way home, he pulled his truck over on the side of the highway. He got out and crawled underneath as if he was examining the truck. Satisfied with the privacy, he undid his pants and started to masturbate. He closed his eyes and thought of his lover. As he grew closer to orgasm, he felt a quick tug at the bottom of his pants. Not wanting to lose his mental fantasy or the orgasm, he kept his eyes shut and said, "What?"

He heard, "This is the police. What's going on here?"

The man replied, "I'm checking out the rear axle, it's busted."

"Well, you might as well check your brakes too while you're down there because your truck rolled down the hill five minutes ago."

Sunday School Daze

Mary can't stand Sunday school, but her brother William doesn't have a problem with it. So one day in Sunday school, Mary thinks, "The hell with it," and decides to go to sleep. The teacher sees this and asks Mary a question to keep her awake.

"Mary, who created the heavens and the earth?"

William, who is sitting behind Mary, pokes her in the butt with his pencil. Mary wakes up and shouts, "God almighty!"

And the teacher says, "Yes. That's correct, Mary."

Mary goes back to sleep and the teacher asks her another question.

"Who died on the cross for our sins?"

William pokes Mary again. She wakes up and shouts, "Jesus Christ!"

Once again, she goes back to sleep. This time the teacher asks, "Mary, what was the first thing Eve said to Adam?"

William pokes her again. Mary wakes up and shouts, "If you don't stop poking me with that thing, I'm gonna break it off!"

Temper and the Farmer's Wife

Through the kitchen window a farmer's wife sees her son coming home from school. The boy's in a bad mood, and as he crosses the field he kicks a pig. He walks a little further and kicks a cow.

Once inside, his mother says, "I saw what you did, young man! For kicking the pig you'll get no bacon for a week, and for kicking the cow, no milk for a week."

Just at that moment, the boy's father walks through the door and boots the cat halfway across the room.

The boy looks at his mother and says, "Do you wanna tell him, or should I?"

Ten Minutes to Go

A well dressed business man was walking down the street when a little kid covered in soot said to him respectfully, "Sir, can you tell me the time?"

The portly man stopped, carefully unbuttoned his coat and jacket, removed a large watch from a vest pocket, looked at it and said, "It is a quarter to three, young man."

"Thanks," said the boy. "At exactly three o'clock you can kiss my ass."

With that, the kid took off running, and with an angry cry, the outraged businessman started chasing him.

He had not been running long when an old friend stopped him. "Why are you running like this at your age?" asked the friend.

Gasping and almost incoherent with fury, the business man said, "That little brat asked me the time and when I told him it was quarter to three he told me that at exactly three, I should kiss his ass!"

"So what's your hurry," said the friend. "You still have ten minutes."

Tennessee State Troopers Don't Have Balls

A young woman was pulled over in Nashville, Tennessee for speeding. As the Tennessee State Trooper walked to her car window, flipping open his ticket book, she said, "I bet you are going to sell me a ticket to the Tennessee State Police Ball."

He replied, "Tennessee State Troopers don't have balls."

There was a moment of silence while she smiled and he realized what he'd just said. He then closed his book, got back in his patrol car and left.

She was laughing too hard to start her car.

Test of Time

A young boy was looking through the family album and asked his mother, "Who's this guy on the beach with you with all the muscles and curly hair?"

"That's your father."

"Then who's that old bald-headed fat man who lives with us now?"

Texas Baby

A man from Texas buys a round of drinks for everyone in the bar as he announces his wife has just produced "A typical Texas baby boy weighing twenty pounds." Congratulations shower all around, and many exclamations of 'wow!' are heard.

Two weeks later he returns to the bar. The bartender says, 'Say, you're the father of the typical Texas baby that weighed twenty pounds at birth, aren't you? How much does the baby weigh now?'

The proud father answers, 'fifteen pounds.'

The bartender is puzzled. 'Why? What happened? He already weighed twenty pounds at birth.'

The Texas father takes a slow sip from his beer, wipes his lips on his shirt sleeve, leans over to the bartender and proudly announces, 'Had him circumcised.'

THE GUNFIGHTER

A young man in the Old West wanted to be the best gunfighter alive. He practiced every day, but knew he was still missing something that would make him the best.

One night, as he was sitting in a saloon, he spotted an old man who had the reputation of being the greatest gunfighter in his day. So the young fella went over to the old man and told him his dream. The old man looked him up and down and said, "I have a suggestion that is sure to help."

"Tell me, tell me," said the young man.

"Tie the bottom of your holster lower onto your leg."

"Will that make me a better gunfighter?"

"Definitely," said the old man.

The young gunman did what he was told, then in a flash he drew his gun and shot the bow tie off the piano player. "Wow, that really helped. Do you have any more suggestions?"

"Yeah, if you cut a notch in the top of your holster where the hammer hits, the gun will come out smoother."

"Will that make me a better gunfighter?"

"It sure will," said the old man.

The young guy did what he was told, drew his gun in a blur and shot the cufflink off the piano player. "This is really helping me. Is there anything else you can share with me?"

"One more thing," said the old man, "Get that can of axle grease over there in the corner and rub it all over your gun." The young man didn't hesitate but started putting the grease just on the barrel of the gun.

"No, the whole gun, handle and everything," said the old man.

"Will that make me a better gunfighter?"

"No," said the old man, "but when Wyatt Earp gets done playing that piano he's going to shove that gun up your ass, and it won't hurt as much."

The Old NAVY CHIEF

A circus owner runs an ad for a lion tamer and two people show up. One is a good looking, older retired Navy Chief in his late sixties and the other is a gorgeous blond in her mid-twenties.

The circus owner tells them, "I'm not going to sugar coat it. This is one ferocious lion. He ate my last tamer so you two had better be good or you're history. Here's your equipment -- chair, whip and a gun. Who wants to try out first?"

The girl says, "I'll go first.." She walks past the chair, the whip and the gun and steps right into the lion's cage. The lion starts to snarl and pant and begins to charge her. About halfway there, she throws open her coat revealing her beautiful naked body.

The lion stops dead in his tracks, sheepishly crawls up to her and starts licking her feet and ankles. He continues to lick and kiss her entire body for several minutes and then rests his head at her feet.

The circus owner's jaw is on the floor. He says, "I've never seen a display like that in my life." He then turns to the retired Navy Chief and asks, "Can you top that?"

The tough old Chief replies, "No problem, just get that lion out of there."

The Power of Alcohol

A man is waiting for his wife to give birth. The doctor comes in and informs the dad that his son was born without torso, arms or legs. The son is just a head! But the dad loves his son and raises him as well as he can, with love and compassion.

After 21 years, the son is now old enough for his first drink. Dad takes him to the bar, tearfully tells the son he is proud of him and orders up the biggest, strongest drink for his boy. With all of the bar patrons looking on curiously and the bartender shaking his head in disbelief, the boy takes his first sip of alcohol.

Swoooosh! Plop!! A torso pops out! The bar is dead silent; then bursts into whoops of joy. The father, shocked, begs his son to drink again. The patrons chant 'Take another drink!'

The bartender continues to shake his head in dismay . Swoooosh!

Plip! Plop!! Two arms pop out.

The bar goes wild. The father, crying and wailing, begs his son to drink again. The patrons chant, 'Take another drink! Take another drink!!' The bartender ignore s the whole affair and goes back to polishing glasses, shaking his head, clearly unimpressed by the amazing scenes.

By now the boy is getting tipsy, but with his new hands he reaches down, grabs his drink and guzzles the last of it. Plop! Plip!! Two legs pop out. The bar is in chaos.

The father falls to his knees and tearfully thanks God. The boy stands up on his new legs and stumbles to the left then staggers to the right through the front door, into the street, where a truck runs over him and kills him instantly. The bar falls silent.

The father moans in grief.   The bartender sighs and says,

(Wait for it)

(It's coming)

(Ya ready?)

(Don't hate me)

(You're gonna hate me)

(Take a deep breath)

'He should've quit while he was a head'

The Smiths Were Unable to Conceive

The Smiths were unable to conceive children and decided to use a surrogate father to start their family. On the day the surrogate father was to arrive, Mr. Smith kissed his wife and said, "I'm off. The man should be here soon"

Half an hour later, just by chance a door-to-door baby photographer rang the doorbell, hoping to make a sale. "Good morning, madam. I've come to...."

"Oh, no need to explain. I've been expecting you," Mrs. Smith cut in.

"Really?" the photographer asked. "Well, good. I've made a specialty of babies"

"That's what my husband and I had hoped. Please come in and have a seat"

After a moment, she asked, blushing, "Well, where do we start?"

"Leave everything to me. I usually try two in the bathtub, one on the couch and perhaps a couple on the bed. Sometimes the living room floor is fun too; you can really spread out!"

"Bathtub, living room floor? No wonder it didn't work for Harry and me"

"Well, madam, none of us can guarantee a good one every time. But, if we try several different positions and I shoot from six or seven different angles, I'm sure you'll be pleased with the results"

"My, that's a lot of....." gasped Mrs. Smith.

"Madam, in my line of work, a man must take his time. I'd love to be in and out in five minutes, but you'd be disappointed with that, I'm sure"

"Don't I know it," Mrs. Smith said quietly.

The photographer opened his briefcase and pulled out a portfolio of his baby pictures. "This was done on the top of a bus in downtown London"

"Oh my God!" Mrs. Smith exclaimed, tugging at her handkerchief.

"And these twins turned out exceptionally well, when you consider their mother was so difficult to work with"

"She was difficult?" asked Mrs. Smith.

"Yes, I'm afraid so. I finally had to take her to Hyde Park to get the job done right. People were crowding around four and five deep, pushing to get a good look"

"Four and five deep?" asked Mrs. Smith, eyes widened in amazement.

"Yes," the photographer said, "And for more than three hours too. The mother was constantly squealing and yelling. I could hardly concentrate. Then darkness approached and I began to rush my shots. Finally, when the squirrels began nibbling on my equipment; I just packed it all in."

Mrs. Smith leaned forward. "You mean squirrels actually chewed on your, um......equipment?"

"That's right. Well, madam, if you're ready, I'll set up my tripod so we can get to work."

"Tripod?????"

"Oh yes, I have to use a tripod to rest my Canon on. It's much too big for me to hold for very long. Madam? Madam? .... Good Lord, she's fainted!!"

The Tearful Bride

A new young bride calls her mother in tears. She sobs, "Robert doesn't appreciate what I do for him."

"Now, now," her mother comforted, "I am sure it was all just a misunderstanding."

"No, mother, you don't understand. I bought a frozen turkey roll and he yelled and screamed at me about the price!"

"Well, the nerve of that lousy cheapskate!" says her mom. "Those turkey rolls are only a few dollars."

"No, mother it wasn't the price of the turkey, it was the airplane ticket."

"Airplane ticket.... What did you need an airplane ticket for?"

"Well mother, when I went to fix it, I looked at the directions on the package and it said - 'Prepare from a frozen state,' so I flew to Alaska!"

The Top 5 Men in a Woman's life are:

1. Doctor.
2. Dentist
3. Coal man.
4. Decorator.
5. Bank manager.

A Doctor says to take off your clothes.
A Dentist says open wide.
A Coal man asks "where do you want it, front or back?"
A Decorator says "how do you like it now that it's up?"
A Bank manager says "don't take it out you'll lose interest"!

The Whole Truth

At school, a boy was told by a classmate that most adults are hiding at least one dark secret, and that this makes it very easy to blackmail them by saying, "I know the whole truth." The boy decides to go home and try it out.

He goes home and as he is greeted by his mother he says, "I know the whole truth."

His mother quickly hands him $20 and says, "Just don't tell your father."

Quite pleased, the boy waits for his father to get home from work and greets him with, "I know the whole truth."

The father promptly hands him $40 and says, "Please don't say a word to your mother."

Very pleased, the boy is on his way to school the next day, when he sees the mailman at his front door. The boy greets him by saying, "I know the whole truth."

The mailman drops the mail, opens his arms, and says, "Then come give your father a big hug."

This Could Happen to You.

I was barely sitting down when I heard a voice from the other stall saying: "Hi, how are you?"

I'm not the type to start a conversation in the restroom but I don't know what got into me, so I answered, somewhat embarrassed, "Doin' just fine!"

And the other person says: "So what are you up to?"

What kind of question is that? At that point, I'm thinking this is too bizarre so I say: "Uhhh, I'm like you, just traveling!"

At this point I am just trying to get out as fast as I can when I hear another question. "Can I come over?"

Ok, this question is just too weird for me but I figured I could just be polite and end the conversation. I tell them "No........I'm a little busy right now!!!"

Then I hear the person say nervously...

"Listen, I'll have to call you back. There's an idiot in the other stall who keeps answering all my questions."

Cell phones, don't you just love them

Tiffany's ..Ha Ha

A lady walks into Tiffany's. She looks around, spots a beautiful diamond bracelet and walks over to inspect it. As she bends over to look more closely, she unexpectedly farted. Very embarrassed, she looks around nervously to see if anyone noticed her little whoops and prays that a salesperson wasn't anywhere near.

As she turns around, her worst nightmare materializes in the form of a salesman standing right behind her. Good looking as well.

Cool as a cucumber, he displays all of the qualities one would expect of a professional in a store like Tiffany's, he politely greets the lady with, "Good day, Madam. How may we help you today?"

Blushing and uncomfortable, but still hoping that the salesman somehow missed her little 'incident', she asks, "Sir, what is the price of this lovely bracelet?"

He answers, "Madam... if you farted just looking at it -- you're going to shit when I tell you the price."

Two Brothers

Once upon a time there were two brothers. One brother was very mischievous, always getting into trouble. The other brother, however, was very good. He was always kind to animals, helped elderly neighbors, and led an exemplary life.

As time went on, the brothers stayed in touch but were never close. The evil brother became a heavy drinker and a womanizer. The other brother was a devoted husband and father and supported many charities.

One day the evil brother died. Then, after a few years, the good brother passed away. He went to heaven and was rewarded with a happy afterlife. One day he went to God and asked, "Where is my brother? He died before me, but I have not seen him here in heaven."

God replied, "As you know, your brother led an evil life, so he is not spending eternity here in heaven. He has been sent elsewhere."

"I'm sorry to hear that," the good brother replied. "But I do miss him and wish I could see him again."

"You can see him if you wish," God said. "I will give you the power to gaze into hell."

So the power was granted and the good brother gazed into hell. Before long he saw his brother sitting on a bench. In one arm he held a keg of beer, and in the other he cradled a gorgeous young blonde.

The good brother turned to God and said, "I can't believe what I'm seeing. I have found my brother, and he has a keg of beer in one arm and a beautiful woman in the other. Surely, hell cannot be that bad."

God explained. "Things are not always as they seem.

The keg has a hole in it.

The blonde doesn't."

Two Ladies Talking In Heaven

1st woman: Hi! My name is Sherry.
2nd woman: Hi! I'm Sylvia. How'd you die?

1st woman: I froze to death.
2nd woman: How horrible!

1st woman: It wasn't so bad. After I quit shaking from the cold, I began to get warm & sleepy, & finally died a peaceful death. What about you?

2nd woman: I died of a massive heart attack. I suspected that my husband was cheating, so I came home early to catch him in the act. But instead, I found him all by himself in the den watching TV.

1st woman: So, what happened?

2nd woman: I was so sure there was another woman there somewhere that I started running all over the house looking. I ran up into the attic & searched, & down into the basement. Then I went through every closet & checked under all the beds. I kept this up until I had looked everywhere, & finally I became so exhausted that I just keeled over with a heart attack & died.

1st woman: Too bad you didn't look in the freezer---we'd both s till be alive.

PRICELESS!

Wake Up for School

Early one morning, a mother went in to wake up her son. "Wake up, son. It's time to go to school!"

"But why, Mom? I don't want to go."

"Give me two reasons why you don't want to go."

"Well, the kids hate me for one, and the teachers hate me, too!"

"Oh, that's no reason not to go to school. Come on now and get ready."

"Give me two reasons why I should go to school."

"Well, for one, you're 52 years old. And for another, you're the Principal!"

Wedding Vows

During the wedding rehearsal, the groom approached the pastor with an unusual offer.

"Look, I'll give you $100 if you'll change the wedding vows. When you get to me and the part where I'm to promise to 'love, honor and obey' and 'forsaking all others, be faithful to her forever,' I'd appreciate it if you'd just leave that part out." He passed the minister a $100 bill and walked away satisfied.

It is now the day of the wedding, and the bride and groom have moved to that part of the ceremony where the vows are exchanged. When it comes time for the groom's vows, the pastor like the young man in the eye and says:

"Will you promise to prostrate yourself before her, obey her every command and wish, serve her breakfast in bed every morning of your life and swear eternally before God and your lovely wife that you will not ever even look at another woman, as long as you both shall live?"

The groom gulped and looked around, and said in a tiny voice, "Yes."

The groom leaned toward the pastor and hissed, "I thought we had a deal!"

The pastor put the $100 bill into his hand and whispered back, "She made me a much better offer."

Welfare vs Job

A guy walks into the local welfare office, marches straight up to the counter and says, "Hi...You know, I just HATE drawing welfare. I'd really rather have a job."

The social worker behind the counter says, "Your timing is excellent. We just got a job opening from a very wealthy old man who wants a chauffeur and bodyguard for his nymphomaniac daughter. You'll have to drive around in his Mercedes, but he'll supply all of your clothes.

Because of the long hours, meals will be provided. You'll be expected to escort her on her overseas holiday trips. You will have to satisfy her sexual urges. You'll have a two-bedroom apartment above the garage. The starting salary is $200,000 a year".

The guy says, "You're bullshittin' me!"

The social worker says, "Yeah, well... you started it."

What's Good For the Goose is Good For The Gander

A man went into a store and began looking around. He saw a washer and dryer, but there was no price listed on them. He asked the sales person "How much are the washer and dryer?"

"Five dollars for both of them," the salesman said.

"Yeah right, you've got to be kidding me!" the man replied sarcastically.

"No, that's the price," the salesman said, "Do you want to buy them or not?"

"Yeah, I'll take them!" the customer responded.

He continued to look around and saw a car stereo system with a detachable face cassette player, a CD changer, amplifier, speakers, and subwoofers. "How much?" he asked.

"Five dollars for the system," the salesman answered.

"Is it stolen?" the guy asks.

"No," said the salesman, "It's brand new, do you want it or not?"

"Sure," the customer replied. He looked around some more.

Next he found a top of the line computer with printer and monitor. "How much?"

"Five dollars," was the familiar response.

"I'll take that too!" the man said.

As the salesperson is ringing up the purchases, the man asked him, "Why are your prices so cheap?"

The salesman said, "Well, the owner of the store is at my house right now with my wife. What he's doing to her, I'm doing to his business!"

Where are You Going

"I'm reminded of Albert Einstein, the great physicist who was once traveling from Princeton on a train when the conductor came down the aisle, punching the tickets of every passenger. When he came to Einstein, Einstein reached in his vest pocket. He couldn't find his ticket, so he reached in his trouser pockets. It wasn't there. He looked in his briefcase but couldn't find it. Then he looked in the seat beside him. He still couldn't find it.

"The conductor said, 'Dr. Einstein, I know who you are. We all know who you are. I'm sure you bought a ticket. Don't worry about it.'

"Einstein nodded appreciatively. The conductor continued down the aisle punching tickets. As he was ready to move to the next car, he turned around and saw the great physicist down on his hands and knees looking under his seat for his ticket.

"The conductor rushed back and said, 'Dr. Einstein, Dr. Einstein, don't worry, I know who you are; no problem. You don't need a ticket. I'm sure you bought one.' Einstein looked at him and said, 'Young man, I too, know who I am. What I don't know is where I'm going."

Which is Faster?

A hip young man goes out and buys the best car available: a 2005 Bugatti Veyron. It is the best and most expensive car in the world, and it sets him back $1.24M. He takes it out for a spin and, while doing so, stops for a red light. An old man on a moped (both looking about 90 years old) pulls up next to him. The old man looks over the sleek, shiny surface of the car and asks, "What kind of car ya got there, sonny?"

The young man replies "A 2005 Bugatti Veyron. It cost $1.24M."

"That's a lot of money" says the old man, shocked. "Why does it cost so much?

"Because this car can do up to 320 miles an hour!" states the cool dude proudly.

The moped driver asks, "Can I take a look inside?" "Sure," replies the owner.

So, the old man pokes his head in the window and looks around. Leaning back on his moped, the old man says "That's a pretty nice car, all right!"

Just then, the light changes, so the guy decides to show the old man what his car can do. He floors it, and within 30 seconds the speedometer reads 320 MPH.

Suddenly, he notices a dot in his rear view mirror. It seems to be getting closer! He slows down to see what it could be and suddenly, whoooosh! Something whips by him, going much faster!

"What on earth could be going faster than my Bugatti?" the young man asks himself.

Then, ahead of him, he sees a dot coming toward him. Whoooooosh! It goes by again, heading the opposite direction! And, it almost looked like the old man on the moped! "Couldn't be," thinks the guy. "How could a moped outrun a Bugatti?"

Again, he sees a dot in his rear view mirror! Whooooosh!

Ka-bbblammm! It plows into the back of his car, demolishing the rear end. The young man jumps out, and good grief, it is the old man!!! Of course the moped and the old man are hurting for certain. He runs up to the dying old man and says, "You're hurt bad! Is there anything I can do for you?"

The old man groans and replies "Yes. Unhook my suspenders from your side-view mirror!"

Who's The Boss?

All the organs of the body were having a meeting, trying to decide who was the one in charge.

"I should be in charge," said the BRAIN, "Because I run all the body's systems, so without me nothing would happen."

"I should be in charge," said the BLOOD, "because I circulate oxygen all over so without me you'd all waste away."

"I should be in charge," said the STOMACH, "because I process food and give all of you energy."

"I should be in charge," said the LEGS, "because I carry the body wherever it needs to go."

"I should be in charge," said the EYES, "Because I allow the body to see where it goes."

"I should be in charge," said the RECTUM, "Because I'm responsible for waste removal."

All the other body parts laughed at the RECTUM and insulted him, so in a huff, he shut down tight.

Within a few days, the BRAIN had a terrible headache, the STOMACH was bloated, the LEGS got wobbly, the EYES got watery, and the BLOOD was toxic.

They all decided that the RECTUM should be the boss.

The Moral of the story? The ASS HOLE is usually in charge!

Why English is So Hard to Learn

1) The bandage was wound around the wound.

2) The farm was used to produce produce.

3) The dump was so full that it had to refuse more refuse.

4) We must polish the Polish furniture.

5) He could lead if he would get the lead out.

6) The soldier decided to desert his dessert in the desert.

7) Since there is no time like the present, he thought it was time to present the present.

8) A bass was painted on the head of the bass drum.

9) When shot at, the dove dove into the bushes.

10) I did not object to the object.

11) The insurance was invalid for the invalid.

12) There was a row among the oarsmen about how to row.

13) They were too close to the door to close it.

14) The buck does funny things when the does are present.

15) A seamstress and a sewer fell down into a sewer line.

16) To help with planting, the farmer taught his sow to sow.

17) The wind was too strong to wind the sail.

18) After a number of injections my jaw got number.

19) Upon seeing the tear in the painting I shed a tear.

20) I had to subject the subject to a series of tests.

21) How can I intimate this to my most intimate friend?

Why I Fired My Secretary

I woke up early, feeling depressed because it was my birthday, and I thought, "I'm another year older," but decided to make the best of it. So I showered and shaved, knowing when I went down to breakfast my wife would greet me with a big kiss and say, "Happy birthday, dear." All smiles, I went in to breakfast, and there sat my wife, reading her newspaper, as usual. She didn't say one word. So I got myself a cup of coffee, made some toast and thought to myself, "Oh well, she forgot. The kids will be down in a few minutes, smiling and happy, and they will sing 'Happy Birthday' and have a nice gift for me." There I sat, enjoying my coffee, and I waited. Finally, the kids came running into the kitchen, yelling, "Give me a slice of toast! I'm late! Where is my coat? I'm going to miss the bus!" Feeling more depressed than ever, I left for the office.

When I walked into the office, my secretary greeted mc with a great big smile and a cheerful "Happy birthday, boss." She then asked if she could get me some coffee. Her remembering my birthday made me feel a whole lot better.

Later in the morning, my secretary knocked on my office door and said, "Since it's your birthday, why don't we have lunch together?" Thinking it would make me feel better, I said, "That's a good idea." So we locked up the office, and since it was my birthday, I said, "Why don't we drive out of town and have lunch in the country instead of going to the usual place?" So we drove out of town and went to a little out-of-the-way inn and had a couple of martinis and a nice lunch. We started driving back to town, when my secretary said, "Why don't we go to my place, and I will fix you another martini." It sounded like a good idea, since we didn't have much to do in the office. So we went to her apartment, and she fixed us some martinis. After a while, she said, "If you will excuse me, I think I will slip into something more comfortable," and she left the room.

In a few minutes, she opened her bedroom door and came out carrying a big birthday cake. Following her were my wife and all my kids. And there I sat with nothing on but my socks.

Why I'm Tired

For a couple years I've been blaming it on lack of sleep, not enough sunshine, too much pressure from my job, earwax build-up, poor blood, or anything else I could think of. But now I found out the real reason: I'm tired because I'm overworked. Here's why: The population of this country is 273 million.

140 million are retired.

That leaves 133 million to do the work.

There are 85 million in school, which leaves 48 million to do the work.

Of this there are 29 million employed by the federal government, leaving 19 million to do the work.

2.8 million are in the armed forces preoccupied with killing Saddam Hussein. Which leaves 16.2 million to do the work.

Take from that total the 14,800,000 people who work for state and city governments, and that leaves 1.4 million to do the work.

At any given time there are 188,000 people in hospitals, leaving 1,212,000 to do the work.

Now, there are 1,211,998 people in prisons.

That leaves just two people to do the work. You and me. And there you are sitting, at your computer, reading jokes.

Nice, real nice.

Wisdom of the Phrases

- If you're too open minded, your brains will fall out.
- Age is a very high price to pay for maturity.
- Going to church doesn't make you a Christian any more that going to a garage makes you a mechanic.
- Artificial intelligence is no match for natural stupidity.
- If you must choose between two evils, pick the one you've never tried before.
- My idea of housework is to sweep the room with a glance.
- Not one shred of evidence supports to notion that life is serious.
- It is easier to get forgiveness that permission.
- For every action, there is an equal and opposite government program.
- If you look like your passport picture, you probably need the trip.
- Bills travel through the mail at twice the speed of checks.

- A conscience is what hurts when all your other parts feel so food.

Woman of His Dreams

A young man called his mother and announced excitedly that he had just met the woman of his dreams. Now what should he do?

His mother had an idea: "Why don't you send her flowers, and on the card invite her to your apartment for a home- cooked meal?"

He thought this was a great strategy, and arranged a date for a week later. His mother called the day after the big date to see how things had gone.

"The evening was a disaster," he moaned.

"Why, didn't she come over?" asked his mother.

"Oh, she came over, but she refused to cook...."

World's Toughest Cowboy

Three cowboys are sitting around a campfire, out on the lonesome prairie, each with the bravado for which cowboys are famous.

A night of tall tales commences.

The first says, "I must be the meanest, toughest cowboy there is. Why, just the other day, a bull got loose in the corral and gored six men before I wrestled it to the ground, by the horns, with my bare hands."

The second chimes in, "Why that's nothing. I was walking down the trail yesterday and a fifteen foot rattler slid out from under a rock and made a move for me. I grabbed that snake with my bare hands, bit its head off, and sucked the poison down in one gulp. And I'm still here today."

The third cowboy remained silent, slowly stirring the coals with his penis.

You Got To Do The Pots

A guy wins the lottery and decides to buy himself a Harley Davidson, he goes down to his local bike shop and after purchasing a top of the range bike, the owner of the shop tells him to coat the bike in Vaseline every time it looks like raining.

That night he goes and picks his girlfriend up on his new toy and heads over to her parents house for the first time. As they arrive there, she explains to him that whenever they have dinner, don't talk. "If you talk," she tells him, "you have to do the pots."

The man is astounded as he walks into the house as it is a complete mess. Anyway, the family all sit down for dinner not saying a word. The man decides to take advantage of the situation by groping his girlfriend's tits, yet there is not a sound from anyone.

So he decides to screw his girlfriend on the table, and still there is not a word. He then proceeds to do his girlfriend's mum over the table, but still, amazingly, there's not a word from anyone.

Just at that moment he notices the rain on the kitchen window and remembers his precious motorbike, so he reaches into his pocket and flops the Vaseline out. At which point his girlfriend's dad leaps up and shouts, "Okay! Okay! I'll do the fucking pots!"

Yugo Envy

A guy driving a Yugo pulls up at a stoplight next to a Rolls-Royce. The driver of the Yugo rolls down his window and shouts to the driver of the Rolls, "Hey, buddy, that's a nice car. You got a phone in your Rolls? I've got one in my Yugo!"

The driver of Rolls looks over and says simply, "Yes I have a phone."

The driver of the Yugo says, "Cool! Hey, you got a fridge in there too?

I've got a fridge in the back seat of my Yugo!"

The driver of the Rolls, looking annoyed, says, "Yes, I have a refrigerator."

The driver of the Yugo says, "That's great, man! Hey, you got a TV in there, too? You know, I got a TV in the back seat of my Yugo!"

The driver of the Rolls, looking very annoyed by now, says, "Of course I have a television. A Rolls-Royce is the finest luxury car in the world!"

The driver of the Yugo says, "Very cool car! Hey, you got a bed in there, too? I got a bed in the back of my Yugo!" Upset that he did not have a bed, the driver of the Rolls-Royce sped away, and went straight to the dealer, where he promptly ordered that a bed be installed in the back of the Rolls.

The next morning, the driver of the Rolls picked up the car, and the bed looked superb, complete with silk sheets and brass trim. It was clearly a bed fit for a Rolls-Royce.

So the driver of the Rolls begins searching for the Yugo, and he drove all day. Finally, late at night, he finds the Yugo parked, with all the windows fogged up from the inside. The driver of the Rolls got out and knocked on the Yugo.

When there wasn't any answer, he knocked and knocked, and eventually the owner stuck his head out, soaking wet. "I now have a bed in the back of my Rolls-Royce," the driver of the Rolls stated arrogantly.

The driver of the Yugo looked at him and said, "You got me out of the shower to tell me THIS?"

Hunting

Aged Hunter at the Home for the Aged

A young reporter went to a retirement home to interview an aged but legendary explorer. The reporter asked the old man to tell him the most frightening experience he had ever had.

The old explorer said, "Once I was hunting Bengal tigers in the jungles of India. I was on a narrow path and my faithful native gun bearer was behind me. Suddenly the largest tiger I have ever seen leaped onto the path in front of us. I turned to get my weapon only to find the native had fled. The tiger leapt toward me with a mighty ROARRRR! I soiled myself."

The reporter said, "Under those circumstances anyone would have done the same."

The old explorer said, "No, not then - just now when I went 'ROARRRR!'"

Bear Hunting

Two men went bear hunting. While one stayed in the cabin, the other went out looking for a bear. He soon found a huge bear, shot at it but only wounded it. The enraged bear charged toward him, he dropped his rifle and started running for the cabin as fast as he could. He ran pretty fast but the bear was just a little faster and gained on him with every step. Just as he reached the open cabin door, he tripped and fell flat.

Too close behind to stop, the bear tripped over him and went rolling into the cabin.

The man jumped up, closed the cabin door and yelled to his friend inside, "You skin this one while I go and get another!"

Did You See That?

Two guys are out hunting deer. The first guy says, "Did you see that?"

"No," the second guy says.

"Well, a bald eagle just flew overhead," the first guy says.

"Oh," says the second guy.

A couple of minutes later, the first guy says, "Did you see that?"

"See what?" the second guy asks.

"Are you blind? There was a big, black bear walking on that hill, over there."

"Oh."

A few minutes later the first guy says: "Did you see that?"

By now, the second guy is getting aggravated, so he says, "Yes, I did!"

And the first guy says: "Then why did you step in it?"

Montana Grizzly Bear Notice...

In light of the rising frequency of human/grizzly bear conflicts, the Montana Department of Fish and Game is advising hikers, hunters, and fishermen to take extra precautions and keep alert for bears while in the field.

Outdoorsmen Alert Notice

"We advise that outdoorsmen wear noisy little bells on their clothing so as not to startle bears that aren't expecting them. We also advise outdoorsmen to carry pepper spray with them in case of an encounter with a bear. It is also a good idea to watch out for fresh signs of bear activity. Outdoorsmen should recognize the difference between black bear and grizzly bear poop. Black bear poop is smaller and contains lots of berries and squirrel fur. Grizzly bear poop has little bells in it and smells like pepper."

Moose Call

Two hunters went moose hunting every winter without success. Finally, they came up with a fool-proof plan. They got a very authentic cow moose costume and learned the mating call of a cow moose. The plan was to hide in the costume, lure the bull, then come out of the costume and shoot the bull.

They set themselves up on the edge of a clearing, donned their costume, and began to give the moose love call. Before long, their call was answered as a bull came crashing out of the forest and into the clearing.

When the bull was close enough, the guy in front said, "Okay, let's get out and get him." After a moment that seemed like an eternity, the guy in the back shouted, "The zipper is stuck! What are we going to do!?" The guy in the front says, "Well, I don't know how about you but I'm going to start nibbling grass."

Husband and Wife

A Different Look At Things

A married couple has been stranded on a deserted island for many years. One day another man washes up on shore. He and the wife become attracted to each other right away, but realize they must be creative if they are to engage in any hanky-panky. The husband, however, is very glad to see the second man there. "Now we will be able to have three people doing eight hour shifts in the watchtower, rather than two people doing 12-hour shifts."

The newcomer is only too happy to help and in fact volunteers to do the first shift. He climbs up the tower to stand watch. Soon, the couple on the ground are placing stones in a circle to make a fire to cook supper. The second man yells down, "Hey, no screwing!" They yell back, "We're not screwing!"

A few minutes later they start to put driftwood into the stone circle. Again the second man yells down, "Hey, no screwing!" Again they yell back, "We're not screwing!" Later they are putting palm leaves on the roof of their shack to patch leaks. Once again the second man yells down, "Hey, I said no screwing!" They yell back, "We're not screwing!"

Eventually the shift is over and the second man climbs down from the tower to be replaced by the husband. He's not even halfway up before the wife and her new friend are hard at it. The husband looks out from the tower and says, "Son-of-a-gun. From up here it DOES look like they're screwing.

A Married Couple

Tom was in his usual place in the morning sitting at the table, reading the paper after breakfast. He came across an article about a beautiful actress that was about to marry a football player who was known primarily for his lack of IQ and common knowledge.

He turned to his wife Linda, with a look of question on his face.

"I'll never understand why the biggest smocks get the most attractive wives."

His wife replies, "Why, thank you, dear!"

A Testing Question

This guy's wife asks, "Honey if I died would you remarry?"

He replies, "Well, after a considerable period of grieving, we all need companionship, I guess I would."

She says, "If I died and you remarried, would she live in this house?"

He replies, "We've spent a lot of time and money getting this house just the way we want it. I'm not going to get rid of my house, I guess she would."

So she asks, "If I died and you remarried, and she lived in this house, would she sleep in our bed?"

He says, "That bed is brand new, we just paid two thousand dollars for it, it's going to last a long time, I guess she would."

So she asks, "If I died and you remarried, and she lived in this house, and slept in our bed, would she use my golf clubs?"

He says, "Oh no, she's left handed."

And That's How the Fight Started.....

One year, I decided to buy my mother-in-law a cemetery plot as a Christmas gift.... The next year, I didn't buy her a gift. When she asked me why, I replied, "Well, you still haven't used the gift I bought you last year!"

And that's how the fight started.....

I asked my wife, 'Where do you want to go for our anniversary?' It warmed my heart to see her face melt in sweet appreciation. 'Somewhere I haven't been in a long time!' she said. So I suggested, 'How about the kitchen?'

And that's when the fight started...

My wife and I are watching Who Wants To Be A Millionaire while we were in bed. I turned to her and said, 'Do you want to have Sex?' 'No,' she answered. I then said, 'Is that your final answer?' She didn't even look at me this time, simply saying 'Yes...' So I said, 'Then I'd like to phone a friend.'

And that's when the fight started...

I took my wife to a restaurant. The waiter, for some reason, took my order first. 'I'll have the rump steak, medium rare, please.' He said, 'Aren't you worried about the mad cow?' 'Nah, she can order for herself.'

And that's when the fight started.....

My wife sat down on the couch next to me as I was flipping the channels. She asked, 'What's on TV?' I said, 'Dust'

And then the fight started..

My wife was hinting about what she wanted for our upcoming anniversary. She said, 'I want something shiny that goes from 0 to 200 in about 3 seconds.' I bought her a set of bathroom scales.

And then the fight started....

My wife and I were sitting at a table at her high school reunion, and she kept staring at a drunken man swigging his drink as he sat alone at a nearby table. I asked her, 'Do you know him?'

'Yes,' she sighed, 'He's my old boyfriend.... I understand he took to drinking right after we split up those many years ago, and I hear he hasn't been sober since.'

'My God!' I said, 'Who would think a person could go on celebrating that long?'

And then the fight started...

I rear-ended a car this morning.. So, there we were alongside the road and slowly the other driver got out of his car.

You know how sometimes you just get soooo stressed and little things just seem funny? Yeah, well I couldn't believe it... he was a DWARF!!! He stormed over to my car, looked up at me, and shouted, 'I AM NOT HAPPY!'

So, I looked down at him and said, 'Well, then which one are you?'

And then the fight started...

Aspirin for the Wife

A husband walks into the bedroom holding two aspirin and a glass of water. His wife asks, "What's that for?"

"It's for your headache."

"I don't have a headache."

He replies, "Gotcha!"

Bedside Manners

Susie's husband had been slipping in and out of a coma for several months. Things looked grim, but she was by his bedside every single day. One day as he slipped back into consciousness, he motioned for her to come close to him. She pulled the chair close to the bed and leaned her ear close to be able to hear him.

"You know" he whispered, his eyes filling with tears, "you have been with me through all the bad times. When I got fired, you stuck right beside me. When my business went under, there you were. When we lost the house, you were there. When I got shot, you stuck with me. When my health started failing, you were still by my side. "And you know what?"

"What, dear?" she asked gently, smiling to herself.

"I think you're bad luck."

Coffee?

Well here's a clever one...(sarcasm intended)

A man and his wife were having an argument about who should brew the coffee each morning. The wife said, "You should do it, because you get up first, and then we don't have to wait as long to get our coffee."

The husband said, "You are in charge of cooking around here and you should do it, because that is your job, and I can just wait for my coffee."

Wife replies, "No, you should do it, and besides, it is in the Bible that the man should do the coffee."

Husband replies, "I can't believe that, show me."

So she fetched the Bible, and opened the New Testament and showed him at the top of several pages, that it indeed says..........

"Hebrews"

Confessions of the Newlyweds

A young couple were on their honeymoon. The husband was sitting in the bathroom on the edge of the bathtub saying to himself, "Now how can I tell my wife that I've got really smelly feet and that my socks absolutely stink? I've managed to keep it from her while we were dating, but she's bound to find out sooner or later that my feet stink. Now how do I tell her?"

Meanwhile, the wife was sitting in the bed saying to herself, "Now how do I tell my husband that I've got really bad breath? I've been very lucky to keep it from him while we were courting, but as soon as he's lived with me for a week, he's bound to find out. Now how do I tell him gently?"

The husband finally plucks up enough courage to tell his wife and so he walks into the bedroom. He walks over to the bed, climbs over to his wife, puts his arm around her neck, moves his face very close to hers and says, "Darling, I've a confession to make."

And she says, "So have I, love." To which he replies, "Don't tell me, you've eaten my socks."

Deathbed Confession

A women on her deathbed called her husband and instructed him to look under their bed and open the wooden box he found. He was puzzled by the 3 eggs and $7,000 in cash he found in the box, so he asked his wife what the eggs were for.

"Oh those", she replied, "every time we had unsatisfactory marital relations, I put an egg in the box".

Not bad, the husband thought to himself, after 35 years of marriage, then he asked, "But what about the $7,000?"

"Oh that", she replied, "every time I got a dozen I sold them."

Drinking Solution

A man drinks a shot of whiskey every night before bed. After years of this, the wife wants him to quit; she gets two shot glasses, filling one with water and the other with whiskey. After getting him to the table that had the glasses, she brings his bait box. She says I want you to see this. She puts a worm in the water it, and it swims around. She puts a worm in the whiskey, and the worm dies immediately. She then says, feeling that she has made her point clear, "what do you have to say about this experiment?"

He responds by saying: "If I drink whiskey, I won't get worms!"

Give Him What He Wants

An escaped convict broke into a house and tied up a young couple who had been sleeping in the bedroom.

As soon as he had a chance, the husband turned to his voluptuous young wife, bound up on the bed in a skimpy nightgown, and whispered, "Honey, this guy hasn't seen a woman in years. Just cooperate with anything he wants. If he wants sex with you, just go along with it and pretend you like it. Our lives depend on it!" "Dear," the wife hissed, spitting out her gag, "I'm so relieved you feel that way, because he just told me that he thinks you're really cute!"

Going Camping

Ed, Ted and their wives went out camping one weekend. Ed and Ted slept in one tent while the wives used the other.

At about three in the morning, Ted woke up and yelled, "Wow, unbelievable!"

Which woke Ed. "What's going on?" said Ed.

"I've got to go to the other tent and find my wife." said Ted.

"How come?" said Ed.

"To have sex! I just woke up with the biggest hard-on I've ever had in my life!" said Ted.

After a pause, Ed said, "Do you want me to come with you?"

"Hell, no! Why would I want you to do that?" said Ted.

"Because that's my dick you're holding," said Ed.

Golf Balls

A young couple gets married, and the groom asks his bride if he can have a dresser drawer of his own that she will never open. The bride agrees. After 30 years of marriage, she notices that his drawer has been left open. She peeks inside and sees 3 golf balls and $1,000.

She confronts her husband and asks for an explanation. He explains "Every time I was unfaithful to you, I put a golf ball in the drawer." She figures 3 times in 30 years isn't bad and asks "But what about the $1,000?" He replied "Whenever I got a dozen golf balls, I sold them"

Golf or Porn

A man is watching a game of golf on TV, But he keeps switching channels to a dirty movie featuring a lusty couple having raucous sex.

"I don't know whether to watch them or the game", he says to his wife.

"For Heaven's sake, watch them," his wife says. "You already know how to play golf!!!

Golfing Groom

The bride came down the aisle and when she reached the altar, the groom was standing there with his golf bag and clubs at his side.

She said:" What are your golf clubs doing here"?

He looked her right in the eye and said, "This isn't going to take all day, is it?"

Heads Up

The widow takes a look at her dear departed one right before the funeral and, to her horror, finds that he's in his brown suit. She'd specifically said to the undertaker that she wanted him buried in his blue suit; she'd brought it especially for that occasion, and she was distressed that the mortician had left him in the same brown suit he'd been wearing when the lightning bolt hit him.

She demanded that the corpse be changed into the blue suit she'd brought especially for that purpose. The undertaker said, "But madam! It's only a minute or two until the funeral is scheduled to begin! We can't possibly take him out and get him changed in that amount of time.

The lady said, "Who's paying for this?" Seeing the logic to this argument, a very reluctant mortician wheeled the coffin out, but then wheeled it right back in a moment later. Miraculously, the corpse was in a blue suit.

After the ceremony, a well-satisfied widow complimented the undertaker on the smooth and speedy service. She especially wanted to know how he'd been able to get her husband into a blue suit so fast. The funeral director said, "Oh, it was easy. It happens that there was another body in the back room and he was already dressed in a blue suit. All we had to do was switch heads!

Hooker In Training

Harry and his wife are having hard financial times, so they decide she'll become a hooker.

She's not quite sure what to do, so Harry says, "Stand in front of that bar and pick up a guy and tell him it'll be a hundred bucks. If you've got a question, I'll be parked around the corner."

She's not there five minutes when a guy pulls up and asks, "How much?"

She says, "A hundred dollars."   He says, "Shit. All I've got is thirty."

She says, "Hold on." She runs back to Harry and says, "What can he get for thirty dollars?"
Harry says, "A hand job."

She runs back and tells the guy all he gets for thirty dollars is a hand job.   He says, "Okay."

She gets in the car; he unzips his pants, and out pops a HUGE PENIS. She stares at it for a minute, and then says, "I'll be right back."

She runs back around the corner and says breathlessly, "Harry, can you lend this guy seventy bucks?"

Husband Compliment

A woman is standing nude looking in the bedroom mirror... She is not happy with what she sees and says to her husband, "I feel horrible; I look old, fat and ugly... I really need you to pay me a compliment."

The husband replies, "Your eyesight's damn near perfect."

Husband Dies While Making Love

A guy dies while making love to his wife. A few days later the undertaker calls her and says, "Your husband still has a hard-on, what shall I do with it?" The wife replies, "Cut it off and shove it up his ass!" The undertaker does as he is told. On the day of the funeral the wife visits her husband for the last time and sees a tear rolling down his face, so she whispers in his ear, "It fucking hurts doesn't it!"

Husband Goes Fishing

Saturday morning I got up early, put on my long johns, dressed quietly, made my lunch, grabbed the dog, slipped quietly into the garage to hook the boat up to the truck, and proceeded to back out into a torrential downpour.

There was snow mixed with the rain and the wind was blowing 50 mph. I pulled back into the garage, turned on the radio, and discovered that the weather would be bad throughout the day.

I went back into the house, quietly undressed, and slipped back into bed. There I cuddled up to my wife's back, now with a different anticipation, and whispered, "The weather out there is terrible."

She sleepily replied,

"Can you believe my stupid husband is out fishing in that shit."

Male Assertiveness

A mild-mannered man was tired of being bossed around by his wife so he went to a psychiatrist.

The psychiatrist said he needed to build his self-esteem, and so gave him a book on assertiveness, which he read on the way home.

He had finished the book by the time he reached his house.

The man stormed into the house and walked up to his wife.

Pointing a finger in her face, he said, "From now on, I want you to know that I am the man of this house, and my word is law! I want you to prepare me a gourmet meal tonight, and when I'm finished eating my meal, I expect a sumptuous dessert afterward. Then, after dinner, you're going to draw me my bath so I can relax. And when I'm finished with my bath, guess who's going to dress me and comb my hair?"

"The funeral director," said his wife.

Man in the Mirror

A woman came home one day with a mirror and told her husband it was magic. Her husband told her to prove it.

She said watch, "Mirror, mirror on the wall, make my boobs biggest of all."

Sure enough, they grew huge.

The husband was amazed and said, "Ooh, oooh, let me try! Mirror, mirror show me more, make my dick touch the floor."

His legs fell off.

Me Too!!!!

A man walks into his bedroom and sees his wife packing a suitcase. He asks, 'What are you doing?'

She answers, I'm moving to Nevada. I heard that the prostitutes there get paid $400 for doing what I do for you for free.

Later that night, on her way out, the wife walks into the bedroom and sees her husband packing his suitcase.

When she asks him where he's going, he replies,

I'm coming too. I want to see how you live on $800 a year.

Most Shocking

There's an old couple, both in their 70's, on a sentimental holiday back to the place where they first met. They're sitting in a pub and he says to her, "Do you remember the first time we had sex together over fifty years ago? We went behind the barn. You leaned against the fence and I made love to you from behind."

"Yes, she says, I remember it well." she replies.

"OK, he says, How about taking a stroll round there again and we can do it for old times sake?"

Smiling his wife responds, "Oh Henry, you devil, that sounds like a good idea, she answers."

There's a man sitting at the next table listening to all this, having a chuckle to himself. He thinks, I've got to see this, two old timers having sex against a fence. So he follows them.

They walk haltingly along, leaning on each other for support, aided by walking sticks. Finally they get to the back of the barn and make their way to the fence. The old lady lifts her skirt, takes her knickers down and the old man drops his trousers. She turns around and hangs on to the fence and the old man moves in. Suddenly they erupt into the most furious sex the watching man has ever seen. They are bucking and jumping like eighteen-year-olds. This goes on for about forty minutes. She's yelling Ohhh God! He's hanging on to her hips for dear life.

This is the most athletic sex imaginable. Finally, they both collapse panting on the ground. The guy watching is amazed. He thinks he has learned something about life that he didn't know. He starts to think about his own aged parents and wonders whether they still have sex like this.

 After about half an hour of lying on the ground recovering, the old couple struggle to their feet and put their clothes back on. The guy, still watching thinks, that was truly amazing, he was going like a train. I've got to ask him what his secret is.

As the couple pass, the guy says to them, "That was something else, you must have been shagging for about forty minutes. How do you manage it? Is there some sort of secret?"

"No, there's no secret, the old man says, except fifty years ago that fucking fence wasn't electrified."

Mixed Emotions

A husband and wife were sitting watching a TV program about psychology and explaining the phenomenon of "mixed emotions". The husband turned to his wife and said, "Honey, that is a bunch of crap. I bet you can't tell me anything that will make me happy and sad at the same time.

She said: "Out of all your friends, you have the biggest dick".

Mutual Attraction

In the middle of an argument a man said to his wife, "I don't know how you can be so stupid and so beautiful all at the same time!"

The wife responded calmly, "Allow me to explain...the good Lord made me beautiful so you would be attracted to me; and he made me stupid so I would be attracted to you!"

Newlyweds on Their Honeymoon

The newlyweds are in their honeymoon room and the groom decides to let the bride know where she stands right from the start of the marriage. He proceeds to take off his trousers and throw them at her. He says, "Put those on."

The bride replies, "I can't wear your trousers."

He replies, "And don't forget that! I will always wear the pants in the family!"

The bride takes off her panties and throws them at him with the same request, "Try those on!"

He replies, "I can't get into your panties!"

"And you never will if you don't change your attitude."

Penny Scale

A husband stepped on one of those penny scales that tell you your fortune and weight and dropped in a coin.

"Listen to this," he said to his wife, showing her a small, white card. "It says I'm energetic, bright, resourceful and a great lover."

"Yeah," his wife nodded, "and it has your weight wrong, too."

Picture Perfect

On their first night together, a newlywed couple go to change. The new bride comes out of the bathroom showered and wearing a beautiful robe. The proud husband says, "My dear, we are married now, you can open your robe." The beautiful young woman opens her robe, and he is astonished. "Oh, oh, aaaahhh," he exclaims, "My God you are so beautiful, let me take your picture. Puzzled she asks, "My picture?" He answers, "Yes my dear, so I can carry your beauty next to my heart forever".

She smiles and he takes her picture, and then he heads into the bathroom to shower. He comes out wearing his robe and the new wife asks, "Why do you wear a robe? We are married now." At that the man opens his robe and she exclaims, "OH, OH, OH MY, let me get a picture". He beams and asks why and she answers, "So I can get it enlarged!"

Questions of Prior Activity

A man and a woman had been married some time when the woman began to question her husband. "I know you've been with a lot of woman before. How many were there?" The husband replied, "Look, I don't want to upset you, there were many. Let's just leave it alone." The wife continued to beg and plead. Finally, the husband gave in. "Let's see." he said "There was one, two, three, four, five, six, **YOU**, eight, nine..."

Sam & Becky on Their 50th Anniversary

Sam and Becky are celebrating their 50th wedding anniversary. Sam says to her, "Becky, I was wondering - have you ever cheated on me?"

Becky replies, "Oh Sam, why would you ask such a question now? You don't want to ask that question..."

"Yes, Becky, I really want to know. Please..."

"Well, all right. Yes, 3 times..."

"Three? Well, when were they?" he asked.

"Well, Sam, remember when you were 35 years old and you really wanted to start the business on your own and no bank would give you a loan? Remember, then one day the bank president himself came over the house and signed the loan papers, no questions asked?"

"Oh, Becky, you did that for me! I respect you even more than ever, to do such a thing for me. So, when was number 2?"

"Well, Sam, remember when you had that last heart attack and you were needing that very tricky operation, and no surgeon would touch you? Then remember how Dr. DeBakey came all the way up here, to do the surgery himself, and then you were in good shape again?"

"I can't believe it! Becky, you should do such a thing for me, to save my life. I couldn't have a more wonderful wife. To do such a thing, you must really love me darling. I couldn't be more moved. So, all right then, when was number 3?"

"Well, Sam, remember a few years ago, when you really wanted to be president of the golf club and you were 17 votes short..?"

Sell All My Stuff When I Die

One lazy Sunday morning the wife and I were quiet and thoughtful, sitting around the breakfast table when she said to me unexpectedly, "When I die, I want you to sell all my stuff, immediately."

"Now why would you want me to do something like that?" I asked.

"I figure a man as fine as yourself would eventually remarry and I don't want some other asshole using my stuff."
I looked at her intently and said: "What makes you think I'd marry another asshole?"

Sex for $25

George and Harriet decided to celebrate their 25th Wedding Anniversary with a trip to Las Vegas. When they entered the hotel/casino and registered, a sweet young woman dressed in a very short skirt became very friendly. George brushed her off. Harriet objected, "George, that young woman was nice, and you were so rude."

"Harriet, she's a prostitute."

"I don't believe you. That sweet young thing?"

"Let's go up to our room and I'll prove it."

In their room, George called down to the desk and asked for 'Bambi' to come to room 1217. "Now," he said, "you hide in the bathroom with the door open just enough to hear us, OK?" Soon, there was a knock on the door. George opened it and Bambi walked in, swirling her hips provocatively. George asked, "How much do you charge?" "$125 basic rate, $100 tips for special services." Even George was taken aback. "$125! I was thinking more in the range of $25." Bambi laughed derisively. "You must really be a hick if you think you can buy sex for that price."

"Well," said George, "I guess we can't do business. Goodbye." After she left, Harriet came out of the bathroom. She said, "I just can't believe it!" George said, "Let's forget it. We'll go have a drink, then eat dinner."

At the bar, as they sipped their cocktails, Bambi came up behind George, pointed slyly at Harriet, and said, "See what you get for $25?"

She's A Liar

"That wife of mine is a liar," said the angry husband to a sympathetic pal seated next to him in the bar.

"How do you know?" the friend asked.

"She didn't come home last night, and when I asked her where she'd been, she said she'd spent the night with her sister, Shirley."

"So?" the friend replied.

"So, she's a liar. I spent the night with her sister Shirley!"

Social Security Benefits

The man went to the social security office to claim his social security benefits. When he got there, he took a number and waited. As he waited through the long line of applicants, he realized that he had forgotten his birth certificate. His name was called. He told the counselor that he had forgotten his birth certificate. She said that was okay, just take off his shirt. He did and displayed a chest of gray hair. His claim was approved.

When he got home, he told his wife what happened. She remarked, "You should have dropped your pants and gotten disability too!"

Tell Me

A very elderly couple is having an elegant dinner to celebrate their 75th wedding anniversary.

The old man leans forward and says softly to his wife . . . "Dear, there is something that I must ask you. It has always bothered me that our 10th child never quite looked like the rest of our children. Now I want to assure you that these 75 years have been the most wonderful experience I could have ever hoped for, and your answer cannot take that all away. But, I must know, did he have a different father?"

The wife drops her head, unable to look her husband in the eye. She paused for moment and then confessed. "Yes. Yes he did."

The old man is much shaken, the reality of what his wife was admitting hit him harder than he had expected. With a tear in his eye he asks "Who? Who was he? Who was the father?"

Again the old woman drops her head, saying nothing at first as she tried to muster the courage to tell the truth to her husband. Then, finally, she says. . . . . . . "You."

The Broken Lawn Mower:

When our lawn mower broke and wouldn't run, my wife kept hinting to me that I should get it fixed. But, somehow I always had something else to take care of first, the shed, the Ute, making beer.. Always something more important to me.

Finally she thought of a clever way to make her point.

When I arrived home one day, I found her seated in the tall grass, busily snipping away with a tiny pair of sewing scissors. I watched silently for a short time and then went into the house. I was gone only a minute, and when I came out again I handed her a toothbrush. I said, 'When you finish cutting the grass, you might as well sweep the driveway.'

The doctors say I will walk again, but I will always have a limp.

Three Couples, No Sex

Three couples went in to see the minister about becoming new members of his church. The minister said that they would have to go without sex for two weeks and then come back and tell him how it went.

The first couple was retired, the second couple was middle aged and the third couple was newly married.

Two weeks went by, and the couples returned to the minister.

The retired couple said it was no problem at all.

The middle-aged couple said it was tough for the first week, but after that it was no problem.

The newlyweds said it was fine until she dropped the can of paint.

"Can of PAINT!" exclaimed the minister.

"Yeah," said the newlywed man. "She dropped the can and when she bent over to pick it up I had to have her right there and then. Lust took over."

The minister just shook his head and said that they were not welcome in the church.

"That's okay," said the man. "We're not welcome in Home Depot either."

Touchdown

A man and his wife have gone to bed. After laying in bed for a few minutes the man cuts a fart.
His wife rolls over and asks, "What in the world was that?"

The man says, "Touchdown, I'm ahead, seven zip."

A few minutes later the wife lets one loose. The man says to her, "What was that?"
She replies, "Touchdown, tied the score."

The man lays there for about ten minutes trying to work one up. He tries so hard that he craps the bed.

The wife asks, "Now what in the world was that?"
He replies, "Half time. Switch sides."

Who Wants To Be A Millionaire

So, a husband and wife are in bed watching Who Wants to be a Millionaire and the husband says, "Would you like to make love?"

The wife says, "No."

The husband says, "Is that your final answer?"

The wife says, "Yes."

The husband says, "Then I'd like to call a friend."

Who's Linda?

A guy goes down for breakfast and it is quite obvious that his wife upset with him. He asks, "What is the matter?"

She replies, "Last night you were talking in your sleep and I want to know who Linda is?"

Thinking quickly on his feet he tells her that Linda was 'Lucky Linda' and was actually a name of a horse that he bet on that day and won $40.

She seemed quite happy with the explanation and he went off to work.

When he got home that night, his wife was upset with him again. Asking her what the matter was now, she replied "Your horse phoned."

Who's Wife?

A man walks into a bar, late one night completely exhausted and dripping with sweat and orders 5 whiskies.

"What's wrong with you?" The barman says.

"In my car I've got a nymphomaniac - you couldn't satisfy her if you were there 'til Christmas," he replies.

"We'll see about that," says the barman and goes out to the car parking lot.

He has been in the car with the woman for a while when there is a knock on the window and a policeman shines in his flashlight. The barman jumps up and winds down the window to talk to the policeman.

"It's all right officer, I'm just fucking my wife," he says.

"Oh, I'm sorry sir, I didn't know it was your wife" replies the cop.

The barman replies -"Neither did I 'til you shone your flashlight!"

Wife and Sex

A wife went in to see a therapist and said, "I've got a big problem doctor. Every time we're in bed and my husband climaxes, he lets out this earsplitting yell."

"My dear," the shrink said, "that's completely natural. I don't see what the problem is."

"The problem," she complained, "is that it wakes me up."

Words

A husband read an article to his wife about how many words women use a day... 30,000 to a man's 15,000. The wife replied, "The reason has to be because we have to repeat everything to men...

The husband then turned to his wife and asked,

"What?"

Wrong Number

A woman suspects her husband is cheating on her. One day, she dials her home and a strange woman answers. The woman says, "Who is this?"

"This is the maid," answered the woman.

"We don't have a maid" , said the woman. The maid says, "I was hired this morning by the man of the house. The woman says, "Well, this is his wife. Is he there?"

The maid replied, "he is upstairs in the bedroom with someone who I figured was his wife."

The woman is fuming. She says to the maid, "Listen, would you like to make $50,000?"

The maid says, "What will I have to do?"

The woman tells her, "I want you to get my gun from the desk, and shoot the jerk and the witch he's with."

The maid puts the phone down; the woman hears footsteps and the gun shots. The maid comes back to the phone, "What do I do with the bodies?"

The woman says, "Throw them in the swimming pool."

Puzzled, the maid answers, "But there's no pool here."

A long pause and the woman says, "Is this 555-4821?"

Lawyer

Dishonest Lawyer

Murphy, a dishonest lawyer, bribed one of his client's jurors to hold out for a charge of manslaughter, fearing the murder charge being brought by the state. The jury was out for days before returning with the verdict:

"Manslaughter!"

Later, as Murphy paid off the corrupt juror, he asked him if he had a hard time convincing the other jurors to see things his way.

"Boy, did I!" said the juror. "They kept voting to acquit!"

Do You Know Me?

A prosecuting attorney called his first witness, a grandmotherly, elderly woman, to the stand. He approached her and asked, "Mrs. Jones, do you know me?"

She responded, "Why, yes, I do know you Mr. Williams. I've known you since you were a young boy. And frankly, you've been a big disappointment to me. You lie, you cheat on your wife, you manipulate people and talk about them behind their backs. You think you're a rising big shot when you haven't the brains to realize you never will amount to anything more than a two-bit paper pusher. Yes, I know you."

The lawyer was stunned. Not knowing what else to do he pointed across the room and asked, "Mrs. Williams, do you know the defense attorney?"

She again replied, "Why, yes I do. I've known Mr. Bradley since he was a youngster, too. I used to baby-sit him for his parents. And he, too, has been a real disappointment to me. He's lazy, bigoted, he has a drinking problem. The man can't build a normal relationship with anyone and his law practice is one of the shoddiest in the entire state. Yes, I know him."

At this point, the judge rapped the courtroom to silence and called both counselors to the bench. In a very quiet voice, he said with menace, "If either of you asks her if she knows me, you'll be jailed for contempt!"

Generous Lawyer

A local United Way office realized the organization had never received a donation from the town's most successful lawyer. The person in charge of contributions called him to persuade him to contribute.

"Our research shows that out of a yearly income of at least $500,000, you give not a penny to charity. Wouldn't you like to give back to the community in some way?"

The lawyer mulled this over for a moment and replied, "First did your research also show that my mother is dying after a long illness, and has medical bills that are several times her annual income?"

Embarrassed, the United Way rep mumbled, "Um…no."

The lawyer interrupts, "or that my brother, a disabled veteran, is blind and confined to a wheelchair?"

The stricken United Way rep began to stammer out an apology, but was interrupted again.

"or that my sister's husband died in a traffic accident," the lawyer's voice rising in indignation, leaving her penniless with three children?!"

The humiliated United Way rep, completely beaten, said simply, "I had no idea…"

On a roll, the lawyer cut him off once again, "So if I don't give any money to them, why should I give any to you?"

Two Lawyers Walking Down The Street

Two lawyers were walking down Rodeo Drive, and saw a beautiful model walking towards them. "What a babe," one said, "I'd sure like to fuck her!"

"Really?" the other responded, "Out of what?"

Magic Genie

A Modern Day Cowboy

A modern day cowboy has spent many days crossing the Texas plains without water. His horse has already died of thirst. He's crawling through the sand, certain that he has breathed his last breath, when all of a sudden he sees an object sticking out of the sand several yards ahead of him. He crawls to the object, pulls it out of the sand, and discovers what looks to be an old briefcase. He opens it and out pops a genie. But this is no ordinary genie. She is wearing a FEMA (Federal Emergency Management Agency) ID badge and a dull gray dress. There's a calculator in her pocketbook. She has a pencil tucked behind one ear.

"Well, cowboy," says the genie... "You know how I work....You have three wishes."

"I'm not falling for this." said the cowboy... "I'm not going to trust a FEMA genie."

"What do you have to lose? You've got no transportation, and it looks like you're a goner anyway!"

The cowboy thinks about this for a minute, and decides that the genie is right. "OK!, I wish I were in a lush oasis with plenty of food and drink." *****POOF*****

The cowboy finds himself in the most beautiful oasis he has ever seen, and he is surrounded with jugs of wine and platters of delicacies.

"OK, cowpoke, what's your second wish."

"My second wish is that I was rich beyond my wildest dreams." *****POOF*****

The cowboy finds himself surrounded by treasure chests filled with rare gold coins and precious gems.

"OK, cowpuncher, you have just one more wish. Better make it a good one!"

After thinking for a few minutes, the cowboy says... "I wish that no matter where I go, beautiful women will want and need me." ***POOF***

He was turned into a tampon.

The moral of the story: If the government offers you anything, there's going to be a string attached.

Kidney Transplant

A salesman walking along the beach found a bottle. When he rubbed it, lo and behold, a genie appeared. "I will grant you three wishes," announced the genie. "But since Satan still hates me, for every wish you make, your rival gets the wish as well -- only double."

The salesman thought about this for a while. "For my first wish, I would like ten million dollars," he announced. Instantly the genie gave him a Swiss bank account number and assured the man that $10,000,000 had been deposited. "But your rival has just received $20,000,000," the genie said.

"I've always wanted a Ferrari," the salesman said. Instantly a Ferrari appeared. "But your rival has just received two Ferraris," the genie said.

"And what is your last wish?" "Well," said the salesman, "I've always wanted to donate a kidney for transplant."

Speaking Clearly

One evening this drunk walks into a bar, sits down, and happens to notice a 12" tall man standing on the bar. Astonished, the man asks the guy next to him; "What the hell is that?" The guy next to him replies "He's a pianist!", to which the drunk replied "Horse shit, your pulling my leg" So the guy next to him picks up the 12" man , grabs some books, and props the little man up to the piano. Sure enough, this little man started hammering out all the favorite tunes of the bars' patrons.

Stunned, the drunk asks "That little guy is cool, where the hell did you get him"? The fella told the drunk how he had found a genie bottle out in the alley, rubbed it 'til a genie appeared, and was granted one wish.

All of a sudden the drunk hauls ass out the back door, finds the bottle, and starts rubbing it: when all of a sudden a genie pops out and grants him one wish. In a slur, the drunk asks "I wish for a million bucks". Suddenly, the sky turns black and overhead a million ducks come flying overhead shittin' all over him.

Angrily, the drunk runs back inside, slams the door and begins cursing "You son of a bitch, I found that genie bottle and wished for a million bucks and all of a sudden there are a million ducks shitting all over my new suit." The fella started laughing and wildly exclaimed "You don't really think I wished for a 12" pianist do you?"

Tiny Wish

A man is sitting in a pub, when a guy with an incredibly small head walks in and sits down next to him.

The first guy looks up and bursts out laughing. He asks, "What on earth happened to your head?"

The second man replies, "I was stranded on an island and a bottle floated up. I opened it and out came a female genie. She was by far the most beautiful woman I had ever seen. She told me I had one wish - so I took my time and thought long and hard about what I wanted. Finally, I told her that I wanted to spend the rest of our lives making passionate love to each other. She told me that was the one wish she couldn't fulfill."

"So, then what happened?" asked the first guy.

"Well, before I could think, I blurted out, 'So I suppose a little head is out of the question?'"

Medical

A Cardiologist's Funeral

A very prestigious cardiologist died, and was given a very elaborate funeral by the hospital he worked for most of his life... A huge heart... covered in flowers stood behind the casket during the service as all the doctors from the hospital sat in awe. Following the eulogy, the heart opened, and the casket rolled inside. The heart then closed, sealing the doctor in the beautiful heart forever..

At that point, one of the mourners just burst into laughter. When all eyes stared at him, he said, 'I am so sorry, I was just thinking of my own funeral... I'm a gynecologist.'

A Dental Appointment

One day, a man walks into a dentist's office and asks how much it will cost to extract wisdom teeth.

"Eighty dollars," the dentist says.

"That's a ridiculous amount," the man says. "Isn't there a cheaper way?"

"Well," the dentist says, "if you don't use an aesthetic, I can knock the price down to $60."

Looking annoyed the man says, "That's still too expensive!"

"Okay," says the dentist. "If I save on anesthesia and simply rip the teeth out with a pair of pliers, I can knock the price down to $20."

"Nope," moans the man, "it's still too much."

"Well," says the dentist, scratching his head, "if I let one of my students do it, I suppose I can knock the price down to $10."

"Marvelous," says the man, "book my wife for next Tuesday!"

A Doctor And His Wife At Breakfast...

A doctor and his wife were having a big argument at breakfast. "You aren't so good in bed either!", he shouted and stormed off to work. By mid morning, he decided he'd better make amends and called home.

"What took you so long to answer?"

"I was in bed."

"What were you doing in bed this late?"

"Getting a second opinion."

A Man Buys a Condom

A man walks into a pharmacy, buys a condom, then walks out of the store laughing hysterically. The pharmacist thinks this is weird, but, hey, there's no law preventing weird people from buying condoms. Maybe it's a good thing.

The next day, the man comes back to the store, purchases another condom, and once again he leaves the store laughing wildly. This piques the interest of the pharmacist. What's so funny about buying a rubber, anyway?

So he tells his clerk, "If this guy ever comes back, I want you to follow him to see where he goes."

Sure enough, the next day the laugher is back. He buys the condom, starts cracking up, then leaves. The pharmacist tells his clerk to go follow the guy.

About an hour later, the clerk comes back to the store. "Did you follow him? Where did he go?" asks the pharmacist.

The clerk replies "Your house."

A Nutty Game

A doctor at an (insane) asylum decided to take his inmates to a baseball game. For weeks in advance, he coached his patients to respond to his commands. When the day of the game arrived, everything seemed to be going well.

As the national anthem started, the doctor yelled, "Up nuts!"

And the inmates complied by standing up. After the anthem he yelled, "Down nuts!" And they all sat.

After a home run he yelled, "Cheer nuts!" And they all broke into applause and cheers.

Thinking things were going very well; he decided to go get a beer and a hot dog, leaving his assistant in charge.

When he returned there was a riot in progress. Finding his assistant, he asked what happened.

The assistant replied, "Well... everything was fine until some guy walked by and yelled, 'PEANUTS'

A Professor is Giving the First Year Medical Students...

A professor is giving the first year medical students their first lecture on autopsies, and decides to give them a few basics before starting.

"You must be capable of two things to do an autopsy. The first thing is that you must have no sense of fear." At this point, the lecturer sticks his finger into the dead man's anus, and then licks it.
He asks all the students to do the same thing with the corpses in front of them.

After a couple of minutes silence, they follow suit.

"The second thing is that you must have an acute sense of observation: I stuck my middle finger into the corpse's anus, but I licked my index finger.

Annual Checkup

An 80 year old man is having his annual checkup. The doctor asks him how he's feeling. "I've never been better!" he replies. "I've got an eighteen-year-old bride who's pregnant with my child! What do you think about that?"

The doctor considers this for a moment, then says, "Well, let me tell you a story. I know a guy who's an avid hunter. He never misses a season. But one day he's in a bit of a hurry and he accidentally grabs his umbrella instead of his gun. So he's walking in the woods near a creek and suddenly spots a beaver in some brush in front of him! He raises up his umbrella, points it at the beaver and squeezes the handle. 'BAM' The beaver drops dead in front of him."

"That's impossible!" said the old man in disbelief, "Someone else must have shot that beaver."

"Exactly," said the Doctor

Doctor and Mental Patient

Three patients in a mental institution prepare for an examination given by the head psychiatrist. If the patients pass the exam, they will be free to leave the hospital. However, if they fail, the institution will detain them for five years.

The doctor takes the three patients to the top of a diving board looking over an empty swimming pool, and asks the first patient to jump.

The first patient jumps head first into the pool and breaks both arms.

Then the second patient jumps and breaks both legs.

The third patient looks over the side and refuses to jump. "Congratulations! You're a free man. Just tell me why didn't you jump?" asked the doctor.

To which the third patient answered, "Well Doc, I can't swim!"

Doctors Visit

A man went to the Doctor's office to get a double dose of Viagra.

The Doctor told him that he couldn't prescribe him a double dose.

"Why not?" asked the man.

"Because it's not safe," replied the Doctor.

"But I need it really bad," said the man.

"Well, why do you need it so badly?" asked the Doctor.

The man said, "My girlfriend is coming into town on Friday; my ex-wife will be here on Saturday; and my wife is coming home on Sunday. Can't you see? I must have a double dose."

The Doctor finally relented saying, "Okay, I'll give it to you, but you have to come in on Monday morning so that I can check you to see if there were any side effects."

On Monday, the man dragged himself in, his right arm in a sling.

The Doctor asked, "What happened to you?"

The man said, "No one showed up!"

Going About His Business

A Doctor is going about his business, with a rectal thermometer tucked behind his ear.

He goes into a staff meeting to discuss the day's activities, when a co-worker asks why he has a thermometer behind his ear?

In a wild motion he grabs for the thermometer, looks at it and exclaims: "Damn, some asshole has my pen!"

Good Eyes

This woman rushes to see her doctor, looking very much worried and all strung out. She rattles off, "Doctor, take a look at me. When I woke up this morning, I looked at myself in the mirror and saw my hair all wiry and frazzled up.

"My skin was all wrinkled and pasty, my eyes were blood-shot and bugging out, and I had this corpse-like look on my face! What's wrong with me, Doctor?"

The doctor looks her over for a couple of minutes, then calmly says, "Well, I can tell you that there ain't nothing wrong with your eyesight."

Guy Falls Asleep on the Beach

A guy falls asleep on the beach for several hours and gets a horrible sunburn. He goes to the hospital, and is promptly admitted after being diagnosed with second-degree burns. With his skin already starting to blister, and the severe pain he was in, the Doctor prescribes continuous intravenous feeding with saline, electrolytes, a sedative, and a Viagra pill every four hours.

The nurse, who is rather astounded, says, "What good will Viagra do for him, Doctor?

The Doctor replied, "It will keep the sheets off his legs."

Hickory Dickery Dock

A flat-chested young lady went to Dr. Smith for advice about breast enlargements. He told her, "Every day when you get out of the shower, rub the top of your nipples and say, 'Scooby dooby dooby, I want bigger boobies.'

She did this every day faithfully. After several months, it worked! She grew great boobs! One morning she was running late, and in her rush to leave for work, she realized she had forgotten her morning ritual. At this point she loved her boobs and didn't want to lose them, so she got up in the middle of the bus and said, "Scooby dooby dooby, I want bigger boobies."

A guy sitting nearby asked her, "Do you go to Dr. Smith by any chance?"

"Why yes, I do. How did you know?"

The man stood up and cupped his balls and said, "Hickory dickery dock..."

I Just Did

Patient: "Doc, you gotta help me. I'm under a lot of stress. I keep losing my temper with people."

Doctor: "Tell me about your problem."

Patient: "I just did, you fucking jackass!"

I Was The Third Girl

Mr. Geraldo says to his doctor, "Doc, I had the worst dream of my life last night. I dreamed I was with twelve of the most beautiful chorus girls in the world. Blondes, brunettes, redheads, and they were all dancing in a row."

The psychiatrist says, "Now hold on, Mr. Geraldo. That doesn't sound so terrible."

Mr. Geraldo says, "Oh, yeah? I was the third girl from the end."

Jack Went to the Doctor

Jack went to the Doctor and said, "Doc, I'm having trouble getting my penis erect. Can you help me?"

After a complete examination the Doctor told Jack, "Well, the problem with you is that the muscles around the base of your penis are damaged. There's really nothing I can do for you except if you're willing to try an experimental treatment."

Jack asked sadly, "What is this treatment?"

"Well," the Doctor explained, "what we would do is take the muscles from the trunk of a baby elephant and implant them in your penis."

Jack thought about it silently, and then said, "Well, the thought of going through life without ever having sex again is too much. Let's go for it."

A few weeks after the operation, Jack was given the green light to use his improved equipment. He planned a romantic evening for his girlfriend and took her to one of the nicest restaurants in the city. In the middle of dinner he felt a stirring between his legs that continued to the point of being painful. To release the pressure Jack unzipped his fly. His penis immediately sprung from his pants, went to the top of the table, grabbed a bun and then returned to his pants.

His girlfriend was stunned at first, but then said with a sly smile, "That was incredible! Can you do it again?"

Jack replied with his eyes watering, "Well, I guess so, but I don't think I can fit another bun in my ass."

Making Love to A Ghost

A psychiatrist is addressing a group of people who have all had experiences with the supernatural. He asks: "Who here has seen a ghost?"

Everyone puts up their hands.

He then asks: "Who here has spoken with a ghost?"

Half the audience puts up their hands.

"And who here has touched a ghost?"

Ten percent of the crowd puts up their hands. He asks: "And who here has made love with a ghost?"

One little man in the back row puts up his hand...

The psychiatrist looks down from the podium at the little man and says: "Do you mean to tell me that you have made love with a ghost?"

The man replies, "Oh No! I'm sorry. I couldn't hear you correctly. I thought you said 'goat'."

Marriage JOKE

A psychiatrist visited a California mental institution and asked a patient, "How did you get here? What was the nature of your illness?" He got the following reply.

"Well, it all started when I got married and I guess I should never have done it. I married a widow with a grown daughter who then became my stepdaughter. My dad came to visit us, fell in love with my lovely stepdaughter, then married her. And so my stepdaughter was now my stepmother. Soon, my wife had a son who was, of course, my daddy's brother-in-law since he is the half-brother of my stepdaughter, who is now, of course, my daddy's wife. So, as I told you, when my stepdaughter married my daddy, she was at once my stepmother! Now, since my new son is brother to my stepmother, he also became my uncle. As you know, my wife is my step-grandmother since she is my stepmother's mother. Don't forget that my stepmother is my stepdaughter. Remember, too, that I am my wife's grandson. But hold on just a few minutes more. You see, since I'm married to my step-grandmother, I am not only the wife's grandson and her hubby, but I am also my own grandfather. Now can you understand how I got put in this place?"

After staring blankly with a dizzy look on his face, the psychiatrist replied: "Move over!"

Mental Asylum

During a visit to the mental asylum, a visitor asked the Director what the criterion was which defined whether or not a patient should be institutionalized.

"Well," said the Director, "we fill up a bathtub, then we offer a teaspoon, a teacup and a bucket to the patient and ask him or her to empty the bathtub."

"Oh, I understand," said the Visitor.

"A normal person would use the bucket because it's bigger than the spoon or the teacup."

"No." said the Director, "A normal person would pull the plug. Do you want a bed near the window?"

Mental Hospital

I was walking past the mental hospital the other day, and all the patients were shouting, "13....13.. ..13"

The fence was too high to see over but I saw a little gap in the planks and looked through to see what was going on.

Some bastard poked me in the eye with a stick.

Then they all started shouting "14....14... .14"...

Mental Release

A man who had been in a mental home for some years finally seemed to have improved to the point where it was thought he might be released.

The head of the institution, in fit of commendable caution, decided, however, to interview him first.

"Tell me," said he, "It would be wonderful to get back to real life and if I do, I will certainly refrain from making my former mistake. I was a nuclear physicist, you know, and it was the stress of my work in weapons research that helped put me here. If I am released, I shall confine myself to work in pure theory, where I trust the situation will be less difficult and stressful."

"Marvelous," said the head of the institution.

"Or else," ruminated the inmate, "I might teach. There is something to be said for spending life in bringing up a new generation of scientists."

"Absolutely," said the head.

"Then again, I might write. There is considerable need for books on science for the general public. Or I might even write a novel based on my experiences in this fine institution."

"An interesting possibility," said the head.

"And finally, if none of these things appeal to me, I can always continue to be a teakettle."

Mistaken Identity

Tommy was playing in the house with his balloon. Throwing it this way and that, punching it up in the air, bouncing it off the walls until the balloon floated into the bathroom and into the toilet bowl. Tommy looked at this, pulled a face of disgust and left the balloon where it landed.

A little while later his father entered the bathroom and promptly, without looking, sat down, with his magazine to do his "business". On standing he looked with horror at the toilet bowl!!! The excrement had totally covered the balloon and the picture was of an immense and absurd gigantic mountain of shit.

Not wanting to believe what had just happened he quickly phoned his friend who was a doctor.

"Gerald, I had a shit that just filled up the whole toilet. I've never seen so much shit in one sitting. It's almost overflowing. I must have a very serious problem."

"Heck John you are most probably exaggerating!"

"What exaggeration. I am looking at all that shit now. It's absurd. I must be very ill".

"OK. I'm on my way home but I'll pop in as it's on my way."

The doctor arrived and went directly to the toilet where his friend was standing at the door waiting.

"Hello John, where's this business that you ……GOOD HEAVENS SWEET MOTHER OF GOD!!!!!!!!!!!!!!!! What is this????? For heavens sake what have you eaten?"

"Didn't I tell you? Now you believe me, hey?"

"This is un-be-lie-va-ble!!!!"

"So you think I have a serious problem?"

"Well to start with I am going to take a sample"

Gerald, the doctor proceeded to take a small sterilized bottle out of his medical bag and when he pricked the "cake" to take his specimen

………..POW!!!!!!!!! The balloon popped and shit went flying to every crevice within the four walls of the bathroom!!!!!!!

Absolute silence follows the eruption. Both men encased in shit look at each other and the doctor shouts   "Son of a bitch! I thought I had seen it all in this life, but a fart with a shell….. never! ! !

My Wife's Hearing

A man goes to his doctor and says, "I don't think my wife's hearing isn't as good as it used to be. What should I do?"

The doctor replies, "Try this test to find out for sure. When your wife is in the kitchen doing dishes, stand fifteen feet behind her and ask her a question, if she doesn't respond keep moving closer asking the question until she hears you."

The man goes home and sees his wife preparing dinner. He stands fifteen feet behind her and says, "What's for dinner, honey?" He gets no response, so he moves to ten feet behind her and asks again. Still no response, so he moves to five feet. Still no answer. Finally he stands directly behind her and says, "Honey, what's for dinner?"

She replies, "For the forth time, I SAID CHICKEN!"

No Laughing Matter

A guy goes to see a doctor and when they get into the private room the doctor says to the patient, "What seems to be the problem?" The patient answers, "You have to promise not to laugh."

The doctors said fine, and the patient pulls down his pants and the doctor tried not to laugh at his small penis.

The doctor managed to ask, "What's the problem?"

The patient then said, "It's swollen."

Nurse Jenny is Confused

Two doctors were in a hospital hallway one day complaining about Nurse Jenny. "She's incredibly dumb. She does everything absolutely backwards." said one doctor. "Just last week, I told her to give a patient 2 milligrams of Percocet every 10 hours. She gave him 10 milligrams every 2 hours. He nearly died on us!"

The second doctor said, "That's nothing. Earlier this week, I told her to give a patient an enema every 24 hours. She tried to give him 24 enemas in one hour! The guy nearly exploded!"

Suddenly, they hear this blood-curdling scream from down the hall. "Oh my God!" said the first doctor, "I just realized I told Nurse Jenny to prick Mr. Smith's boil!"

Test Results

A male patient is lying in bed in the hospital, wearing an oxygen mask over his mouth and nose, still heavily sedated from a difficult, four hour, surgical procedure.

A young, student nurse appears to give him a partial sponge bath.

"Nurse", he mumbles, from behind the mask. "Are my testicles black?"

Embarrassed, the young nurse replies, "I don't know, Sir. I'm only here to wash your upper body and feet."

He struggles to ask again, "Nurse, are my testicles black?"

Concerned that he may elevate his blood pressure and heart rate from worry about his testicles, she overcomes her embarrassment and sheepishly pulls back the covers. She raises his gown, holds his penis in one hand and his testicles in the other. Then, she takes a close look and says, "There's nothing wrong with them, Sir!"

The man pulls off his oxygen mask, smiles at her and says very slowly, "Thank you very much. That was wonderful, but, listen very, very closely...... A r e - m y - t e s t - r e s u l t s - b a c k?

The Urologist Appointment

An older gentleman had an appointment to see the urologist who shared offices with several other doctors.

The waiting room was filled with patients. As he approached the receptionist's desk, he noticed that the receptionist was a large un-friendly woman who looked like a Sumo wrestler.

He gave her his name.

In a very loud voice, the receptionist said, **"YES, I HAVE YOUR NAME HERE; YOU WANT TO SEE THE DOCTOR ABOUT IMPOTENCE, RIGHT?"**

All the patients in the waiting room snapped their heads around to look at the very embarrassed man.

He recovered quickly, and in an equally loud voice replied, **"NO, I'VE COME TO INQUIRE ABOUT A SEX CHANGE OPERATION, BUT I DON'T WANT THE SAME DOCTOR THAT DID YOURS."**

The Wife

A woman accompanied her husband to the doctor's office.

After his checkup, the doctor called the wife into his office alone. He said, "Your husband is suffering from a very severe stress disorder. If you don't follow my instructions carefully, your husband will surely die.

"Each morning, fix him a healthy breakfast. Be pleasant at all times. For lunch make him a nutritious meal. For dinner prepare an especially nice meal for him.

"Don't burden him with chores. Don't discuss your problems with him;

it will only make his stress worse. Do not nag him. Most importantly, make love to him regularly.

"If you can do this for the next 10 months to a year, I think your husband will regain his health completely."

On the way home, the husband asked his wife, "What did the doctor say?"

"He said you're going to die," she replied.

Military

Army Pilot Taking a Physical

An Army pilot goes to his doctor for his physical and gets sent to the urologist as a precaution. When he gets there, he discovers the urologist is a very pretty female

The female doctor says, "I'm going to check your prostate today, but this new procedure is a little different from what you are probably used to. I want you to lie on your right side, bend your knees, then while I check your prostate, take a deep breath and say, '99' ."

The guy obeys and says,"99".

The doctor says, "Great. Now turn over on your left side and again, while repeat the check, take a deep breath and say, '99'."

Again, the guy says, '99'.

The doctor said, "Very good. Now then, I want you to lie on your back with your knees raised slightly. I'm going to check your prostate with this hand, and with the other hand I'm going to hold on to your penis to keep it out of the way. Now take a deep breath and say, '99'."

The guy begins, "One .. Two ..Three".

Honor in the line of Fire

The officer shouted orders to a nearby soldier. With considerable bravery, the GI ran directly onto the field of battle, in the line of fire, to retrieve a dispatch case from a dead soldier. In a hail of bullets, he dove back to safety. "Private," the officer said, "I'm recommending you for a medal. You risked your life to save the locations of our secret warehouses."

"Warehouses!?" the private shouted. "I thought you said whorehouses!"

'It's The Box Office.'

While the C-5 was turning over its engines, a female crewman gave the GI's on board the usual information regarding seat belts, emergency exits, etc.

Finally, she said, 'Now sit back and enjoy your trip while your captain, Judith Campbell, and crew take you safely to Afghanistan."

An old MSgt. sitting in the eighth row thought to himself, "Did I hear her right? Is the captain a woman?"

When the attendant came by he said, "Did I understand you right? Is the captain a woman?"

"Yes," said the attendant, "In fact, this entire crew is female."

"My God," he said, "I wish I had two double scotch and sodas. I don't know what to think with only women up there in the cockpit."

"That's another thing, Sergeant," said the crew member. "We No Longer Call It 'The Cockpit'.

"It's The Box Office."

Major and Sex

A young , attractive woman thought she might have some fun with a stiff-looking military man at a cocktail party, so she walked over and asked him, "Major, when was the last time you had sex?"

"1956," was his reply.

"No wonder you look so uptight!" she exclaimed. "Major, you need to get out more!"

"I'm not sure I understand you," he answered, glancing at his watch, ..."It's only 2014 now."

Navy Navigation

This is the transcript of an alleged radio conversation of a U. S. naval ship with Canadian authorities off the coast of Newfoundland in October, 1995. Radio conversation released by the Chief of Naval Operations on 10-10-95 was subsequently denied by the U.S. navy.

Americans: "Please divert your course 15 degrees to the North to avoid a collision."

Canadians: "Recommend you divert YOUR course 15 degrees to the South to avoid a collision."

Americans: "This is the Captain of a US Navy ship. I say again, DIVERT YOUR course."

Canadians: "No. I say again, you divert YOUR course."

Americans: "This is the aircraft carrier USS Lincoln, the second largest ship in the United States Atlantic Fleet. We are accompanied by three destroyers, three cruisers, and numerous support vessels. I demand that you change your course 15 degrees north...that's one-five-degrees North, or counter-measures will be undertaken to ensure the safety of this ship."

Canadians: "This is a lighthouse. Your call."

Not Done

While practicing auto-rotations during a military night training exercise, a Huey Cobra messes up and lands on its tail rotor.

The landing is so hard it breaks off the tail boom. However, the chopper fortunately remains upright on its skids, sliding down the runway, doing 360s.

As the Cobra slides past the tower, trailing a brilliant shower of sparks, this radio exchange takes place: Tower: "Sir, do you need any assistance?"

Cobra: "I don't know, Tower, we ain't done crashin' yet."

Photo Finish

The soldier servicing overseas and far from home was annoyed and upset when his girl wrote breaking off their engagement and asking for her photograph back.

He went out and collected from his friends all the unwanted photographs of women that he could find, bundled them all together and sent them to her with a note: "Regret can not remember which one is you. Please keep your photo and return the others."

The Doctor's Receptionist

An 86 year old Veteran walked into a crowded waiting room and approached the desk.... The Receptionist said, "Yes sir, what are you seeing the Doctor for today?"

"There's something wrong with my dick", he replied.

The Receptionist became irritated and said, "You shouldn't come into a crowded waiting room and say things like that."

"Why not, you asked me what was wrong and I told you," he replied.

The Receptionist replied; "Speaking like that you have caused much embarrassment to the people in this room. You should have said there is something wrong with your ear and discussed the problem further with the Doctor in private."

The Veteran replied, "You shouldn't ask people questions in a room full strangers, if the answer could embarrass anyone."

The receptionist then said "I suggest that you leave the room and come back and rephrase your answer." The Veteran walked out, waited several minutes and then re-entered.

The Receptionist smiled smugly and asked, "Yes?"

"There's something wrong with my ear," he stated.

The Receptionist nodded approvingly and smiled, knowing he had taken her advice. "And what is wrong with your ear?" she asked.

"I can't piss out of it," he replied.

The waiting room erupted in laughter. Mess with a Veteran and you will lose!

The Lieutenant and the Sergeant

The Lieutenant and the Sergeant were on maneuvers. As they lay down for the night, The Lieutenant said: "Sergeant, look up into the sky and tell me what you see".

The Sergeant: "I see millions and millions of stars".

The Lieutenant: "And what does that tell you?"

The Sergeant: "Astronomically, it tells me that there are millions of galaxies and potentially billions of planets. Theologically, it tells me that God is great and that we are small and insignificant. Meteorologically, it tells me that we will have a beautiful day tomorrow. What does it tell you?"

The Lieutenant: "Somebody stole our tent."

The Young Officer and the Camel

A young officer was posted to a British army detachment in the desert. On tour of the facility with the master sergeant, he noticed a group of camels. "What are those for?" he asked. "The men use them when they want to have sex." "Don't say another word, sergeant. That is the most disgusting thing I have ever heard. Get rid of those camels immediately!" "Yes Sir."

A few weeks went by and the young officer began to get rather horny. He called the sergeant over and asked, "Where are the camels we used to have?" The sergeant replied that he had sold them to a Bedouin that camped nearby. "Take me to them, please."

The officer and the sergeant went over to the Bedouin camp and found the camels. The officer told the sergeant to leave him alone with the camels, then picked out the most attractive one, and proceeded to have sex with the camel.

On the way back to the camp, the officer asked, "Sergeant, do the men actually enjoy sex with the camels?" The sergeant looked at the officer in astonishment and exclaimed, "I don't know! They use them to ride into town to where the girls are."

One Liners

Clean Short Jokes, Funny One Line Jokes

An onion can make people cry but there has never been a vegetable invented to make them laugh. ~ Will Rogers

All reports are in. Life is now officially unfair.

If all is not lost, where is it?

The first rule of holes: If you are in one, stop digging.

I went to school to become a wit, only got halfway through.

It was all so different before everything changed.

Some days you're the dog, some days you're the hydrant.

I wish the buck stopped here. I could use a few.

It's hard to make a comeback when you haven't been anywhere.

The only time the world beats a path to your door is if you're in the bathroom.

If God wanted me to touch my toes, He would have put them on my knees.

When you're finally holding all the cards, why does everyone else decide to play chess?

Health is merely the slowest possible rate at which one can die.

It's not hard to meet expenses. They're everywhere.

Girlie Wisdom

1 - One of the mysteries of life is that a two pound box of chocolates can make you gain five pounds.

2 - The reason women over 50 don't have babies is because we would put them down and forget where we put them.

3 - It's time to give up jogging for your health when your thighs keep rubbing togothor and ctarting your pantc on firo.

4 - What happens if you confuse your Valium with your birth control pills?
You have 12 kids, but you don't really care.

5 - Skinny people bug me. They say things like, "Sometimes I forget to eat." Now, I've forgotten my keys, my glasses, my address and my mother's maiden name. But I have never forgotten to eat! You have to be a special kind of stupid to forget to eat!

6 - What is the best way to forget your troubles? Wear tight clothes.

7 - Why is it harder to lose weight as you get older? Because by that time your body and your fat have become really good friends.

8 - My mind doesn't wander, it leaves completely.

9 - What happens when you leave an outfit hanging in your closet for a while? It shrinks two sizes.

10 - It's nice to live in a small town, because if you don't know what you are doing, someone else does.

11 - I read some article which said that the symptoms of stress are impulse buying, eating too much and driving too fast. Are they kidding? That's what I call a perfect day.

Good Comebacks

Man: "Haven't we met before?"
Woman: "Perhaps. I'm the receptionist at the VD Clinic."

Man: "Haven't I seen you someplace before?
Woman: "Yeah, that's why I don't go there anymore."

Man: "Is this seat empty?"
Woman: "Yes, and this one will be too if you sit down."

Man: "So, wanna go back to my place?"
Woman: "Well, I don't know. Will two people fit under a rock?"

Man: "Your place or mine?"
Woman: "Both. You go to yours and I'll go to mine."

Man: "I'd like to call you. What's your number?"
Woman: "It's in the phone book."

Man: "But I don't know your name."
Woman: "That's in the phone book too."

Man: "So what do you do for a living?"
Woman: "I'm a female impersonator."

Man: "Hey, baby, what's your sign?"
Woman: "Do not Enter"

Man: "How do you like your eggs in the morning?"
Woman: "Unfertilized!"

Man: "Hey, come on, we're both here at this bar for the same reason"
Woman: "Yeah! Let's pick up some chicks!"

Man: "I know how to please a woman."
Woman: "Then please leave me alone."

Man: "I want to give myself to you."
Woman: "Sorry, I don't accept cheap gifts."

Man: "If I could see you naked, I'd die happy:
Woman: "Yeah, but if I saw you naked, I'd probably die laughing".

Man: "Your body is like a temple."
Woman: "Sorry, there are no services today."

Man: "I'd go through anything for you."
Woman: "Good! Let's start with your bank account."

Man: "I would go to the end of the world for you.
Woman: "Yes, but would you stay there?

HAVE YOU HEARD: Puns for the educated?

- The roundest knight at King Arthur's round table was Sir Cumference . He acquired his size from too much pi.
- I thought I saw an eye doctor on an Alaskan island, but it turned out to be an optical Aleutian.
- She was only a whisky maker, but he loved her still.
- A rubber band pistol was confiscated from algebra class because it was a weapon of math disruption.
- The butcher backed into the meat grinder and got a little behind in his work.
- No matter how much you push the envelope, it'll still be stationery.
- A dog gave birth to puppies near the road and was cited for littering.
- A grenade thrown into a kitchen in France would result in Linoleum Blownapart.
- Two silk worms had a race. They ended up in a tie.
- Time flies like an arrow. Fruit flies like a banana.
- A hole has been found in the nudist camp wall. The police are looking into it.

- Atheism is a non-prophet organization.
- Two hats were hanging on a hat rack in the hallway. One hat said to the other, "You stay here; I'll go on a head."
- I wondered why the baseball kept getting bigger. Then it hit me.
- A sign on the lawn at a drug rehab center said: "Keep off the Grass."
- A small boy swallowed some coins and was taken to a hospital. When his grandmother telephoned to ask how he was, a nurse said, "No change yet."
- A chicken crossing the road is poultry in motion.
- The short fortune-teller who escaped from prison was a small medium at large.
- The man who survived mustard gas and pepper spray is now a seasoned veteran.
- A backward poet writes inverse.
- In democracy it's your vote that counts. In feudalism it's your count that votes.
- When cannibals ate a missionary, they got a taste of religion.
- Don't join dangerous cults: Practice safe sects!

Insults

1. I like your approach ….. Let's see your departure.

2. His antenna doesn't pick up all the channels.

3. Not the sharpest knife in the drawer, is he?

4. Doesn't have his belt through all the lopes.

5. Got an IQ that's about room temperature.

6. The wheel's spinning, but the hamster's asleep.

7. He forgot to pay his brain bill.

8. The gates are down, the lights are flashing, but the train just isn't coming.

9. I think he rode the Tilt-a-Whirl too long.

10. Hard to believe that he beat out a million other sperm.

11. He keeps a coat hanger in the backseat in case he locks the keys in his car.

12. Definitely has a bad brains-to-testosterone ratio.

Quick One Liners

1 What's the difference between chopped beef and pea soup?
Everyone can chop beef, but not everyone can pea soup!

2 Why don't aliens eat clowns.
Because they taste funny.

3 Two snowmen are standing in a field. One says to the other :
"Funny, I smell carrots too".

4 What's the difference between erotic and kinky?
Erotic = using a feather
Kinky = using the whole chicken

5 A man and a woman started to have sex in the middle of a dark forest.

After 15 minutes of this, the man finally gets up and says, "Damn, I wish I had a flashlight."

The woman says, "So do I. You've been eating grass for the past ten minutes!"

6 (insult) I'd like to see things from your <u>point of view</u> but I can't seem to get my head that far up my ass.

7 (insult) Pardon me, but you've obviously mistaken me for someone who gives a damn.

8 (insult) I don't know what makes you so stupid, but it really works!

9 (insult) I thought of you all day today. I was at the zoo.

10 If you take a Oriental person and spin him around several times, does he become disoriented?

11 What hair color do they put on the driver's license of a bald man?

12 Why do you need a driver's license to buy liquor when you can't drink and drive?

13 You know how most packages say "Open here". What is the protocol if the package says, "Open somewhere else"?

14 If corn oil comes from corn, where does baby oil come from?

15 If a turtle doesn't have a shell, is he homeless or naked?

16 I thought about how mothers feed their babies with tiny little spoons and forks so I wondered what do Chinese mothers use? Toothpicks?

17 "Life is all about ass. You're either covering it, laughing it off, kicking it, kissing it, busting it or trying to get a piece of it."

18 Some days you're the dog, some days you're the hydrant.

19 Beware of the toes you step on today. They could be attached to the ass you may have to kiss tomorrow.

20 The difference between the Pope and your boss. The Pope only expects you to kiss his ring.

21 If someone with multiple personalities threatens to kill himself, is it considered a hostage situation?

22 If you try to fail, and succeed, which have you done?

23 I intend to live forever - so far, so good.

24 Energizer Bunny arrested, charged with battery.

25 If at first you don't succeed, then skydiving definitely is not for you.

26 Hard work pays off in the future. Laziness pays off now.

27 What disease did cured ham have?

28 What's the difference between unique and very unique?

29 We put in our two cents, but only get a penny for our thoughts. Who gets the extra penny?

30 When do you become important enough to be considered assassinated and not just murdered?

31 Can you cry under water?

32 Who decided that a round pizza should be put in a square box?

33 When you get to heaven, are you stuck for eternity wearing the same clothes you were buried in?

34 Why did we put a man on the moon before we realized it would be a good idea to make luggage with wheels?

35 Why are actors IN movies but ON television?

36 Why do toasters always have a setting that burns the toast?

37 Why does grass grow where you do not want it and not grow where you do?

38 Why do we say we slept like a baby when they wake up every two hours?

39 Why do we pay to get to the top of tall buildings, then pay to use binoculars to look at things on the ground?

40 If a deaf person goes to court, do they call it a hearing?

41 What is a Japanese maple tree called in Japan? (Ans: Baby's Palm)

42 We say, "It's Greek to me." What do the Greeks say? (Ans: It's Chinese to me.)

43 If we don't care that Jimmy cracked corn, why do we still sing about it?

44 Why does Goofy stand upright and Pluto stand on all four feet? They're both dogs.

45 Do "Twinkle, Twinkle Little Star" and "The Alphabet Song" have the same tune?

46 On Gilligan's Island, the professor could make a radio out of a coconut. Why couldn't he fix the hole in the boat?

47 If Wile E. Coyote has enough money to buy all that stuff from ACME, why doesn't he just buy himself dinner?

48 Can you drive in the car pool lane if you're driving a hearse with a corpse in it?

49 It is hard to understand how a cemetery raised its burial cost and blamed it on the cost of living.

50 Eight qualities of a PERFECT boyfriend... Brave, Intelligent, Gentle, Polite, Energetic, Non-alcoholic, Industrious, Self-organized. In short, B.I.G.P.E.N.I.S.

51 Be nice to your kids . . . they'll be the ones choosing your nursing home.

52 He met a lady while browsing. She unzipped his dotcom when downloading. Since he was virus free he slotted his floppy disk into her hotmail she screamed yahoo!

53 Did you have Campbell's soup today? (she answers yes/no) Because you're lookin' mmm... mmm... good!

54 I have the body of a god... Buddha!

55 My luck is so bad that if I bought a cemetery, people would stop dying.

56 I'm in shape ... round's a shape isn't it?

57 I'm a nobody.. nobody's perfect.. therefore, I'M PERFECT!!!

58 I Don't Know What Makes You So Dumb, But It Really Works.

59 I was so ugly that my Mom fed me with a sling shot.

60 I was so ugly that my Mom use to tie a steak around my neck just so the dog would play with me.

61 How does AVON find so many women willing to take orders?

62 Why do we drive on parkways when we park on driveways?

63 Did you hear about the blind prostitute? Well, you got to hand it to her.

64 Sex is like poker... if you don't have a good partner you better have a good hand.

65 He who runs behind a car is exhausted.

66 He who stands on the toilet is high on pot.

Phone Jokes

Q. What do you get when you cross a telephone with a pair of pants?
A. Bell-bottoms!

Q. How is a telephone like a dirty bathtub?
A. They both have rings!

Q. What happened to the little frog who sat on the telephone?
A. He grew up to be a bellhop!

Q. What do you get if you cross a telephone with an iron?
A. A smooth operator!

Q. What do you call a large person who constantly calls up people, pretending to be somebody else?
A. A big phone-y!

Q. Why didn't the skeleton need a telephone?
A. He had no body to talk with!

Q. How does a cheerleader answer the phone?
A. H-E-L-L-O!

Q. What do you get if you cross a phone with a pair of glasses?
A. A television.

Q. What is the cheapest time to call your friends long distance?
A. When they're not home!

Q. How does Ebenezer Scrooge make phone calls?
A. Collect!

Q. What do you get if you cross a phone with a birthday celebration?
A. A party line!

Q. How does a barber make phone calls?
A. He cuts them short.

Q. Why didn't the mummy want a telephone?
A. He always got too wrapped up in his calls!

Results from Email Information

1 -I want to thank all of you for your educational e-mails over the past years. I am totally screwed up now and have little chance of recovery.

2 - I no longer open a bathroom door without using a paper towel, or have the waitress put lemon slices in my ice water without worrying about the bacteria on the lemon peel.

3 - I can't use the remote in a hotel room because I don't know what the last person was doing while flipping through the adult movie channels.

4 - I can't sit down on the hotel bedspread because I can only imagine what has happened on it since it was last washed.

5 - I have trouble shaking hands with someone who has been driving because the number one pastime while driving alone is picking one's nose.

6 - Eating a little snack sends me on a guilt trip because I can only imagine how many gallons of trans-fats I have consumed over the years.

7 - I can't touch any woman's purse for fear she has placed it on the floor of a public bathroom.

8 - I MUST SEND MY SPECIAL THANKS to whoever sent me the one about rat poop in the glue on envelopes because I now have to use a wet sponge with every envelope that needs sealing.

9 - ALSO, now I have to scrub the top of every can I open for the same reason.

10 - I no longer have any money, but that will change once I receive the $15,000 that Bill Gates/Microsoft and AOL are sending me for participating in their special e-mail program.

11 - I no longer worry about my soul because I have 3,000 angels looking out for me, and St. Theresa's Novena has granted my every wish.

12 - I can't have a drink in a bar because I'll wake up in a bathtub full of ice with my kidneys gone.

13 - I can't eat at KFC because their chickens are actually horrible mutant freaks with no eyes, feet or feathers.

14 - I can't use cancer-causing deodorants even though I smell like a water buffalo on a hot day.

15 - THANKS TO YOU I have learned that my prayers only get answered if I forward an e-mail to seven of my friends and make a wish within five minutes.

16 - BECAUSE OF YOUR CONCERN, I no longer drink Coca Cola because it can remove toilet stains.

17 - I no longer buy gas without taking someone along to watch the car so a serial killer doesn't crawl in my back seat when I'm filling up.

18 - I no longer drink Pepsi or Fanta since the people who make these products are atheists who refuse to put 'Under God' on their cans.

19 - I no longer use Cling Wrap in the microwave because it causes seven different types of cancer.

20 - AND THANKS FOR LETTING ME KNOW I can't boil a cup of water in the microwave anymore because it will blow up in my face ... Disfiguring me for life.

21 - I no longer go to the movies because I could be pricked with a needle infected with AIDS when I sit down.

22 - I no longer go to shopping malls because someone will drug me with a perfume sample and rob me.

23 - I no longer receive packages from UPS or Fed Ex since they are actually Al Qaeda agents in disguise. And I no longer answer the phone because someone will ask me to dial a number for which I will get a phone bill with calls to Jamaica , Uganda , Singapore , and Uzbekistan.

24 - I no longer buy cookies from Neiman-Marcus since I now have their recipe.

25 - THANKS TO YOU I can't use anyone's toilet but mine because a big black snake could be lurking under the seat and cause me instant death when it bites my butt.

26 - AND THANKS TO YOUR GREAT ADVICE I can't ever pick up a coin dropped in the parking lot because it probably was placed there by a sex molester waiting to grab me as I bend over.

27 - I no longer drive my car because buying gas from some companies supports Al Qaeda, and buying gas from all the others supports South American dictators.

28 - I can't do any gardening because I'm afraid I'll get bitten by the wood spider and my hand will fall off.

29 - If you don't send this e-mail to at least 144,000 people in the next 70 minutes, a large dove with diarrhea will land on your head at 5:00 p.m. tomorrow afternoon, and the fleas from 120 camels will infest your back, causing you to grow a hairy hump. I know this will occur because it actually happened to a friend of my next door neighbor's ex-mother-in-law's second husband's cousin's best friend's beautician.

30 - Oh, by the way, a German scientist from Argentina, after a lengthy study, has discovered that people with insufficient brain activity read their e-mail with their hand on the mouse.

Don't bother taking it off now, it's too late.

31 - PS: I now keep my toothbrush in the living room, because I was told by e-mail that water splashes over 6 ft. out of the toilet.

The Things That Drive A Sane Person Mad

❏   You have to try on a pair of sunglasses with that stupid little plastic thing in the middle of them.

❏   The person behind you in the supermarket runs his cart into the back of your ankle.

❏   The elevator stops on every floor and nobody gets on.

❏   There's always a car riding your tail when you're slowing down to find an address.

❏   You open a can of soup and the lid falls in.

❏   There's a dog in the neighborhood that barks at EVERYTHING.

❏   You can never put anything back in a box the way it came.

❏   Your tire gauge lets out half the air while you're trying to get a reading.

❏   A station comes in brilliantly when you're standing near the radio but buzzes, drifts and spits every time you move away.

❏   There are always one or two ice cubes that won't pop out of the tray.

❏   You wash a garment with a tissue in the pocket and your entire laundry comes out covered with lint.

❏   The car behind you blasts its horn because you let a pedestrian finish crossing.

❏   A piece of foil candy wrapper makes electrical contact with your filling (or braces).

❏   You set the alarm on your digital clock for 7pm instead of 7am.

❏   The radio station doesn't tell you who sang that song.

❏   You rub on hand cream and can't turn the bathroom doorknob to get out.

❏ People behind you on a supermarket line dash ahead of you to a counter just opening up.

❏ Your glasses slide off your ears when you perspire.

❏ You can't look up the correct spelling of a word in the dictionary because you don't know how to spell it.

❏ You have to inform five different sales people in the same store that you're just browsing.

❏ You had that pen in your hand only a second ago and now you can't find it.

❏ You reach under the table to pick something off the floor and smash your head on the way up.

Think about this - Oneliners

❏ The Government wants more money? Why don't they try selling candy bars like the Boy Scouts do?

❏ Many people will spend the summer occupied with fishing and politics. In fishing you use a worm, and in politics a worm uses you.

❏ A person that learns from their mistakes is smart. A person that learns from other people's mistakes is smarter.

❏ Why be difficult? Put some effort in and be impossible.

❏ I am extraordinarily patient, provided I get my own way in the end.

❏ I'm learning to speak Spanish by calling my bank and pressing the #2 button.

❏ It takes less time to do something right than to explain why you did it wrong.

❐ The things you tell your teenagers don't reach them 'til they're in their 40s.

❐ He who lives without discipline dies without honor.

❐ I have a speech impediment . . . my foot.

❐ I need some duck tape . . . my duck has a quack in it

❐ I was thinking of becoming a doctor. I have the handwriting for it.

❐ The more you say, the less people remember.

❐ 98% of the time I am right. Why worry about the other 3%.

❐ With proper diet, rest, and exercise a healthy body will last a lifetime.

❐ Thesaurus: ancient reptile with an excellent vocabulary.

❐ Practice courtesy. You never know when it might become popular again.

❐ Any sports fan can tell you the most brutal thing about professional football is the price of the tickets.

❐ It's discouraging to think how many people are shocked by honesty and how few by deceit.

❐ The measure of success is not how much money you have in the bank, but rather how much money the bank will lend you.

❐ Anyone who starts a sentence "With all due respect..." is about to insult you.

❐ Don't count your fish until they're on dry land.

❐ Don't judge, you idiot.

❐ Marriage is like a tourniquet; it stops your circulation.

❑ Everything on land is within walking distance.

❑ The road to success is marked with many tempting parking places.

❑ We're not truly happy until we focus on others.

❑ Sarcasm: an ingenious way of making intelligent people feel stupid.

❑ Love isn't blind . . . it just has Attention Deficit Disorder.

❑ Life is a bowl of cherries . . . overpriced and only available at certain times.

❑ A lot of good-looking faces are wasted on ugly people.

❑ Funny that most of our best-sellers are written at a 9th-grade reading level.

❑ Small talk is one step down from no talk.

❑ If it weren't for humor, we might never get at the truth.

❑ To understand politics, we must read between the lies.

Parrot

It's the plumber

A man had a parrot that he taught to speak. He taught the bird to say 'Who is it?' whenever the doorbell rang.

One day the man's wife told him: "The bathroom sink is clogged up and I can't get it to come loose, you need to call a plumber." So the man went to work and after he got to the office he had his secretary call a plumber for him. After trying three different shops, she found a plumber to fix the main drain. The secretary gave the plumber the address and added that the wife would be home to let him in.

Meanwhile the wife had left for lunch and her card club and forgot that her husband was going to call the plumber out to the house.

So after a while the plumber shows up at the man's house and rings the bell. The parrot says, "Who is it?" The man at the door says: "It's the plumber." Nobody comes to the door. He rings the bell again. "Who is it?" says the parrot. "It's the plumber!" the man calls out, louder this time. Still, no one comes to the door.

He rings the bell again. "Who is it?" says the parrot. "It's the plumber!!" calls out the man, angry now. But still, no one comes to the door. One more time, the man rings the bell. "Who is it?" says the parrot. The man bellows out: **"It's the plumber!!!!"**

Then the man clutches his chest and has a heart attack right there on the front porch, and dies. About 5:30 the wife and husband arrive home at the same time and notice a man lying on the front porch. They drag him into the living room and the wife says to the husband: "I wonder who it is?" "It's the plumber!" says the parrot.

Moses and Jesus

A burglar breaks into a house. He sees a CD player that he wants so he takes it. Then he hears a voice "JESUS is watching you". He looks around with his flashlight wandering "What The HELL Was That?".

He spots some $ on a table and takes it......Once again he hears a voice "JESUS is watching you". He hides in a corner trying to find where the voice came from. He spots a birdcage with a parrot in it! He goes over and asks "Was that your voice?".

The parrot said "YES". He then says "What's your name?" The parrot answered, "MOSES".

The burglar says "What kind of person names his bird Moses?"

The parrot replies, "THE SAME PERSON THAT NAMES HIS ROTWEILER 'JESUS'."

Parrot and a Flight Passenger

In reaching his plane seat, a man is surprised to see a parrot strapped into the seat next to him. The man asks the stewardess for a cup of coffee and the parrot squawks, "And why don't you get me a whisky you bitch."

The stewardess, flustered by the parrot's outburst, brings back a whisky for the parrot but inadvertently forgets the man's cup of coffee.

As the man nicely points out the omission of his coffee to the stewardess, the parrot downs his drink and shouts, "And get me another whisky you slut."

Visibly shaken, the stewardess comes back with the parrot's whisky but still no coffee for the man.

Unaccustomed to such slackness, the man decides that he is going to try the parrots approach, "I've asked you twice for a cup of coffee wench, I expect you to get it for me right now or I'm going to slap that disgustingly ugly face of yours!"

Next thing they know, both the man and the parrot are wrenched up and thrown out of the emergency exit by 2 burly stewards.

Plunging downwards to the ground the parrot turns to the man and says, "For someone who can't fly, you sure are a lippy bastard... "

Parrot For Mom

Three sons left home, went out on their own and prospered. Getting back together, they discussed the gifts they were able to give their elderly mother.

The first said, "I built a big house for our mother."

The second said, "I sent her a Mercedes with a driver."

The third smiled and said, "I've got you both beat. You remember how mom enjoyed reading the Bible? And you know she can't see very well. So I sent her a remarkable parrot that recites the entire Bible. It took elders in the church 12 years to teach him. He's one of a kind. Mama just has to name the chapter and verse, and the parrot recites it."

Soon thereafter, mom sent out her letters of thanks: "Milton," she wrote one son, "The house you built is so huge. I live in only one room, but I have to clean the whole house."

"Gerald," she wrote to another, "I am too old to travel. I stay most of the time at home, so I rarely use the Mercedes. And the driver is so rude!"

"Dearest Donald," she wrote to her third son, "You have the good sense to know what your mother likes. The chicken was delicious."

Talking Parrots

A lady goes to her parish priest one day and tells him, "Father, I have a problem. I have two female parrots but they only know how to say one thing." "What do they say?" the priest inquired. "They say, 'Hi, we're prostitutes. Do you want to have some fun?" "That's obscene!" the priest exclaimed, "I can see why you are embarrassed."

He thought a minute and then said, "You know, I may have a solution to this problem. I have two male parrots that I have taught to pray and read the Bible. Bring your two parrots over to my house and we will put them in the cage with Francis and Job. My parrots can teach your parrots to praise and worship. I'm sure your parrots will stop saying that...that phrase in no time."

"Thank you," the woman responded, "this may very well be the solution."

The next day, she brought her female parrots to the priest's house. As he ushered her in, she saw this two male parrots were inside their cage, holding their rosary beads and praying. Impressed, she walked over and placed her parrots in with them. After just a couple of seconds, the female parrots exclaimed out in unison, "Hi, we're prostitutes. Do you want to have some fun?"

There was a stunned silence. Finally, one male parrot looked over at the other male parrot and said, "Put the beads away, Francis, our prayers have been answered!"

The Magician and the Parrot

There was a magician on a cruise ship, and he was really good. As he was performing the highlight of his show, a parrot walked onstage and squawked, "It's in his sleeve!" The magician chased the bird away.

The next day the magician was performing his highlight again (in front of a smaller audience) when the parrot walked onstage and declared, "It's in his pocket!"

The next day, as he was performing the highlight trick, he saw the parrot in the crowd. But before the parrot could ruin the magic trick, the boat crashed into a rock and sank.

The magician was lucky enough to find a board to hang on to. On the other end of the board was the parrot.

They stared at each other for three full days, neither of them saying anything, when suddenly the parrot said, "I give up, what'd you do with the ship?"

Police

Deputy Gomer

The local sheriff was looking for a deputy, so Gomer went in to try out for the job.

"Okay," the sheriff drawled, "Gomer, what is 1 and 1?"

"11" he replied.

The sheriff thought to himself, "That's not what I meant, but he's right."

"What two days of the week start with the letter 'T'?"

"Today and tomorrow."

The sheriff was again surprised that Gomer supplied a correct answer that he had never thought of himself.

"Now Gomer, listen carefully: Who killed Abraham Lincoln?"

Gomer looked a little surprised himself, then thought really hard for a minute and finally admitted, "I don't know."

"Well, why don't you go home and work on that one for a while?"

So, Gomer wandered over to the barbershop where his pals were waiting to hear the results of the interview. Gomer was exultant. "It went great! First day on the job and I'm already working on a murder case!"

Drunk Driver

A female officer arrests a drunk. She warns him, "You have the right to remain silent. Anything you say can and will be held against you."

The drunk replies, "Boobs."

Glasses

A policeman stops a lady and asks for her license. He says "Lady, it says here that you should be wearing glasses."

The woman answered "Well, I have contacts."

The policeman replied "I don't care who you know! You're getting a ticket!"

Juggling Test

A juggler who was driving to his next performance was stopped by the police. "What are those knives doing in your car?" asked the officer.

"I juggle them in my act."

"Oh yeah?" says the cop. "Let's see you do it." So the juggler starts tossing and juggling the knives.

A guy driving by sees this and says, "Wow, am I glad I quit drinking. Look at the test they're making you do now!"

Tail Light

"How long have you been driving without a tail light?" asked the policeman after pulling over a motorist. The driver jumped out, ran to the rear of his car and gave a long, painful groan.

He seemed so upset that the cop was moved to ease up on him a bit.

"Come on, now," he said, "you don't have to take it so hard. It isn't that serious."

"It isn't?" cried the motorist.

"Then you know what happened to my boat and trailer?"

Taking a Breathalyzer Test

A cop saw a car weaving all over the road and pulled it over. He walked up to the car and saw a nice-looking woman behind the wheel. There was a strong liquor smell on her breath.

He said, 'I'm going to give you a breathalyzer test to determine if you are under the influence of alcohol.' She blew up the balloon and he walked it back to the police car. After a couple of minutes, he returned to her car and said, 'It looks like you've had a couple of stiff ones.'

She replied, 'You mean it shows that, too?'

Tennessee State Troopers Don't Have Balls

A young woman was pulled over in Nashville, Tennessee for speeding. As the Tennessee State Trooper walked to her car window, flipping open his ticket book, she said, "I bet you are going to sell me a ticket to the Tennessee State Police Ball."

He replied, "Tennessee State Troopers don't have balls."

There was a moment of silence while she smiled and he realized what he'd just said. He then closed his book, got back in his patrol car and left.

She was laughing too hard to start her car.

Truth or Consequences

Police officers George and Mary had been assigned to walk the beat. They had only been out a short while when Mary said, "Damn, I was running late this morning after my workout and after I showered, I forgot to put on my panties! We have to go back to the station to get them." George replied, "We don't have to go back, just give the K-9 unit, Fido, one sniff, and he will go fetch them for you."

It was a hot day and Mary didn't feel like heading back to the station, so she lifted her skirt for the dog. Fido's nose shoots between her legs, sniffing and snorting. After 10 seconds of sniffing, Fido's ears pick up, he sniffs the wind, and he is off in a flash towards the station house. Five minutes go by and no sign of Fido. Ten minutes pass, and the dog is nowhere to be seen. Fifteen minutes pass, and they are starting to worry.

Twenty minutes pass, and they hear sirens in the distance. The sirens get louder and louder. Suddenly, followed by a dozen police cars, Fido rounds the corner with the Desk Sergeant's balls in his mouth.

Political

A Bronze Rat

A tourist from the Midwest walked into a Chinese curio shop in San Francisco. While looking around at the exotic merchandise, he noticed a very lifelike, life-sized, bronze statue of a rat. It had no price tag, but was so incredibly striking the tourist decided he must have it. He took it to the old shop owner and asked, "How much for the bronze rat?"

"Ahhh, you have chosen wisely! It is $12 for the rat, and $100 for the story," said the wise old Chinaman. The tourist quickly pulled out twelve dollars. "I'll just take the rat, you can keep the story", he said.

As he walked down the street carrying his bronze rat, the tourist noticed that a few real rats had crawled out of the alleys and sewers and had begun following him down the street. This was a bit disconcerting so he began walking faster.

A couple blocks later he looked behind him and saw to his horror the herd of rats behind him had grown to hundreds, and they began squealing.

Sweating now, the tourist began to trot toward the Bay. After a couple more blocks, he looked around only to discover that the rats now numbered in the THOUSANDS, and were squealing and coming toward him faster and faster.

Terrified, he ran to the edge of the Bay and threw the bronze rat as far as he could into the Bay. Amazingly, the thousands of rats all jumped into the Bay after the bronze rat, and were all drowned.

The man walked back to the curio shop in Chinatown. "Ahhh," said the owner, "You have come back for story, yes?

"Are you kidding ?" said the man,

"I came back to see if you have a bronze Democrat!"

ABOUT AS GOOD AS IT GETS FOR ME!

Having arrived at the Gates of Heaven, Barrack Obama meets a man with a beard. "Are you Mohammed?" he asks. "No my son, I am St. Peter; Mohammed is higher up." Peter then points to a ladder that rises into the clouds.

Delighted that Mohammed should be higher than St. Peter, Obama climbs the ladder in great strides, climbs up through the clouds and comes into a room where he meets another bearded man. He asks again, "Are you Mohammed?"

"Why no," he answers, "I am Moses, Mohammed is higher still."

Exhausted, but with a heart full of joy he climbs the ladder yet again, he discovers a larger room where he meets an angelic looking man with a beard. Full of hope, he asks again, "Are you Mohammed?" "No, I am Jesus Christ....you will find Mohammed higher up."

Mohammed higher than Jesus! Man, oh man! Obama can hardly contain his delight and climbs and climbs ever higher. Once again, he reaches an even larger room where he meets this truly magnificent looking man with a silver white beard and once again repeats his question: "Are you Mohammed?" he gasps as he is by now, totally out of breath from all his climbing. "No, my son.... I am Almighty God, the Alpha and the Omega, but you look exhausted. Would you like a cup of coffee?"

Obama says, "Yes please!" As God looks behind him, he claps his hands and yells out: "Hey Mohammed - two coffees!"

Keep your trust in God...your president is an idiot.........;

 In God I Trust

Air Force One Crashes

Air Force One crashed in the middle of rural America. Panic stricken, the local sheriff mobilized and descended on the farm in force. When they got there, the disaster was clear. The aircraft was totally destroyed with only a burned hulk left smoldering in a tree line that bordered a farm. The sheriff and his men entered the smoking mess but could find no remains of anyone, including the President.

They spotted the local farmer plowing a field not too far away as if nothing at all happened. They hurried over to the man's tractor.

"Hank," the sheriff yelled, panting and out of breath. "Did you see this terrible accident happen?"

"Yep. sure did." the farmer mumbled unconcernedly, cutting off the tractor's engine.

"Do you realize that is the airplane of the President of the United States?"

"Yep."

"Were there any survivors?"

"Nope. They's all kilt straight out," the farmer answered. "I done buried them all myself. Took me most of the morning..."

"President Obama is dead?" the sheriff shouted.

"Well," the farmer grumbled, restarting his tractor. "He kept a-saying he wasn't... But you know how that sumbitch lies."

Apology is in Order

We must apologize; your shipment is back ordered.

We simply cannot keep up with the demand of this very popular item.

180 million are on back order. We will complete your delivery as soon as possible.

Barack Obama has a heart-attack

One day in the future, Barack Obama has a heart-attack and dies.

He immediately goes to hell, where the devil is waiting for him.
"I don't know what to do here," says the devil. "You are on my list, but I have no room for you. You definitely have to stay here, so I'll tell you what I'm going to do. I've got a couple of folks here who weren't quite as bad as you. I'll let one of them go, but you have to take their place. I'll even let YOU decide who leaves."

Obama thought that sounded pretty good, so the devil opened the door to the first room. In it was Ted Kennedy and a large pool of water. Ted kept diving in, and surfacing, empty handed. Over, and over, and over he dived in and surfaced with nothing. Such was his fate in hell.

"No," Obama said. "I don't think so. I'm not a good swimmer, and I don't think I could do that all day long."

The devil led him to the door of the next room. In it was Al Gore with a sledgehammer and a room full of rocks. All he did was swing that hammer, time after time after time.

"No, this is no good; I've got this problem with my shoulder. I would be in constant agony if all I could do was break rocks all day," commented Obama.

The devil opened a third door. He saw GW Bush crawling through the Iraqi desert, his hands and knees were raw and bloody. He kept muttering: "I know those WMD's are here somewhere..."

Obama said: "No thanks, I cannot handle a dry climate very well."

The devil opened a 4th door. Through it, Obama saw Bill Clinton, lying on the bed, his arms tied over his head, and his legs restrained in a spread-eagle pose. Bent over him was Monica Lewinsky, doing what she does best.

Obama looked at this in shocked disbelief, and finally said, "Yeah man, I can handle this."

The devil smiled and said .. . . . .
(This is priceless...)

"OK, Monica, you're free to go."

Barack's Bingo

Try this the next time you hear the President speak... It will keep you awake!

Please follow the rules before watching. I used to avoid listening to his speeches. Now, I look forward to the next one.

Here is something to help make Obama's speeches almost tolerable.

Just print out this page, distribute it to friends, and listen. (be sure to read directions at the bottom)

BARACK'S BULLSHIT

LET ME BE CLEAR	HELD ACCOUNTABLE	HISTORIC	MAKE NO MISTAKE	I'VE SAID TIME AND TIME AGAIN
UH, I, UH, UMMM	CRISIS	PAHK-EE-STAHN	WORST ECONOMY SINCE THE GREAT DEPRESSION	SAVED OR CREATED
GAME CHANGER	THERE ARE THOSE WHO SAY	PREVIOUS ADMINISTRATION	INHERITED	BACK FROM THE BRINK
UNPRECEDENTED	FISCAL RESPONSIBILITY	I, ME, MY	NOT ONE DIME	TRANSPARENT
THAT'S SIMPLY NOT TRUE	THE SYSTEM IS BROKEN	YOU CAN KEEP YOUR PRESENT PLAN	RESTORE OUR REPUTATION	CHOICE AND COMPETITION

Rules for Bullshit Bingo:
1. Before Barrack Obama's next televised speech, print your "Bullshit Bingo"
2. Check off the appropriate block when you hear one of those words/phrases.
3. When you get five blocks horizontally, vertically, or diagonally, stand up and shout "BULLSHIT!"

Bush and Obama at the Barber Shop

George Bush and Barack Obama somehow ended up at the same barber shop.

As they sat there, each being worked on by a different barber, not a word was spoken. The barbers were even afraid to start a conversation, for fear it would turn to politics.

As the barbers finished their shaves, the one who had Obama in his chair reached for the aftershave. Obama was quick to stop him saying, 'No thanks, my wife Michelle will smell that and think I've been in a whorehouse,'

The second barber turned to Bush and said, 'How about you sir?' Bush replied, 'Go ahead; my wife doesn't know what the inside of a whorehouse smells like.'

Bush, Cheney, and the Buck

Bush and Cheney went hunting, killed a giant buck, and were dragging it by the legs back to their car, when they were approached by a seasoned old hunter.

"Hello, Mr. President and Vice President. If I may please make a suggestion... it would be much easier for you to drag your deer in the other direction. Then the antlers won't dig into the ground."

The leaders of the free world thanked the man and tried his suggestion. A while later Cheney said, "You know, that was good thinking. This is a lot easier!"

"Yes sir," agreed Bush. "But durn it! We're gettin' farther away from our truck!"

Clinton and the Beer Cans

Back when Bill Clinton and Hillary got married Bill told her, "There's one thing I want you to know. There's a box under my bed and I don't want you to look in it until I die."

Hillary agreed to this but, over the years, the curiosity got the better of her and she finally looked in it. She found three beer cans and 1.5 million dollars in cash.

When she asked Bill what the beer cans were for, he replied, "Well, those are for all the times I've cheated on you."

Hillary said, "Well, that's not bad after all these years and you being a politician and traveling and all."

She was about to leave, but then she said, "Hey, Bill, what about the 1.5 million dollars?"

Bill replied, "That's for all the times the box got full and I had to cash the cans in."

Coded Message from Bin Laden to Bush

After numerous rounds of 'We don't know if Osama Bin Laden is still alive', Osama decided to personally send President Bush a letter in his own handwriting to let him know he was 'still in the game'.

Mr. Bush opened the letter, which contained a single line of 'coded' message:

370HSSV-0773H

Mr. Bush was baffled, so he sent copies to his Chief of Staff, and several Secretaries, including Condi Rice and Donald Rumsfeld. Their assistants and aides had no clue as to the meaning or translation of the code, so it was sent to the Federal Bureau of Investigation, then to the CIA and also to NASA. With no clue to the translation, they eventually asked Israel's MOSAD for help.

Within a minute, MOSAD cabled the White House with this reply:

"Tell the President he is holding the message upside down."

Drinking Politics

A man wearing a Democratic pin walks into a bar and sees a picture of President Bush hanging behind the bartender. He calls the bartender over and says, "You should take that picture down. George Bush is a blight upon this nation. He should be impeached."

The bartender, a life-long Republican, is completely offended. "Why you liberal piece of garbage. How dare you come into my bar and tell me how to run my business!"

"Listen, I'm the customer, so I'm always right." the man says. "That picture offends me, so I want you to take it down."

"That it," the bartender says, "How would you like it if I came into your bar and told you what to do?"

"Well, you'd be the customer, so you'd be right," the man says.

"Fine, then let's switch places," the bartender says.

So, they do. The man takes the bartender's place behind the bar, and the bartender walks outside, waits a moment, and then comes back inside. The bartender sits at the bar and says to the bar, "You should take that pin off. The Democrats are destroying our country with their liberal agenda."

"Sorry," the man says, "but we don't serve Republicans here."

EX-President Bush goes into a Bar

Ex-President Bush, decides to leave the Ranch and go out to sit in a local Crawford bar. A guy walks in and asks the barman, 'Isn't that Bush sitting at the end of the bar?'

The bartender says, "Yep, that's him." So the guy walks over and says, "Wow, this is a real honor! What are you doing in here?"

Bush says, "I'm planning WW III."

The guy says, "Really? What's going to happen?"

Bush says, "Well, I'm going to kill 140 million Muslims and one blonde with big Boobs."

The guy exclaimed, "A blonde with big boobs? Why kill a blonde with big boobs?"

Bush turns to the bartender and says, "See I told you no one gives a shit about the 140 million Muslims."

Explanation of Just What is the Government

A five year old little boy asked his dad to explain the government to him. The father said: "Okay, son, I'll explain it the best way I can. "See, me, I'm like the government, because everything has to come through me in order for this house to work smoothly. Your mother is like the people, because she has some say, but I can override it. The maid is the working class, because she works for us. Your baby brother is the future."

Needless to say, the little boy was very confused. That night after he went to bed, he happened to wake up because he heard his little brother crying. He went to his parents' room to get his mom but when he opened the door his mother was asleep, and his dad wasn't there. So, he went to get the maid, but when he opened her door, he saw his dad and the maid, in a lather of sweat and screwing madly. He went to check on his brother himself. He opened his diaper to find that it was full of shit.

The next morning he went up to his dad and said, "Dad, I think I understand the government." His dad replied, "Oh, really, tell me."

So the little boy said, "While the people are sleeping, the government is busy screwing the working class and the future is full of shit!"

Great Haircut

A priest walked into a barber shop in Washington, D.C. After he got his haircut, he asked how much it would be. The barber said, "No charge. I consider it a service to the Lord." The next morning, the barber came to work and there were 12 prayer books and a thank you note from the priest in front of the door.

Later that day, a police officer came in and got his hair cut. He then asked how much it was. The barber said, "No charge. I consider it a service to the community." The next morning, he came to work and there were a dozen donuts and a thank you note from the police officer.

Then, a Senator came in and got a haircut. When he was done he asked how much it was. The barber said, "No charge. I consider it a service to the country." The next morning, the barber came to work and there were 12 Senators in front of the door.

Great Loss

One of the presidential candidates was visiting an elementary school, and the 4th grade class he sat through began a discussion related to words and their meanings.

The teacher asked the candidate if he would like to lead the class in a discussion of the word "tragedy." So, the candidate asked the class for an example of a tragedy.

One boy stood up and said, "If my best friend who lives next door is playing in the street and a car comes along and runs him over, that would be a tragedy."

"No," said the candidate, "that would be an accident."

A girl raised her hand and said, "If a school bus carrying 50 children drove off a cliff, killing everyone on board, that would be a tragedy."

"I'm afraid not," the candidate said. "That's what we would call a Great Loss."

The room went silent. No other children volunteered. The candidate searched the room and asked, "Isn't there someone here who can give me an example of a tragedy?"

Finally, way in the back of the room, Johnny raised his hand, and in a quiet voice, he said, "If your campaign plane, carrying yourself and your running mate, was struck by a missile and blown to smithereens, THAT would be a tragedy."

"That's right! And can you tell me WHY that would be a tragedy?" asked the candidate.

"Well," Johnny said, "because it wouldn't be an accident and it sure as heck wouldn't be a Great Loss..."

Gun Control

Barack Obama at a recent rural elementary school assembly in East Texas, asked the audience for total quiet. Then, in the silence, he started to slowly clap his hands once every few seconds, holding the audience in total silence.

Then he said into the microphone, 'Children, every time I clap my hands together, a child in America dies from gun violence.'

Then, little Richard Earl, with a proud East Texas drawl, pierced the quiet and said: "Well, dumb ass, stop clapping!"

Hillary Clinton speaking to a grade school class

Hillary Clinton goes to a primary school in Ithaca, New York to talk about the world. After her talk she offers question time.
One little boy puts up his hand, and the Senator asks him what his name is. "Kenneth."

"And what is your question, Kenneth?"

"I have three questions: First - whatever happened to your medical health care plan?
Second - why would you run for President after your husband shamed the office?
And third -- whatever happened to all those things you took when you

left the White House?"

Just then the bell rings for recess. Hillary Clinton informs the kiddies that they will continue after recess.
When they resume Hillary says, "Okay where were we? Oh, that's right, question time.

Who has a question?"
A different little boy puts his hand up; Hillary points him out and asks him what his name is.

"Larry." "And what is your question?"

"I have five questions:
First - whatever happened to your medical health care plan?
Second - why would you run for President after your husband shamed the office?
Third - whatever happened to all those things you took when you left the White House?
Fourth - why did the recess bell go off 20 minutes early?
And fifth -- what happened to Kenneth?"

Indian Chief's Observations

Indian Chief 'Two Eagles' was asked by a white government official, 'You have observed the white man for 90 years. You've seen his wars and his technological advances. You've seen his progress, and the damage he's done.' The Chief nodded in agreement.

The official continued, 'Considering all these events, in your opinion, where did the white man go wrong?'

The Chief stared at the government official for over a minute and then calmly replied. 'When white man find land, Indians running it, no taxes, no debt, plenty buffalo, plenty beaver, clean water. Women did all the work; Medicine man free. Indian man spend all day hunting and fishing; all night having sex.'

Then the chief leaned back, puffed his pipe and smiled. "Only white man dumb enough to think he could improve system like that".

JESUS AND THE DEMOCRAT

(I don't care what party you like, this one's funny!!)

A Republican, in a wheelchair, entered a restaurant one afternoon and asked the waitress for a cup of coffee. The Republican looked across the restaurant and asked, "Is that Jesus sitting over there?"

The waitress nodded "yes," so the Republican requested that she give Jesus a cup of coffee, on him.

The next patron to come in was a Libertarian, with a hunched back. He shuffled over to a booth, painfully sat down, and asked the waitress for a cup of hot tea. He also glanced across the restaurant and asked, "Is that Jesus, over there?"

The waitress nodded, so the Libertarian asked her to give Jesus a cup of hot tea, "My treat."

The third patron to come into the restaurant was a Democrat on crutches. He hobbled over to a booth, sat down and hollered, "Hey there honey! How's about getting me a cold glass of wine?" He too looked across the restaurant and asked, "Isn't that God's boy over there?

The waitress nodded, so the Democrat directed her to give Jesus a cold glass of wine. "On my bill," he said loudly.

As Jesus got up to leave, he passed by the Republican, touched him and said, "For your kindness, you are healed." The Republican felt the strength come back into his legs, got up, and danced a jig out the door.

Jesus passed by the Libertarian, touched him and said, "For your kindness, you are healed." The Libertarian felt his back straightening up and he raised his hands, praised the Lord, and did a series of back flips out the door.

Then, Jesus walked towards the Democrat, just smiling.

The Democrat jumped up and yelled, "Don't touch me ... I'm collecting disability."

LOOKING FOR WORK

A doctor from Israel says: "In Israel the medicine is so advanced that we cut off a man's testicles, we put them into another man, and in 6 weeks he is looking for work."

The German doctor comments: "That's nothing, in Germany we take part of the brain out of a person, we put it into another person's head, and in 4 weeks he is looking for work."

A Russian doctor says: "That's nothing either. In Russia we take out half of the heart from a person, we put it into another person's chest, and in 2 weeks he is looking for work."

The U.S. doctor answers immediately: "That's nothing my colleagues, you are way behind us....in the USA (about 2 years ago) we grabbed a person from Kenya with no brains, no heart, and no balls....we made him President of the United States, and now...the whole country is looking for work.

Moses Meets George W.

George W. Bush was getting off of Air Force One in Israel, when he walked passed Moses, who didn't seem to notice him. He turned to Moses and said, "I am George W. Bush, the President of the USA, the most powerful nation on earth. Why didn't you greet me?"

Moses replied, "The last time I spoke to a bush, we starved for 40 years!"

MY NEW CAR

I bought a new Lincoln MKZ but returned to the dealer the next day because I couldn't get the radio to work.

The salesman explained that the radio was voice activated "Nelson," the salesman said to the radio.

The Radio replied, "Ricky or Willie?"

"Willie!" he continued and "On The Road Again" came from the speakers.

Then he said, "Ray Charles!", and in an instant "Georgia On My Mind" replaced Willie Nelson.

I drove away happy, and for the next few days, every time I'd say, "Beethoven," I'd get beautiful classical music. If I said, "Beatles," I'd get one of their awesome songs.

Yesterday, a driver ran a red light and nearly creamed my new MKZ, but I swerved in time to avoid him. I yelled, "Ass Hole!"

Immediately Hail-to-the-Chief began playing.

I LOVE this car!

New Government Seal:

Official Announcement:

The federal government today announced that it is changing its emblem from an Eagle to a CONDOM because it more accurately reflects the government's political stance. A condom allows for inflation, halts production, destroys the next generation, protects a bunch of pricks, and gives you a sense of security while you're actually being screwed!

Damn, it just doesn't get more accurate than that.

New Symbol of the American Presidency

The eagle is gone!

The skunk has replaced the Eagle as the new symbol of the American Presidency. It is half black, half white, and everything it does stinks!

Obama Health Plan

Let me get this straight. We're going to maybe have a health care plan written by a committee whose head says he doesn't understand it, passed by a Congress that hasn't read it but exempts themselves from it, signed by a president that also hasn't read it and who smokes, with funding administered by a treasury chief who didn't pay his taxes, overseen by a surgeon general who is obese, and financed by a country that's nearly broke.

What could possibly go wrong?

If something did go wrong, who would know?

Obama Jokes

The liberals are asking us to give Obama time.
We agree... and think 25 to life would be appropriate.
- *Jay Leno*

America needs Obama-care like Nancy Pelosi needs a Halloween mask.
- *Jay Leno*

Q: Have you heard about McDonald's'
new Obama Value Meal?
A: Order anything you like and the guy behind you has to pay for it.
- *Conan O'Brien*

Q: What does Barack Obama
call lunch with a convicted felon?
A: A fund raiser.
-*Jay Leno*

Q: What's the difference between
Obama's cabinet and a penitentiary?
A: One is filled with tax evaders, blackmailers,
and threats to society. The other is for housing prisoners.
- *David Letterman*

Q: If Nancy Pelosi and Obama were on a boat
in the middle of the ocean and it started to sink,
who would be saved?
A: America!
- *Jimmy Fallon*

Q: What's the difference between
Obama and his dog, Bo?
A: Bo has papers.
- *Jimmy Kimmel*

Q: What was the most positive result of
the "Cash for Clunkers" program?
A: It took 95% of the
Obama bumper stickers off the road.
- *David Letterman*

Jewish Holidays

"Hi. This is President Obama. Is Senator Lieberman in?"

"No, Mr. President. It's Yom Kippur!"

"Well, Hello, Yom. Can I leave a message?"

OBAMA'S CLOCK

A man died and went to heaven. As he stood in front of St. Peter at the Pearly Gates, he saw a huge wall of clocks behind him.

He asked, 'What are all those clocks?'
St. Peter answered, 'Those are Lie-Clocks Everyone on Earth has a Lie-Clock.
Every time you lie the hands on your clock will move.'

'Oh,' said the man, 'whose clock is that?'
'That's Mother Teresa's. The hands have never moved, indicating that she never told a lie.'

'Incredible,' said the man. 'And whose clock is that one?'
St. Peter responded, 'That's Abraham Lincoln's clock. The hands have moved twice, telling us that Abe told only two lies in his entire life.'

'Where's Obama's clock?' asked the man.
'Obama's clock is in Jesus' office.   He's using it as a ceiling fan.

OBAMA WALKS INTO A BAR WITH A PARROT ON HIS SHOULDER.
THE BARTENDER ASKS, "WHERE DID YOU GET THAT?"

"AFRICA . . . THEY'RE ALL OVER THE PLACE!", SAID THE PARROT.

Political Employees

Can you imagine working for a company that has a little more than 500 employees and has the following statistics:

1. 29 have been accused of spousal abuse
2. 7 have been arrested for fraud
3. 19 have been accused of writing bad checks
4. 117 have directly or indirectly bankrupted at least 2 businesses
5. 3 have done time for assault
6. 71 cannot get a credit card due to bad credit
7. 14 have been arrested on drug-related charges
8. 8 have been arrested for shoplifting

9. 21 are currently defendants in lawsuits
10. 84 have been arrested for drunk driving in the last year

Can you guess which organization this is?

Give up yet?

It's the 535 members of the 2011 United States Congress. The same group of idiots that crank out hundreds of new laws each year designed to keep the rest of us in line.

Political Opinion

Having already downed a few power drinks, she turns around, faces him, looks him straight in the eye and says,

"Listen here good looking, I screw anybody, anytime, anywhere, your place, my place, in the car, front door, back door, on the ground, standing up, sitting down, naked or with clothes on; it doesn't matter to me. I just love it!"

Eyes now wide with interest, he responds, "No kidding. I'm in Congress too. What state are you from?"

President Bush with Iraq War Statistics

Donald Rumsfeld briefed the President this morning. He told Bush that three Brazilian soldiers were killed in Iraq. All of the color ran from Bush's face. Then he collapsed onto his desk, head in hands, visibly shaken and was almost whimpering.

Finally, he composed himself and asked Rumsfeld, "Just exactly how many is a brazillion?"

President Clinton Meets With Saddam

President Clinton was in Baghdad talking about the peace accords. Clinton noticed there were 3 buttons on Saddam's chair. He didn't think anything of it at the time.

After a few minutes Saddam pressed the fist button. Immediately a box popped out in front of Clinton and a boxing glove popped up and punched Clinton in the nose. Clinton was a little dazed, but he wanted to continue with the peace accords so he kept talking. After a few minutes Saddam pressed the second button. A boot came out of the floor and kicked Clinton in the shin. Clinton is starting to get angry, but he decides to go on. About 5 minutes later Saddam pressed the last button and another boot came up and kicked Clinton in the balls.

Clinton had it at this point and jumped up and yelled, "That's it, I'll see you in Washington D.C. in 2 weeks!"

Two weeks went by and Saddam came to D.C. He noticed 3 buttons on Clinton's desk and started to get ready for Clinton's revenge. He started talking and after a few minutes Clinton pressed the first button. Saddam ducked and nothing happened. He starts talking again, and after a few minutes Clinton pressed the second button. Saddam moved to the side, but, again, nothing happened. Saddam is starting to get suspicious, but he keeps talking. A few more minutes later Clinton pressed the third button. Saddam jumps up, and still, nothing happens.

At this point Saddam is furious. He yells, "That's it, I'm going back to Baghdad."

Clinton looks straight at him and responds, "What Baghdad?"

Prostitutes in Washington

A hundred prostitutes in Washington D.C. were asked if they would ever sleep with President Clinton. 60% said, 'Never again!'

Republican or Democrat?

A woman in a hot air balloon realized she was lost. She lowered her altitude and spotted a man in a boat below. She shouted to him, "Excuse me, can you help me? I promised a friend I would meet him an hour ago, but I don't know where I am." The man consulted his portable GPS and replied, "You're in a hot air balloon, approximately 30 feet above a ground elevation of 2346 feet above sea level. You are at 31 degrees, 14.97 minutes north latitude and 100 degrees, 49.09 minutes west longitude."

She rolled her eyes and said, "You must be a Republican." "I am," replied the man. "How did you know?" "Well," answered the balloonist, "everything you told me is technically correct, but I have no idea what to do with your information, and I'm still lost. Frankly, you've not been much help to me."

The man smiled and responded, "You must be a Democrat." "I am," replied the balloonist. "How did you know?" "Well," said the man, "you don't know where you are or where you're going. You've risen to where you are, due to a large quantity of hot air. You made a promise that you have no idea how to keep, and you expect me to solve your problem. You're in exactly the same position you were in before we met but, somehow, now it's my fault."

Salesmanship using Government Policies

The kids filed back into class Monday morning. They were very excited. Their weekend assignment was to sell something, then give a talk on productive salesmanship.

Little Sally led off: "I sold girl scout cookies and I made $30," she said proudly, "My sales approach was to appeal to the customer's civil spirit and I credit that approach for my obvious success."

"Very good," said the teacher.

Little Jenny was next: "I sold magazines," she said, "I made $45 and I explained to everyone that magazines would keep them up on current events."

"Very good, Jenny," said the teacher.

Eventually, it was Little Johnny's turn. The teacher held her breath. Little Johnny walked to the front of the classroom and dumped a box full of cash on the teacher's desk. "$2,467" he said.

"$2,467!" cried the teacher, "What in the world were you selling?"

"Toothbrushes," said Little Johnny.

"Toothbrushes!" echoed the teacher, "How could you possibly sell enough tooth brushes to make that much money?

"I found the busiest corner in town," said Little Johnny, "I set up a Dip & Chip stand and gave everybody who walked by a free sample." They all said the same thing, "Hey, this tastes like dog shit!" Then I would say, "It is dog shit. Wanna buy a toothbrush?"   "I used the governmental approach of giving you something shitty for free, and then making you pay to get the shitty taste out of your mouth"

The Canadians

The Canadian government is going to help America with the war on terrorism. They have pledged 2 of their biggest battle ships, 6000 ground troops and 6 fighter jets.

Unfortunately, after the exchange rate conversion, we ended up with 2 canoes, 1 Mountie, and some flying squirrels.

Two Pigs

Last Tuesday, as President Obama got off the Helicopter in front of the White House, he was carrying a baby piglet under each arm.. The squared away Marine guard snaps to attention, Salutes, and says:

"Nice pigs, Sir." The President replies: "These are not pigs. These are authentic Arkansas Razorback Hogs. I got one for Secretary of State Hillary Clinton and I got one for Speaker of the House Nancy Pelosi." The squared away Marine again snaps to attention, Salutes, and says: "Excellent trade, sir."

Puzzles

Brain Teaser

I am only sending this to my smart friends and relatives. I couldn't figure it out till I saw the answers. So see if you can figure out what these words Have In Common...... ??

Banana
Dresser
Grammar
Potato
Revive
Uneven
Assess

Are You Peeking Or Have You Already Given Up?

Give It Another Try....

You'll kick yourself when you discover the answer. Go back and look at them again; think hard.

OK... Here You Go.. Hope You Didn't Cheat.

Answer . . . . . .

In all of the words listed, if you take the first letter, place it at the end of the word, and then spell the word backwards, it will be the same word!!! Told you it was good!

Did you figure it out?

This is a quiz for people who know everything!

These are not trick questions. They are straight questions with straight answers

1. Name the one sport in which neither the spectators nor the participants know the score or the leader until the contest ends.

2. What famous North American landmark is constantly moving backward?

3. Of all vegetables, only two can live to produce on their own for several growing seasons. All other vegetables must be replanted every year. What are the only two perennial vegetables?

4. What fruit has its seeds on the outside?

5. In many liquor stores, you can buy pear brandy, with a real pear inside the bottle. The pear is whole and ripe, and the bottle is genuine; it hasn't been cut in any way. How did the pear get inside the bottle?

6. Only three words in standard English begin with the letters ' dw' and they are all common words. Name two of them.

7. There are 14 punctuation marks in English grammar. Can you name at least half of them?

8. Name the only vegetable or fruit that is never sold frozen, canned, processed, cooked, or in any other form except fresh.

9. Name 6 or more things that you can wear on your feet beginning with the letter 'S.'

Answers To Quiz:

1. The one sport in which neither the spectators nor the participants know the score or the leader until the contest ends **Boxing**

2. North American landmark constantly moving backward . **Niagara Falls** (The rim is worn down about two and a half feet each year because of the millions of gallons of
water that rush over it every minute.)

3. Only two vegetables that can live to produce on their own for several growing seasons
.. **Asparagus and rhubarb**.

4. The fruit with its seeds on the outside .. . **Strawberry**.

5. How did the pear get inside the brandy bottle? **It grew inside the bottle**. (The bottles are placed over pear buds when they are small, and are wired in place on the tree. The bottle is left in place for the en tire growing season. When the pears are ripe, they are snipped off at the stems.)

6. Three English words beginning with dw **Dwarf, dwell and dwindle**.

7. Fourteen punctuation marks in English grammar . **Period, comma, colon, semicolon, dash, hyphen, apostrophe, question mark, exclamation point, quotation marks, brackets, parenthesis, braces, and ellipses.**

8. The only vegetable or fruit never sold frozen, canned, processed, cooked, or in any other form but fresh **Lettuce**.

9. Six or more things you can wear on your feet beginning with 'S' **Shoes, socks, sandals, sneakers, slippers, skis, skates, snowshoes, stockings, stilts.**

Religious

A Blonde in Church

An Alabama preacher said to his congregation, "Someone in this congregation has spread a rumor that I belong to the Ku Klux Klan. This is a horrible lie and one which a Christian community cannot tolerate I am embarrassed and do not intend to accept this Now, I want the party who did this to stand and ask forgiveness from God and this Christian Family."

No one moved.

The preacher continued, "Do you have the nerve to face me and admit this is a falsehood? Remember, you will be forgiven and in your heart, you will feel glory. Now stand and confess your transgression."

Again, all was quiet.

Then slowly, a drop-dead gorgeous blonde with a body that would stop traffic rose from the third pew. Her head was bowed and her voice quivered as she spoke, "Reverend there has been a terrible misunderstanding. I never said you were a member of the Ku Klux Klan. I simply told a couple of my friends that you were a wizard under the sheets."

The preacher fell to his knees, his wife fainted, and the Congregation roared.

A Good Buy

A visitor to the Vatican needs to relieve himself. Imagine his surprise when in the rest rooms he sees the Pope sitting on a toilet masturbating.

As this was a sight few people saw, he quickly took a few photos.

The Pope recovers his composure and buys the camera for $100,000.

As it was a nice camera, the Pope decided to keep it and use it on his travels. One of his entourage sees it and asks how much it cost.

"$100,000" says the Pope.

"Wow! That guy must have seen you coming!"

A Man is Talking to God.

The man: "God, how long is a million years?"
God: "To me, it's about a minute."
The man: "God, how much is a million dollars?"
God: "To me it's a penny."
The man: "God, may I have a penny?"
God: "Wait a minute."

Acts 2:38

 An elderly woman had just returned to her home from an evening of church services when she was startled by an intruder. She caught the man in the act of robbing her home of its valuables and yelled, "STOP! Acts 2:38!" *(Repent and be baptized, in the name of Jesus Christ so that your sins may be forgiven.)*

The burglar stopped in his tracks. The woman calmly called the police and explained what she had done. As the officer cuffed the man to take him in, he asked the burglar, "Why did you just stand there? All the old lady did was yell a Scripture to you."

"Scripture?" replied the burglar. "She said she had an Ax and Two 38's!"

Army of the Lord

Jack was in front of me coming out of church one day, and the preacher was standing at the door as he always is to shake hands. The preacher grabbed Jack by the hand and pulled him aside. The Pastor said to him, "You need to join the Army of the Lord!"

Jack replied, "I'm already in the Army of the Lord, Pastor."

Pastor questioned, "How come I don't see you except at Christmas and Easter?"

Jack whispered back, "I'm in the secret service."

Church Social!

I lost the trivia contest at the church social last night by one point.

The last question was, "Where do most women have curly hair?

Evidently the correct answer is Africa ......I've been asked to find another place to worship.

Come to Confession

A guy goes into the confessional box after years being away from the Church.

He pulls aside the curtain, enters and sits himself down.

There's a fully equipped bar with crystal glasses, the best vestry wine, Guinness on tap, cigars and liqueur chocolates nearby, and on the wall a fine photographic display of buxom ladies who appear to have mislaid their garments.

He hears a priest come in:

"Father, forgive me for it's been a very long time since I've been to confession and I must admit that the confessional box is much more inviting than it used to be".

The priest replies, "Get out, you idiot. You're on my side".

Drunk and Arthritis

A drunk that smelled like a brewery got on a bus one day. He sat down next to a priest. The drunk's shirt was stained, his face was full of bright red lipstick and he had a half-empty bottle of wine sticking out of his pocket. He opened his newspaper and started reading. A couple minutes later, he asked the priest, "Father, what causes arthritis?"

"Mister, it's caused by loose living, being with cheap, wicked women, too much alcohol, and contempt for your fellow man," the priest replied. "Imagine that," the drunk muttered. He returned to reading his paper.

The priest, thinking about what he had said, turned to the man and apologized: "I'm sorry; I didn't mean to come on so strong. How long have you had arthritis?"

"I don't have arthritis, Father," the drunk said, "but I just read in the paper that the Pope does."

Golfing...

Moses and Jesus are part of a Threesome playing golf one day. Moses pulls up to the tee and drives a long one. The ball lands on the fairway, but rolls directly toward a water trap. Quickly, Moses raises his club, the water parts, and the ball rolls to the other side, safe and sound.

Next, Jesus strolls up to the tee and hits a nice long one directly toward the same water trap. It lands right in the center of the pond and kind of hovers over the water. Jesus casually walks out on the water and chips the ball right up onto the green.

Then, the third guy gets up and sort of randomly whacks the ball. It heads out over the fence and into oncoming traffic on a nearby street. It bounces off a truck and hits a nearby tree. From there, it bounces onto the roof of a shack close by and rolls down into the gutter, down the drain spout, out onto the fairway and straight toward the fore mentioned pond.

On the way to the pond, the ball hits a little stone and bounces out over the water and onto a lily pad, where it comes quietly to rest. Suddenly, a very large bullfrog jumps on the lily pad and snatches the ball into his mouth. Just then, an eagle swoops down, grabs the frog and flies away. As they pass over the green, the frog squeals with fright and drops the ball, which bounces right into the hole for a beautiful hole in one.

Moses leans over toward Jesus and whispers, "Do you think your Dad would teach me that shot?"

It's Dark In Here

A woman takes a lover home during the day while her husband is at work. Her 9 year old son comes home unexpectedly, sees them and hides in the bedroom closet to watch. The woman's husband also comes home. She puts her Lover in the closet, not realizing that the little boy is in there already.

The little boy says, "Dark in here." The man says, "Yes, it is." Boy - "I have a baseball." Man - "That's nice." Boy - "Want to buy it?" Man - "No, thanks." Boy - "My dad's outside." Man - "OK, how much?" Boy - "$250"

In the next few weeks, it happens again that the boy and the lover are in the closet together. Boy - "Dark in here." Man - "Yes, it is." Boy - "I have a baseball glove." The lover, remembering the last time, asks the boy, "How much?" Boy - "$750" Man - "Sold."

A few days later, the father says to the boy, "Grab your glove, let's go outside and have a game of catch. The boy says, "I can't, I sold my baseball and my glove." The father asks, "How much did you sell them for?" Boy -"$1,000" The father says, "That's terrible to overcharge your friends like that. That is way more than those two things cost. I'm going to take you to church and make you confess."

They go to the church and the father makes the little boy sit in the confession booth and he closes the door. The boy says, "Dark in here." The priest says, "Don't start that shit again; you're in my closet now."

Midget Nuns

Two guys were at a bar arguing with their friend who was a midget. Sudden out of nowhere, the Pope walks into the bar! "Oh my god its the pope!"

They all say at once "the midget says to the guys 'That's it I'm going ask him."

So he walks up to the Pope and asks "Sir, are there midget nuns in America?"

"No, no, no." says the Pope.

"Are there midget nuns in the entire world?"

"No, no, no." says the Pope.

"Are there even such things as midget nuns?"

"No, no, no." says the Pope.

His friends burst out chanting, "Joe screwed a penguin, Joe screwed a penguin..."

Nookie Green

'Father', he confessed, 'it has been one month since my last confession. I had sex with Nookie Green twice last month.'

The priest told the sinner, 'You are forgiven. Go out and say three Hail Mary's.'

Soon thereafter, another Irish man entered the confessional. 'Father, it has been two months since my last confession. I've had sex with Nookie Green twice a week for the past two months.'

This time, the priest questioned, 'Who is this Nookie Green?'
'A new woman in the neighborhood,' the sinner replied.

'Very well,' sighed the priest. Go and say ten Hail Mary's.;

At mass the next morning, as the priest prepared to deliver the sermon, a tall, voluptuous, drop-dead gorgeous redheaded woman entered the sanctuary. The eyes of every man in the church fell upon her as she slowly sashayed up the aisle and sat down right in front of the priest. Her dress was green and very short, and she wore matching, shiny emerald-green shoes.

The priest and the altar boy gasped as the woman in the green dress and matching green shoes sat with her legs spread slightly apart, but just enough to realize she wasn't wearing any underwear.
The priest turned to the altar boy and whispered, 'Is that Nookie Green?'

The bug-eyed altar boy couldn't believe his ears but managed to calmly reply, 'No Father, I think it's just a reflection from her shoes.

Priest in Absentee

The head priest at a certain church was out for the day, so he asked the deacon to do confession for him. The deacon agrees, and the first person that comes says, "Forgive me, for I just gave a guy a blow job." He says, "You have sinned."

Then he looks at the sheet on the wall that had punishments for certain sins on it, but blow job was not on there, so he went out to ask one of the altar boys what he usually gives for a blow job. The altar boy answered, "Oh, about five dollars."

Praise the Lord

This preacher had a horse that a man wanted to buy, and the preacher says: "Ok, I'll sell him to you." So the man bought him, and the preacher told him: "Now, when you get ready for him to go say 'praise the lord', then when you want to stop say 'amen'."

The man says: "Ok, I got it". So he gets on him and said "praise the lord" and the horse took off. Then the man noticed a deep canyon in front of him and hollered "amen" and the horse stopped. Just before they went over the edge, and the man looked up and said: "Praise the lord."

Priest and His Collar

Johnny is walking along and a priest is coming the other way. Johnny says, "Hey, mister, why are you wearing your collar backwards?"

The priest says, "Because I'm a father."

Johnny says, "Yeah? Well, my old man's got three kids and he don't wear his collar backwards."

The priest says "You don't understand, son. I have thousands of children."

Johnny says, "You should wear your trousers backwards."

SIPPING VODKA

A new priest at his first mass was so nervous he could hardly speak. After mass he asked the monsignor how he had done. The monsignor replied, "When I am worried about getting nervous on the pulpit, I put a glass of vodka next to the water glass. If I start to get nervous, I take a sip."

So next Sunday he took the monsignor's advice. At the beginning of the sermon, he got nervous and took a drink. He proceeded to talk up a storm. Upon his return to his office after the mass, he found the following note on the door:

1) Sip the vodka, don't gulp.
2) There are 10 commandments, not 12.
3) There are 12 disciples, not 10.
4) Jesus was consecrated, not constipated.
5) Jacob wagered his donkey, he did not bet his ass.
6) We do not refer to Jesus Christ as the late J.C.
7) The Father, Son, and Holy Ghost are not referred to as Daddy, Junior and the spook.
8) David slew Goliath; he did not kick the shit out of him.
9) When David was hit by a rock and was knocked off his donkey, don't say he was stoned off his ass.
10) We do not refer to the cross as the 'Big T.'
11) When Jesus broke the bread at the last supper he said, 'Take this and eat it for it is my body.' He did not say 'Eat me'.
12) The Virgin Mary is not called 'Mary with the Cherry'.
13) The recommended grace before a meal is not: Rub-A-Dub-Dub thanks for the grub, Yeah God
14) Next Sunday there will be a taffy pulling contest at St. Peter's not a peter pulling contest at St. Taffy's.

The Archbishop is Your Father

A woman starts dating a doctor. Before too long, she becomes pregnant and they don't know what to do. About nine months later, just about the time she is going to give birth, a priest goes into the hospital for a prostate gland infection.

The doctor says to the woman, "I know what we'll do. After I've operated on the priest, I'll give the baby to him and tell him it was a miracle."

"Do you think it will work?" she asks.

"It's worth a try" he says. So, the doctor delivers the baby and then operates on the priest. After the operation he goes in to the priest and says, "Father, you're not going to believe this."

"What?" asks the priest, "what happened?"

"You gave birth to a child!"

"But that's impossible!" says the priest.

"I just did the operation," insists the doctor, "it's a miracle! Here's your baby."

About fifteen years go by, and the priest realizes he must tell his son the truth. One day, he sits the boy down and says, "Son, I have something to tell you. I'm not your father."

The son says, "What do you mean, you're not my father?"

The priest replies, "I am your mother. The archbishop is your father."

THE MORMON AND THE IRISHMAN...

A Mormon was seated next to an Irishman on a flight from London

.... After the plane was airborne, drink orders were taken.
The Irishman asked for a whiskey, which was promptly brought and placed before him.

The flight attendant then asked the Mormon if he would like a drink.

He replied in disgust, "I'd rather be savagely raped by a dozen whores than let liquor touch my lips."

The Irishman then handed his drink back to the attendant and said, "Me, too, I didn't know we had a choice."

Three Good Reasons That Jesus Was ----

There were 3 good arguments that Jesus was Black:

1. He called everyone brother. .
2. He liked Gospel.
3. He didn't get a fair trial

But then there were 3 equally good arguments that Jesus was Jewish:

1. He went into His Father's business. .
2. He lived at home until he was 33.
3. He was sure his Mother was a virgin and his Mother was sure He was God.

But then there were 3 equally good arguments that Jesus was Italian:

1. He talked with His hands. .
2. He had wine with His meals.
3. He used olive oil

But then there were 3 equally good arguments that Jesus was a Californian:

1. He never cut His hair. .
2. He walked around barefoot all the time.
3. He started a new religion.

But then there were 3 equally good arguments that Jesus was an American Indian:

1. He was at peace with nature. .
2. He ate a lot of fish.
3. He talked about the Great Spirit.

But then there were 3 equally good arguments that Jesus was Irish:

1. He never got married. .
2. He was always telling stories.
3. He loved green pastures.

But the most compelling evidence of all - 3 proofs that Jesus was a woman:

1. He fed a crowd at a moment's notice when there was virtually no food.
2. He kept trying to get a message across to a bunch of men who just didn't get it.
3. And even when He was dead, He had to get up because there was still work to do.

Three Nuns

Three nuns were talking. The first nun said, "I was cleaning in Father's room the other day and do you know what I found? A bunch of pornographic magazines."

"What did you do?" the other nuns asked.

"Well, of course I threw them in the trash."

The second nun said, "Well, I can top that. I was in Father's room putting away the laundry and I found a bunch of condoms!"

"Oh my!" gasped the other nuns. "What did you do?" they asked. "I poked holes in all of them!" she replied.

The third nun fainted.

Traveling Nuns

Two nuns from Ireland must traverse through Transylvania by car. They are a bit on edge. Stopped on the side of the road to rest they are startled when suddenly, out of nowhere, a diminutive Dracula jumps onto the hood of the car and hisses through the windshield.

"Quick, quick!" shouts Sister Marilyn. "Turn the wipers on! That will get rid of the abomination!" Sister Helen switches them on, knocking Dracula about, but he clings on and continues hissing at the nuns.

"What now?" "Switch on the windshield washer! I filled it up with Holy Water before we left," says Sister Marilyn. Dracula screams as the water burns his skin, but he clings on and continues hissing at the nuns.

"My goodness, now what shall we do?" worries Sister Helen.

"Show him your cross," says Sister Marilyn.

"Now you're talking," says Sister Helen as she rolls down the window, leans out and screams, "Get the fuck off our car!"

Two Baptist Ministers

Two Baptist ministers are talking about the immorality of the country today, and one of them says, "I didn't sleep with my wife before I was married. How about you?"

And the other minister says, "I don't know. What was her maiden name?"

Vote for St. Peter

So the voter says to the politician, "I wouldn't vote for you if you were St. Peter himself."

"If I were St. Peter himself, you wouldn't be in my district."

Where's Jesus?

One day in Sunday school, the teacher was talking about where is Jesus to the kids, "Bobby, where is Jesus?" asked the teacher.

"Jesus is in heaven." replied Bobby.

"Very good!", said the teacher. The teacher then asked a little girl," Where is Jesus, Emily?"

Emily said innocently, "Jesus is in my heart!" The teacher beamed at little Emily and said, "How very sweet!!!" The teacher now asked Timmy, "Timmy, where is Jesus?"

"Jesus is in my bathroom." he said assuredly.

"Please elaborate, Timmy." the teacher said.

Timmy then replied, "Well, every morning my dad gets up, bangs on the bathroom door and yells. Jesus Christ, are you still in there!!!"

Restaurant

Hairy Cook

A man walks into a hamburger shop and orders a regular meal. Later, the waitress brings his meal to him. He takes a bite out of it, and notices there's a small hair in the hamburger. He begins yelling frantically at the waitress, "Waitress, there's a hair in my hamburger! I demand to see what is going on!"

So, the waitress takes him back where the cook is and to his demise, he sees the cook take the meat patty and flatten it under his arm pit. He says, "That's disgusting!"

Then the waitress says, "You think that's disgusting you should see him make donuts."

Waiter and the Spoon

A man entered a restaurant and sat at the only open table. As he sat down, he knocked the spoon off the table with his elbow. A nearby waiter reached into his shirt pocket, pulled out a clean spoon, and set it on the table. The diner was impressed. "Do all the waiters here carry spoons in their pockets?"

The waiter replied, "Yes. Ever since an Efficiency Expert visited our restaurant, he determined that 17.8% of our diners knock the spoon off the table. By carrying clean spoons with us, we save trips to the kitchen."

The diner ate his meal. As he was paying the waiter, he commented, "Forgive the intrusion, but do you know that you have a string hanging from your fly?"

The waiter replied, "Yes, we all do. Seems that the same Efficiency Expert determined that we spend too much time washing our hands after using the men's room. So, the other end of that string is tied to my penis. When I need to go, I simply pull the string, do my thing, and then return to work. Having never touched myself, there really is no need to wash my hands. Saves a lot of time."

"Wait a minute," said the diner, "how do you get your penis back in your pants?"

"Well, I don't know about the other guys, but I use the spoon."

Seasonal

A Little Christmas Story

When four of Santa's elves got sick, the trainee elves did not produce toys as fast as the regular ones, and Santa began to feel the Pre-Christmas pressure.

Then Mrs. Claus told Santa her Mother was coming to visit, which stressed Santa even more.

When he went to harness the reindeer, he found that three of them were about to give birth and two others had jumped the fence and were out, Heaven knows where.

Then when he began to load the sleigh, one of the floorboards cracked, the toy bag fell to the ground and all the toys were scattered.

Frustrated, Santa went in the house for a cup of apple cider and a shot of rum. When he went to the cupboard, he discovered the elves had drunk all the cider and hidden the liquor. In his frustration, he accidentally dropped the cider jug, and it broke into hundreds of little glass pieces all over the kitchen floor. He went to get the broom and found the mice had eaten all the straw off the end of the broom.

Just then the doorbell rang, and an irritated Santa marched to the door, yanked it open, and there stood a little angel with a great big Christmas tree.

The angel said very cheerfully, 'Merry Christmas, Santa. Isn't this a lovely day? I have a beautiful tree for you. Where would you like me to stick it?'

And so began the tradition of the little angel on top of the Christmas tree.

Not a lot of people know this.

Christmas Parrot

One day a man walked into a bar and sat down next to a guy with a parrot on his shoulder.

The bartender said, "Cute parrot, does he talk?"

The guy with the parrot says, "He does more than just talk, watch." The guy lit a match and placed it under the parrots left foot. Then the parrot started singing "Jingle Bells", it was a Christmas Parrot. The guy then placed the match under the right foot and the parrot then started to sing "The 12 days of Christmas."

The bartender said, "That's incredible". He then asked, "What does he say when you place them between his feet?"

The guy said, "You know I never tried that, let's see."

When the match was placed between the feet of the parrot the parrot began to sing a familiar tune... "Chestnuts roasting on an open fire."

Christmas Tree

A family is at the dinner table. The son asks his father, 'Dad, how many kinds of boobs are there?

The father, surprised, answers, 'Well, son, there are three kinds of boobs:

1 - In her 20's, a woman's are like melons, round and firm.
2 - In her 30's to 40's, they are like pears, still nice but hanging a bit.
3 - After 50, they are like onions'.

'Onions?'

'Yes, you see them and they make you cry.'

This infuriated his wife and daughter so the daughter said, 'Mom, how many kinds of 'willies' are there?"

The mother, surprised, smiles and answers, 'Well dear, a man goes through three phases:

1 - In his 20's, his willy is like an oak tree, mighty and hard.
2 - In his 30's and 40's, it is like a birch, flexible but reliable.

3 - After his 50's, it is like a Christmas Tree."

"A Christmas tree?"

"Yes - the tree is dead and the balls are just for decoration."

Christmas Tree Cutting

Two Blondes decided that they were going to cut down their own Christmas tree. They went into the woods on this cold winter day and searched for hours for a tree. Finally one blonde said to the other, "I give up. I am going to cut down the very next tree; I don't care if it isn't decorated!"

Clean Christmas Funnies

- Why are ghosts so bad at lying?
  Ans: You can see right through them.
- What kind of tree do fingers grow on?
  Ans: A palm tree.
- What do you call a penguin in the Sahara desert? **Ans:** Lost.
- What did the floor say to the Christmas tree? **Ans:** You've got Nice Balls!
- What do you call a woman who stands between two goal posts?
  Ans: Annette.
- On which side do chickens have most feathers?
  Ans: On the outside.

- What do you call a train loaded with toffee?
  Ans: A chew chew train.
- What must you know to be an auctioneer? **Ans:** Lots.
- Did you hear about the man who bought a paper shop?
  Ans: It blew away.
- What is the vampire's favorite song?
  Ans: Fangs for the memory.

FUNNY CHRISTMAS JOKES

1) Santa's Outfit
How do you know Santa has to be a man?
No woman is going to wear the same outfit year after year.

2) Curious Question
Why does rain drop, but snow fall?

3) Denominations
Maria went to the Post Office to buy stamps for her Christmas cards. "What denomination?" asked the clerk. "Oh! Good heavens! Have we come to this?" said Maria, "Well give me 50 Methodist and 50 Church of England ones please."

4) Christmas Shepherd
One Christmas, Joe and Peter built a skating rink in the middle of a field. A shepherd leading his flock decided to take a shortcut across the rink. The sheep, however, were afraid of the ice and wouldn't cross it. Desperate, the shepherd began tugging them to the other side.

"Look at that," remarked Peter to Joe, "That guy is trying to pull the wool over our ice!"

Funny Christmas Riddles and Puns

Q: What's red and white and black all over?
A: Santa Claus after he slid down the chimney.

Q. Why was Cinderella no good at football?
A. Because her coach was a pumpkin.

Q. Why do reindeer scratch themselves?
A. Because they're the only ones who know where they itch.

Q. Why was Santa's little helper depressed?
A. Because he had low 'elf' esteem.

Q. How do Snowman travel around?
A. By riding an icicle.

Q. Where do Snow-women like to dance?
A. At Snowballs.

Q. Why did the man get the sack from the orange juice factory?
A. Because he couldn't concentrate.

Q. What happened when Guy ate the Christmas decorations?
A. He went down with tinsel-itis.

The 3 stages of man:

1) He believes in Santa Claus.
2) He doesn't believe in Santa Claus.
3) He IS Santa Claus!

More Christmas Riddles

- What do you get if Santa comes down your chimney when the fire is ablaze?
  Answer: Crisp Kringle.
- What do you call people who are frightened of Santa?
  Answer: Claustraphopic.
- What do you get if you team Santa with a detective?
  Answer: Santa Clues!
- What do you get when you cross a vampire and a snowman?
  Answer: Frostbite.
- What is the difference between the Christmas alphabet and the ordinary alphabet?
  Answer: The Christmas alphabet has No L (Noel).

Another Batch of Really Funny Christmas Cracker Jokes

What did the reindeer say before launching into his comedy routine?
This will sleigh you.

What do lions sing at Christmas?
Jungle bells!

What did Adam say to his girlfriend on December 24th?
'It's Christmas! Eve.'

Question and Answer Christmas Jokes

Q: What do elves learn in school?
A: The Elf-abet!

Q: If athletes get athletes foot, what do astronauts get?
A: Missletoe!

Q: Why does Santa have 3 gardens?
A: So he can ho-ho-ho.

Q: Where do polar bears vote?
A: The North Poll.

Q: What do you get when you cross an archer with a gift-wrapper?
A: Ribbon hood.

Q: Why do birds fly south for the winter ?
A: Because it's too far to walk.

Q: What was wrong with the boy's brand new toy electric train set he received for Christmas?
A: Forty feet of track - all straight!

Q: What kind of bird can write?
A: A PENguin.

Q: What do you call a cat on the beach at Christmas time?
A: Sandy Claus!

Q: What nationality is Santa Claus?
A: North Polish.

Q: Why does Santa's sled get such good mileage?
A: Because it has long-distance runners on each side.

Q: What do you call a bunch of grandmasters of chess bragging about their games in a hotel lobby?
A: Chess nuts boasting in an open foyer!

Q: What do you get if you deep fry Santa Claus?
A: Crisp Cringle.

Q: What did the ghosts say to Santa Claus?
A: We'll have a boo Christmas without you.

Q: What did Santa shout to his toys on Christmas Eve?
A: Okay everyone, sack time!!

Q: What do snowmen eat for breakfast?
A: Snowflakes.

Q: If Santa Claus and Mrs. Claus had a child, what would he be called?
A: A subordinate claus.

Q: Why did the elf push his bed into the fireplace?
A: He wanted to sleep like a log.

Q: Why did Santa spell Christmas N-O-E?
A: Because the angel had said, "No L!"

Q: What goes Ho, Ho, Swoosh, Ho, Ho, Swoosh?
A: Santa caught in a revolving door!

Q: Why does Santa Claus go down the chimney on Christmas Eve?
A: Because it "soots" him!

Q: What do you do if Santa gets stuck in your chimney?
A: Pour Santa flush on him.

Q: Did you hear that one of Santa's reindeer now works for Proctor and Gambel?
A: Its true . . . Comet cleans sinks!

Q: Why does Scrooge love Rudolph the Red-Nosed Reindeer?
A: Because every buck is dear to him.

Q: How come you never hear anything about the 10th reindeer "Olive" ?
A: Yeah, you know, "Olive the other reindeer, used to laugh and call him names"

Q: Why is Christmas just like a day at the office?
A: You do all the work and the fat guy with the suit gets all the credit.

Q: What was so good about the neurotic doll the girl was given for Christmas?
A: It was wound up already.

Q: What's a good holiday tip?
A: Never catch snowflakes with your tongue until all the birds have gone south for the winter.

Gift from Santa

On Christmas morning a cop on horseback is sitting at a traffic light, and next to him is a kid on his brand new bike. The cop says to the kid, "Nice bike you got there. Did Santa bring that to you?"

The kid says, "Yeah."

The cop says, "Well, next year tell Santa to put a tail-light on that bike." The cop then proceeds to issue the kid a $20.00 bicycle safety violation ticket.

The kid takes the ticket and before the cop rides off says, "By the way, that's a nice horse you got there. Did Santa bring that to you?"

Humoring the kid, the cop says, "Yeah, he sure did."

The kid says, "Well, next year tell Santa to put the dick underneath the horse, instead of on top."

Halloween Angel

One Halloween this woman opens her door to find the most adorable little girl, with golden blond curly hair and the biggest blue eyes. She was dressed as an Angel, and was just delightful. The woman said, "what are you supposed to say sweetheart?"

The little girl looks up at the woman and says "Twick or Tweat!"

The woman thinks this is just adorable, and she calls her husband to come to the door. The woman say to the child, "Go ahead honey say it just one more time."

Once again the little Angel looks up and says, "Twick or Tweat!"

The husband agrees with his wife, this little Angel is just the cutest thing. The woman picks an apple from the Treat Bowl, shines it up with her apron, and drops it into the little girl's Treat Bag.

The little Angel looks in her bag then looks up at the woman and says, "Thanks a lot lady, you just broke my f**king cookies!"

Mistaken Identity

A couple was invited to a swanky masked Halloween Party. She got a terrible headache and told her husband to go to the party alone. He, being a devoted husband, protested, but she argued and said she was going to take some aspirin and go to bed, and there was no need of his good time being spoiled by not going. So he took his costume and away he went. The wife, after sleeping soundly for one hour, awakened without pain, and as it was still early, she decided to go to the party. In as much as her husband did not know what her costume was, she thought she would have some fun by watching her husband to see how he acted when she was not with him.

She joined the party and soon spotted her husband cavorting around on the dance floor, dancing with every nice chick he could and copping a little feel here and a little kiss there. His wife came up to him and being a rather seductive babe herself, he left his partner high and dry and devoted his time to the new stuff that had just arrived.

She let him go as far as he wished; naturally, since he was her husband. Finally he whispered a little proposition in her ear and she agreed, so off they went to one of the cars and had a little bang. Just before unmasking at midnight, she slipped away and went home and put the costume away and got into bed, wondering what kind of explanation he would make for his behavior.

She was sitting up reading when he came in and asked what kind of a time he had had. He said, "Oh the same old thing. You know I never have a good time when you're not there." The she asked, "Did you dance much?"

Hc replied, "I'll tell you, I never even danced one dance. When I got there, I met Pete, Bill Brown and some other guys, so we went into the den and played poker all evening. But I'll tell you... the guy I loaned my costume to, sure had a real good time!"

Rudolph the Red Nosed Reindeer

A Russian couple was walking down the street in St. Petersburg the other night, when the man felt a drop hit his nose. "I think it's raining," he said to his wife.

"No, that felt more like snow to me," she replied. "No, I'm sure it was just rain, he said." Well, as these things go, they were about to have a major argument about whether it was raining or snowing. Just then they saw a minor communist party official walking toward them. "Let's not fight about it," the man said, "let's ask Comrade Rudolph whether it's officially raining or snowing."

As the official approached, the man said, "Tell us, Comrade Rudolph, is it officially raining or snowing?"

"It's raining, of course," he answered and walked on. But the woman insisted: "I know that felt like snow!" To which the man quietly replied: "Rudolph the Red knows rain, dear!"

The Twelve Days of Christmas
What Really Happened...
(Sanitized for your protection)

On the first day of Christmas...

Miss Agnes McHolstein
69 Cash Avenue
Beaver Valley, Colorado

December 14, 1994

Dearest John:

I went to the door today and the postman delivered a partridge in a pear tree. What a thoroughly delightful gift. I couldn't have been more surprised.

With deepest love and devotion,

Agnes

On the second day of Christmas...

Miss Agnes McHolstein
69 Cash Avenue

Beaver Valley, Colorado

December 15, 1994

Dearest John:

Today the postman brought your very sweet gift. Just imagine two turtle doves. I'm just delighted at your very thoughtful gift. They are just adorable.

All my love,

Agnes

On the third day of Christmas...

Miss Agnes McHolstein
69 Cash Avenue
Beaver Valley, Colorado

December 16, 1994

Dearest John:

Oh! Aren't you the extravagant one. Now I really must protest. I don't deserve such generosity, Three French hens. They are just darling but I must insist, you've been too kind.

Love,

Agnes

On the fourth day of Christmas...

Miss Agnes McHolstein
69 Cash Avenue
Beaver Valley, Colorado

December 17, 1994

Dear John,

Today the postman delivered 4 calling birds. Now really, they are beautiful but don't you think enough is enough. You're being too romantic.

Affectionately,

Agnes

On the fifth day of Christmas...

Miss Agnes McHolstein
69 Cash Avenue
Beaver Valley, Colorado

December 18, 1994

Dearest John.

What a surprise. Today the postman delivered 5 golden rings; one for every finger.
You're just impossible, but I love it. Frankly, all those birds squawking were beginning
to get on my nerves.

All my love,

Anges

On the sixth day of Christmas...

Miss Agnes McHolstein
69 Cash Avenue
Beaver Valley, Colorado

December 19, 1994

Dear John:

When I opened the door there were actually 6 geese a-laying on my front steps. So,
you're back to the birds again, huh? Those geese are huge. Where will I ever keep them?
The neighbors are complaining and I can't sleep through the racket.

Please stop.

Cordially,

Agnes

On the seventh day of Christmas...

Miss Agnes McHolstein
69 Cash Avenue
Beaver Valley, Colorado

December 20, 1994

John:

What's with you and those crazy birds? 7 swans a-swimming. What kind of terrible joke is this? There's bird shit all over the house, and they never stop with the racket. I can't sleep at night and I'm a nervous wreck. It's not funny. So stop sending me all these birds!

Sincerely,

Agnes

On the eighth day of Christmas...

Miss Agnes McHolstein
69 Cash Avenue
Beaver Valley, Colorado

December 21, 1994

O.K. Buster:

I think I prefer the birds. What am I going to do with 8 maids a-milking? It's not enough with all those birds and 8 maids a-milking, but they had to bring their cows! There is shit all over the lawn and I can't move in my own house. Just lay off me, smart ass.

Agnes

On the ninth day of Christmas...

Miss Agnes McHolstein
69 Cash Avenue
Beaver Valley, Colorado

December 22, 1994

Hey! Shithead,

What are you? Some kind of sadist? Now there's 9 pipers playing. And boy, do they play. They've never stopped chasing those maids since they got here yesterday morning. They cows are getting upset, and they're stepping all over those screeching birds. What am I going to do? The neighbors have started a petition to evict me.

You'll get yours,

Agnes

On the tenth day of Christmas...

Miss Agnes McHolstein
69 Cash Avenue
Beaver Valley, Colorado

December 23, 1994

You Rotten Sadist,

Now there's 10 ladies dancing. I don't know why I call those sluts ladies. They've been messing with those pipers all night long. Now the cows can't sleep and they've got the diarrhea. My living room is a river of shit. The Commissioner of Buildings has subpoenaed me to give cause why this building shouldn't be condemned.

I'm sicking the police on you.

One who means it.

On the eleventh day of Christmas...

Miss Agnes McHolstein
69 Cash Avenue
Beaver Valley, Colorado

December 24, 1994

Listen! Looser,

What's with the 11 lords a-leaping on those maids and ladies. Some of those broads will never walk again. Those pipers ran through the maids and have been committing sodomy with the cows. All 23 of the birds are dead. They've been trampled to death in the orgy. I hope you're satisfied, you rotten, vicious swine.

Your sworn enemy,

Agnes

On the twelfth day of Christmas...

Law Offices
Badger, Bender and Cahole
303 Knave Street
Chicago, Illinois

December 25, 1994

Dear Sir:

This is to acknowledge your latest gift of 12 fiddlers fiddling which you have seen fit to inflict on our client, Miss Agnes McHolstein. The destruction, of course, was total. All correspondence should come to our attention. If you should attempt to reach Miss McHolstein at Happy Dale Sanitarium, the attendants have instructions to shoot you on sight. With this letter please find attached warrant for your arrest.

Cordially,

Badger, Bender and Cahole

The Strange Christmas Scene

In a small southern town there was a "Nativity Scene" that showed great skill and talent had gone into creating it. One small feature bothered me.

The three wise men were wearing firemen's helmets.

Totally unable to come up with a reason or explanation, I left. At a "Quik Stop" on the edge of town, I asked the lady behind the counter about the helmets. She exploded into a rage, yelling at me, "You stupid Yankees never do read the Bible!" I assured her that I did, but simply couldn't recall anything about firemen in the Bible.

She jerked her Bible from behind the counter and ruffled through some pages, and finally jabbed her finger at a passage. Sticking it in my face she said "See, it says right c'here, The three wise man came from afar."

Try Before You Buy!

Myra was going to the Christmas office party but needed a new party dress. In the clothing store she asked, 'May I try on that dress in the window, please?'

'Certainly not, madam,' responded the salesgirl, 'You'll have to use the fitting room like everyone else.'

Please Note:

CHISTMAS IS CANCELLED

Apparently, YOU told Santa that you have been GOOD this year ...

He died laughing

Senior

$4000 Hearing Aid

A man was telling his neighbor in Sun City Center, 'I just bought a new hearing aid. It cost me four thousand dollars, but it's state of the art. It's perfect.'

'Really,' answered the neighbor. 'What kind is it?'

'Twelve thirty.'

As Time Passes

We'll be old friends until we are aged and senile. Then we'll be new friends every day thereafter.

Drafting Guys 60 and over...

I am over 60 and the Armed Forces thinks I'm too old to track down terrorists. You can't be older than 42 to join the military. They've got the whole thing backwards. Instead of sending 18-year olds off to fight, they ought to take us old guys. You shouldn't be able to join a military unit until you're at least 35.

For starters: Researchers say 18-year-olds think about sex every 10 seconds. Old guys only think about sex a couple of times a day, leaving us more than 28,000 additional seconds per day to concentrate on the enemy.

Young guys haven't lived long enough to be cranky, and a cranky soldier is a dangerous soldier. 'My back hurts! I can't sleep, I'm tired and hungry.' We are impatient and maybe letting us kill the bad guy, who desperately deserves it, will make us feel better and shut us up for a while.

An 18-year-old doesn't even like to get up before 10 a.m. Old guys always get up early to pee early anyway. Besides, like I said, 'I'm tired and can't sleep and since I'm already up, I may as well be up killing some fanatical terrorist.

If captured we couldn't spill the beans because we'd forget where we put them. In fact, name, rank, and serial number would be a real brainteaser.

Military basic training would be easier for old guys. We're used to getting screamed and yelled at and we're used to soft food. We've also developed an appreciation for guns. We've been using them for years as an excuse to get out of the house, away from the screaming and yelling.   They could lighten up on the obstacle course however. I've been in combat and didn't see a single 20-foot wall with rope hanging over the side, nor did I ever do any pushups after completing basic training.   Actually, the running part is kind of a waste of energy, too. I've never seen anyone outrun a bullet.

An 18-year-old has the whole world ahead of him. He's still learning to shave, to start up a conversation with a pretty girl. He still hasn't figured out that a baseball cap has a brim to shade his eyes, not the back of his head

These are all great reasons to keep our kids at home to learn a little more about life before sending them off into harm's way.

Let us old guys track down those dirty rotten coward terrorists. The last thing an enemy would want to see is a couple million old geezers with attitudes and automatic weapons who know that their best years are already behind them. If nothing else, put us on border patrol....we will have it secured the first night!

Share this with your senior friends. It's purposely in big type so they can read it.

Getting Old

- Long ago when men cursed and beat the ground with sticks, it was called witchcraft. Today, it's called golf.

- Eventually you will reach a point when you stop lying about your age and start bragging about it.

- The older we get, the fewer things seem worth waiting in line for.

- Some people try to turn back their odometers. Not me, I want to people to know "why" I look this way. I've traveled a long way and some of the roads weren't paved.

- How old would you be if you didn't know how old you are?

- When you are dissatisfied and would like to go back to youth, think of Algebra.

- You know you are getting old when everything either dries up or leaks.

- One of the many things no one tells you about aging is that it is such a nice change from being young.

- Ahh, being young is beautiful, but being old is comfortable.

- Old age is when former classmates are so gray and wrinkled and bald, they don't recognize you.

- If you don't learn to laugh at trouble, you won't have anything to laugh at when you are old.

- First you forget names, then you forget faces. Then you forget to pull up your zipper, then...Oh, my goodness, you forgot to pull your zipper down!

- If you jog in a jogging suit, lounge in lounging pajamas, and smoke in a smoking jacket, WHY would anyone want to wear a windbreaker??

And best of all...

- I don't know how I got over the hill without getting to the top.

Great Test

The following Alzheimer's test was developed as a mental age assessment by the School of Psychiatry at Harvard University. Take your time and see if you can read each line aloud without a single mistake. The average person over 50 years of age cannot do it!

1. This is this cat.

2. This is is cat.

3. This is how cat.

4. This is to cat.

5. This is keep cat.

6. This is an cat.

7. This is old cat.

8. This is fart cat.

9. This is busy cat.

10. This is for cat.

11. This is forty cat.

12. This is seconds cat.

Now go back and read the third word in each line from the top down.

HYPNOTIST AT THE SENIOR CENTER

It was entertainment night at the Senior Center. Claude, the hypnotist, exclaimed: "I'm here to put you into a trance; I intend to hypnotize each and every member of the audience."

The excitement was almost electric as Claude withdrew a beautiful antique pocket watch from his coat. "I want you each to keep your eye on this antique watch. It's a very special watch. It's been in my family for six generations"

He began to swing the watch gently back and forth while quietly chanting, "watch the watch, watch the watch, and watch the watch...."

The crowd became mesmerized as the watch swayed back and forth, light gleaming off its polished surface. Hundreds of pairs of eyes followed the swaying watch, until, suddenly... it slipped from the hypnotist's fingers and fell to the floor, breaking into a hundred pieces. "SHIT!" said the Hypnotist.

It took three days to clean up the Senior Center ☺

ID 10 T Error

As we Silver Surfers know, sometimes we have trouble with our computers. I had a problem yesterday, so I called Eric, the 11 year old next door, whose bedroom looks like Mission Control and asked him to come over. Eric clicked a couple of buttons and solved the problem. As he was walking away, I called after him, "So, what was wrong?"

He replied, "It was an ID ten T error."

I didn't want to appear stupid, but nonetheless enquired,

"An, ID ten T error? What's that? In case I need to fix it again."

Eric grinned .... "Haven't you ever heard of an ID ten T error before ?"

"No," I replied.

"Write it down," he said, "and I think you'll figure it out."
So I wrote down:

ID10T

I used to like Eric, the little *******.

LADIES WHO LUNCH

A group of 40-year-old girlfriends discussed where they should meet for lunch. Finally, it was agreed upon that they should meet at the Ocean View restaurant because the waiters there had tight pants and nice bums.

10 years later, at 50 years of age, the group once again discussed where they should meet for lunch. Finally it was agreed that they should meet at the Ocean View restaurant because the food there was very good, the wine selection was good also, and the waiters were cute.

10 years later, at 60 years of age, the group once again discussed where they should meet for lunch. Finally it was agreed that they should meet at the Ocean View restaurant because they could eat there in peace and quiet, the restaurant had a beautiful view of the ocean, and the waiters were sweet boys.

10 years later, at 70 years of age, the group once again discussed where they should meet for lunch. Finally it was agreed that they should meet at the Ocean View restaurant because the restaurant was wheel chair accessible, they even had an elevator, and the waiters were kind.

10 years later, at 80 years of age, the group once again discussed where they should meet for lunch. Finally it was agreed that they should meet at the Ocean View restaurant because they had never been there before.

Perks of Old Age

1. Kidnappers are not very interested in you.

2. In a hostage situation you are likely to be released first.

3. No one expects you to run into a burning building.

4. People call at 9 PM and ask, "Did I wake you?"

5. People no longer view you as a hypochondriac.

6. There is nothing left to learn the hard way.

7. Things you buy now won't wear out.

8. You can eat dinner at 4 P.M.

9. You can live without sex but not without glasses.

10. You enjoy hearing about other people's operations.

11. You get into heated arguments about pension plans.

12. You have a party and the neighbors don't even realize it.

13. You no longer think of speed limits as a challenge.

14. You quit trying to hold your stomach in, no matter who walks into the room.

15. You sing along with elevator music.

16. Your eyes won't get much worse.

17. Your investment in health insurance is finally beginning to pay off.

18. Your joints are more accurate meteorologists than the national weather service.

19. Your secrets are safe with your friends because they can't remember them either.

20. Your supply of brain cells is finally down to manageable size.

Sex and the Ice Cream Truck

On hearing that her elderly grandfather had died, Jenny went straight to visit her grandmother. When she asked how her grandpa had died, her grandma explained, not holding back anything of course, "He had a heart attack during sex, Sunday morning!" Horrified, Jenny suggested that screwing at the age of 94 was surely asking for trouble! "Oh no," her grandma replied. "We had sex every Sunday morning in time with the church bells!" "In with the dings, out with the dongs!" She paused to wipe away a tear, "If it wasn't for that damn ice cream truck, he'd still be alive!!!"

TELL ME This Won't Happen To Us, WILL IT???

DRIVING

Two elderly women were out driving in a large car - both could barely see over the dashboard. As they were cruising along, they came to an intersection. The stoplight was red, but they just went on through The woman in the passenger seat thought to herself 'I must be losing it. I could have sworn we just went through a red light.'

After a few more minutes, they came to another intersection and the light was red Again, they went right through. The woman in the passenger seat was almost sure that the light had been red but was really concerned that she was losing it. She was getting nervous.

At the next intersection, sure enough, the light was red and they went on through. So, She turned to the other woman and said, "Mildred, did you know that we just ran through three red lights in a row? You could have killed us both!"

Mildred turned to her and said, "Oh, crap, am I driving?"

TELL ME THIS WON'T HAPPEN TO US!!!!

Memory

Three sisters, ages 92, 94 and 96, live in a house together. One night the 96-year-old draws a bath. She puts her foot in and pauses. She yells to the other sisters, "Was I getting in or out of the bath?" The 94-year-old yells back, "I don't know. I'll come up and see." She starts up the stairs and pauses "Was I going up the stairs or down?" The 92-year-old is sitting at the kitchen table having tea listening to her sisters, she shakes her head and says, "I sure hope I never get that forgetful, knock on wood..." She then yells, "I'll come up and help both of you as soon as I see who's at the door."

TELL ME THIS WON'T HAPPEN TO US!!!!

I CAN HEAR JUST FINE!

Three retirees, each with a hearing loss, were playing golf one fine March day. One remarked to the other, "Windy, isn't it?" "No," the second man replied, "it's Thursday." And the third man chimed in, "So am I. Let's have a beer."

TELL ME THIS WON'T HAPPEN TO US!!!!

Advertising

A little old lady was running up and down the halls in a nursing home. As she walked, she would flip up the hem of her nightgown and say "Supersex..."
She walked up to an elderly man in a wheelchair. Flipping her gown at him, she said, "Supersex."
He sat silently for a moment or two and finally answered, "I'll take the soup."

TELL ME THIS WON'T HAPPEN TO US!!!!

Who?

Two elderly ladies had been friends for many decades. Over the years, they had shared all kinds of activities and adventures. Lately, their activities had been limited to meeting a few times a week to play cards.

One day, they were playing cards when one looked at the other and said, "Now don't get mad at me ... I know we've been friends for a long time, but I just can't think of your name! I've thought and thought, but I can't remember it. Please tell me what your name is."

Her friend glared at her for at least three minutes she just stared and glared at her. Finally she said, "How soon do you need to know?"

TELL ME THIS WON'T HAPPEN TO US!!!!

SENIOR DRIVING

As a senior citizen was driving down the freeway, his car phone rang. Answering, he heard his wife's voice urgently warning him, "Herman, I just heard on the news that there's a car going the wrong way on Interstate 77. Please be careful!" "Heck," said Herman, "It's not just one car. It's hundreds of them!"

TELL ME THIS WON'T HAPPEN TO US!!!!

Where?

An elderly Floridian called 911 on her cell phone to report that her car has been broken into. She is hysterical as she explains her situation to the dispatcher: "They've stolen the stereo, the steering wheel, the brake pedal and even the accelerator!" she cried. The dispatcher said, "Stay calm, an officer is on the way." A few minutes later, the officer radios in "Disregard." He says. "She got in the back-seat by mistake."

TELL ME THIS WON'T HAPPEN TO US!!!!

The Other Day

The other day I was making toast in our new toaster oven. I noticed that there was only a little butter in the butter dish. Well, I got out another stick of butter and put it in the microware oven to get it soft while the bread was getting toasted. The micro wave was just a small one and we had not adjusted to the temperatures and timing yet so I was playing around with the time. As I was getting the butter soft, the bread was burning. At my age, I am in reverse, trying to get something soft when something is hot and I wind up with a runny mess.

Three old ladies

Three old ladies were sitting side by side on patio chairs at their Orlando retirement home reminiscing. The first lady recalled from years past shopping at the local Piggly Wiggly and demonstrated with her hands, the length and thickness of a cucumber she could buy for a penny.

The second old lady nodded, adding that onions used to be much bigger and cheaper also, and demonstrated the size of two big onions she could buy for a penny a piece.

The third old lady remarked, "I can't hear a word you're saying, but I remember the guy you're talking about."

Truthful Sayings?

Wisdom from Grandpa...

- Whether a man winds up with a nest egg, or a goose egg, depends a lot on the kind of chick he marries.

- Trouble in marriage often starts when a man gets so busy earnin' his salt, that he forgets his sugar.

- Too many couples marry for better, or for worse, but not for good.

- When a man marries a woman, they become one; but the trouble starts when they try to decide which one.

- If a man has enough horse sense to treat his wife like a thoroughbred, she will never turn into an old nag.

- On anniversaries, the wise husband always forgets the past - but never the present.

- A foolish husband says to his wife, "Honey, you stick to the washin', ironin', cookin', and scrubbin'. No wife of mine is gonna work."

- The bonds of matrimony are a good investment, only when the interest is kept up.

- Many girls like to marry a military man - he can cook, sew, and make beds, and is in good health, and he's already used to taking orders.

- Eventually you will reach a point when you stop lying about your age, and start bragging about it.

- The older we get, the fewer things seem worth waiting in line for.

- Some people try to turn back their odometers. Not me, I want people to know "why" I look this way. I've traveled a long way and some of the roads weren't paved.

- How old would you be if you didn't know how old you are?

- When you are dissatisfied and would like to go back to your youth, remember about Algebra.

- I don't know how I got over the hill without getting to the top.

- One of the many things no one tells you about aging is that it is such a nice change from being young.

- Ah, being young is beautiful, but being old is comfortable.

- Old age is when former classmates are so gray and wrinkled and bald, they don't recognize you.

- If you don't learn to laugh at trouble, you won't have anything to laugh at when you are old.

Two Elderly Ladies Smoking

Two elderly ladies were outside their nursing home, having a smoke, when it started to rain. One of the ladies pulled out a condom, cut off the end, put it over her cigarette, and continued smoking.

The lady asked, "What's that?"

"A condom," the other lady responded. "This way my cigarette doesn't get wet."

"Where did you get it?" the other lady asked.

"You can get them at any drugstore."

The next day, the first lady hobbled herself down to the local drugstore and announced to the pharmacist that she wants a box of condoms. The guy looked at her kind of strangely (she is, after all, over 80 years of age), but politely asks what brand she prefers. She said "It doesn't matter as long as it fits a Camel." The pharmacist fainted.

Two Old Men In A Nursing Home

These two old men are in a nursing home. They're talking and realize that it's been years since they have had sex. So they sneak out and go to the closest brothel. Once inside they go to the Madam and ask for the two best girls. The Madam thought "I'm not going to waste my two best girls on these guys I'll just give them inflatable women. They are old and they won't know the difference."

Once the old men finish they leave. On their way back they start talking. The first guy said, "I think mine was dead she didn't move or anything." The second guy said I think mine was a witch because when I nibbled on her neck she farted and flew out the window."

Seniors are Valuable

We have silver in our hair.
We have gold in our teeth.
We have stones in our kidneys.
We have lead in our feet and.
We are loaded with natural gas.

Why I Like Retirement

- Number of days in a week: 6 Saturdays, 1 Sunday
- Bedtime: Three hours after falling asleep on the couch.
- Biggest gripe: There is not enough time to get everything done.
- Benefit of being called a senior: The term comes with a 10% discount.
- What is considered formal attire: Tied shoes.
- Why do retirees count pennies: They are the only ones who have the time.
- Common term for someone who enjoys work and refuses to retire: NUTS!
- Reason retirees are so slow to clean out the basement, attic or garage: They know that as soon as they do, one of their adult kids will want to store stuff there.
- What retirees call a long lunch: Normal .
- Best way to describe retirement: The never ending Coffee Break.
- Biggest advantage of going back to school: If you cut classes, no one calls your parents.
- What do retirees do all week: Monday through Friday, NOTHING. Saturday & Sunday they rest.
- Why doing nothing is hard work: You never know when you're done

You Know You're Growing Older When

- Everything hurts, and what doesn't hurt, doesn't work anyway.

- The gleam in your eyes is from the sun hitting your bifocals.

- You feel like you really hung one on the night before, and you were in bed asleep by eight.

- You get winded playing chess.

- Your children begin to look middle-aged.

- You join a health club and don't go.

- You begin to outlive enthusiasm.

- Your mind makes contracts your body can't meet.

- You know all the answers, but nobody asks the questions.

- You look forward to a dull evening.

- Your favorite part of the newspaper is "25 years ago today!"

- You sit in a rocking chair and can't get it going.

- Your knees buckle and your belt won't.

- You're 17 around the neck and 42 around the waist.

- You stop looking forward to your next birthday.

- Dialing long distance wears you out.

You Know You're Over The Hill When...

1. You find yourself beginning to like accordion music.

2. You're sitting on a park bench and a Boy Scout comes up and

helps you cross your legs.

3. Lawn care has become a big highlight of your life.

4. You tune into the easy listening station...on purpose.

5. You discover that your measurements are now small, medium and large...In that order.

6. You light the candles on your birthday cake and a group of campers form a circle and start singing Cumbaya..

7. You keep repeating yourself.

8. You start video taping daytime game shows.

9. At the airport, they ask to check your bags...and you're not carrying any luggage.

10. You wonder why you waited so long to take up macramé.

11. Your Insurance Company has started sending you their free calendar...a month at a time.

12. At cafeterias, you complain that the gelatin is too tough.

13. Your new easy chair has more options than your car.

14. When you do the "Hokey Pokey" you put your left hip out...and it stays out.

15. One of the throw pillows on your bed is a hot water bottle.

16. Conversations with people your own age often turn into "dueling ailments."

17. It takes a couple of tries to get over a speed bump.

18. You discover the words, "whippersnapper," "scalawag" and "by-cracky" creeping into your vocabulary.

19. You're on a TV game show and you decide to risk it all and go for the rocker.

20. You begin every other sentence with, "Nowadays..."

21. You run out of breath walking DOWN a flight of stairs.

22. You look both ways before crossing a room.

23. Your social security number only has three digits.

24. You come to the conclusion that your worst enemy is gravity.

25. You go to a Garden Party and you're mainly interested in the garden.

26. You find your mouth making promises your body can't keep.

27. The waiter asks how you'd like your steak...and you say "pureed."

28. At parties you attend, "regularity" is considered the topic of choice.

Scotch with Two Drops of Water

A lady goes to the bar on a cruise ship and orders a Scotch with two drops of water. As the bartender gives her the drink she says, "I'm on this cruise to celebrate my 80th birthday and it's today." The bartender says, "Well, since it's your birthday, I'll buy you a drink. In fact, this one is on me."

As the woman finishes her drink, the woman to her right says, "I would like to buy you a drink, too." The old woman says, "Thank you. Bartender, I want a Scotch with two drops of water." "Coming up," says the bartender.

As she finishes that drink, the man to her left says, "I would like to buy you one, too."

The old woman says, "Thank you. Bartender, I want another Scotch with two drops of water." "Coming right up," the bartender says.

As he gives her the drink, he says, "Ma'am, I'm dying of curiosity. Why the Scotch with only two drops of water?" The old woman replies, "Sonny, when you're my age, you've learned how to hold your liquor. Holding your water, however, is a whole other issue."

OLD IS WHEN

'OLD' IS WHEN...Your sweetie says, "Let's go upstairs and make love," and you answer, "Pick one; I can't do both!"

'OLD' IS WHEN...Your friends compliment you on your new alligator shoes and you're barefoot.

'OLD' IS WHEN...A sexy babe catches your fancy and your pacemaker opens the garage door.

'OLD' IS WHEN...Going braless pulls all the wrinkles out of your face.

'OLD' IS WHEN...You don't care where your spouse goes, just as long as you don't have to go along.

'OLD' IS WHEN...You are cautioned to slow down by the doctor instead of by the police.

'OLD' IS WHEN..."Getting a little action" means you don't need to take any fiber today.

'OLD' IS WHEN..."Getting lucky" means you find your car in the parking lot.

'OLD' IS WHEN...An "all nighter" means not getting up to use the bathroom.

AND

'OLD' IS WHEN...You are not sure these are jokes.

Garage Door

The boss walked into the office one morning not knowing his zipper was down and his fly area wide open. His assistant walked up to him and said, "This morning when you left your house, did you close your garage door?" The boss told her he knew he'd closed the garage door, and walked into his office puzzled by the question.

As he finished his paperwork, he suddenly noticed his fly was open, and zipped it up. He then understood his assistant's question about his 'garage door.'

He headed out for a cup of coffee and paused by her desk to ask, "When my garage door was open, did you see my Hummer parked in there?"

She smiled and said, "No, I didn't. All I saw was an old mini van with two flat tires."

An Elderly Gentleman...

An elderly gentleman had serious hearing problems for a number of years. He went to the doctor and the doctor was able to have him fitted for a set of hearing aids that allowed the gentleman to hear 100%

The elderly gentleman went back in a month to the doctor and the doctor said, "Your hearing is perfect. Your family must be really pleased that you can hear again."

The gentleman replied, "Oh, I haven't told my family yet. I just sit around and listen to the conversations. I've changed my will three times!"

Two Elderly Gentlemen

Two elderly gentlemen from a retirement center were sitting on a bench under a tree when one turns to the other and says: "Slim, I'm 83 years old now and I'm just full of aches and pains. I know you're about my age. How do you feel?"

Slim says, "I feel just like a newborn baby."

"Really!? Like a newborn baby!?"

"Yep. No hair, no teeth, and I think I just wet my pants."

An Elderly Couple

An elderly couple had dinner at another couple's house, and after eating, the wives left the table and went into the kitchen.

The two gentlemen were talking, and one said, "Last night we went out to a new restaurant and it was really great. I would recommend it very highly."

The other man said, "What is the name of the restaurant?"

The first man thought and thought and finally said, "What is the name of that flower you give to someone you love? You know... The one that's red and has thorns?"

"Do you mean a rose?"

"Yes, that's the one," replied the man. He then turned towards the kitchen and yelled, "Rose, what's the name of that restaurant we went to last night?"

Wheel Chair Required

Hospital regulations require a wheel chair for patients being discharged. However, while working as a student nurse, I found one elderly gentleman already dressed and sitting on the bed with a suitcase at his feet, who insisted he didn't need my help to leave the hospital. After a chat about rules being rules, he reluctantly let me wheel him to the elevator. On the way down I asked him if his wife was meeting him. "I don't know," he said. "She's still upstairs in the bathroom changing out of her hospital gown."

Remember?

A couple in their nineties are both having problems remembering things. During a checkup, the doctor tells them that they're physically okay, but they might want to start writing things down to help them remember.   Later that night, while watching TV, the old man gets up from his chair, "Want anything while I'm in the kitchen?" he asks.

"Will you get me a bowl of ice cream?"

"Sure."

"Don't you think you should write it down so you can remember it?" she asks.

"No, I can remember it."

"Well, I'd like some strawberries on top, too. Maybe you should write it down, so's not to forget it?"

He says, "I can remember that. You want a bowl of ice cream with strawberries."

"I'd also like whipped cream. I'm certain you'll forget that, write it down?" she asks.

Irritated, he says, "I don't need to write it down, I can remember it! Ice cream with strawberries and whipped cream - I got it, for goodness sake!"

Then he toddles into the kitchen. After about 20 minutes, the old man returns from the kitchen and hands his wife a plate of bacon and eggs. She stares at the plate for a moment.   "Where's my toast?"

She Can Drive

A senior citizen said to his eighty-year old buddy: 'So I hear you're getting married?'

'Yep!'

'Do I know her?'

'Nope!'

'This woman, is she good looking?'

'Not really.'

'Is she a good cook?'

'Naw, she can't cook too well.'

'Does she have lots of money?'

'Nope! Poor as a church mouse.'

'Well, then, is she good in bed?'

'I don't know.'

'Why in the world do you want to marry her then?'

'Because she can still drive!'

Sitting on a Stool

A little old man shuffled slowly into an ice cream parlor and pulled himself slowly, painfully, up onto a stool. After catching his breath, he ordered a banana split.
The waitress asked kindly, "Crushed nuts?"
"No," he replied, "Arthritis."

You Have A Heart Murmur

Morris, an 82 year-old man, went to the doctor to get a physical.
A few days later, the doctor saw Morris walking down the street with a

gorgeous young woman on his arm.

A couple of days later, the doctor spoke to Morris and said, 'You're really doing great, aren't you?"

Morris replied, "Just doing what you said, Doc: 'Get a hot mamma and be cheerful."

The doctor said, "I didn't say that. I said, You've got a heart murmur; be careful."

I Heard You

A man was telling his neighbor, "I just bought a new hearing aid. It cost me four thousand dollars, but it's state of the art. It's perfect."

"Really," answered the neighbor. "What kind is it?"

"Twelve thirty."

Short Jokes

A French Guest

A French guest who was staying in a hotel in Edmonton phoned room service for some pepper.

"Black pepper, or white pepper?" asked the conciergo.

"Toilette pepper!"

Actual Classified Ads

Our experienced Mom will care for your child. Fenced yard, meals, and smacks included.

Dog for sale: eats anything and is fond of children.

Man wanted to work in dynamite factory. Must be willing to travel.

Stock up and save. Limit: one.

Semi-Annual after Christmas Sale

3 year old teacher needed for pre-school. Experience preferred.

Mixing bowl set designed to please a cook with round bottom for efficient beating.

Girl wanted to assist magician in cutting off head illusion. Blue Cross and salary.

Dinner Special -- Turkey $2.35; Chicken or Beef $2.25; Children $2.00

For sale: antique desk suitable for lady with thick legs and large drawers.

Now is your chance to have your ears pierced and get an extra pair to take home, too.

We do not tear your clothing with machinery. We do it carefully by hand.

For sale. Three canaries of undermined sex.

Great Dames for sale.

Have several very old dresses from grandmother in beautiful condition.

Auto Repair Service. Free pick-up and delivery. Try us once, you'll never go anywhere again.

Adam's Night Out

When Adam stayed out late for a few nights, Eve became upset. "You're running around with other women," she accused her mate.

"Eve, honey, you're being unreasonable." Adam responded. "You know you're the only woman on earth."

The quarrel continued until Adam fell asleep, only to be awakened by a strange pain in his side. It was his darling Eve poking him rather vigorously about the torso. "What do you think you're doing?" Adam demanded. "Counting your ribs," said Eve.

Al Qaeda Bingo

How do you play al-Qaeda bingo?
F18….B52….F14…..

Answer Me This

1. Why is it that when you transport something by car, it's called ship-ment but when you transport something by ship it's called cargo?
2. If FedEx and Ups merged, would they call it Fed UP?
3. If you didn't get caught, did you really do it?
4. If you try to fail, and succeed, which have you done?
5. Why are there interstates in Hawaii?
6. Do you need a silencer if you are going to shoot a mine?
7. Is it OK to use my AM radio after NOON?
8. What color is a chameleon on a mirror?
9. If 7-11 is open 24 hours a day, 365 days a year, why are there locks on the doors?
10. Do fish get thirsty?
11. Why don't sheep shrink when it rains?
12. If nothing ever sticks to TEFLON, how do they make TEFLON stick to the pan?
13. If all the nations in the world are in the debt, where did all the money go?
14. Why do we drive on parkways when we park on driveways?
15. Why are they called apartments when they are all stuck together?
16. How does AVON find so many women willing to take orders?
17. If a word in a dictionary were misspelled, how would we know?
18. If olive oil comes from olives, where does baby oil come from?
19. Do vampires get AIDS?
20. Why are cigarettes sold at gas stations when smoking is prohibited there?
21. Do vegetarians eat animal crackers?
22. How come wrong numbers are never busy?
23. You know that little indestructible black box that is used on planes - why can't they make the whole plane out of the same substance?
24. If a fly has no wings would you call him a walk?
25. How much deeper would the ocean be without sponges?
26. If CON is the opposite of PRO, is congress the opposite of progress?

27. If fire fighters fight fire and crime fighters fight crime, what do freedom fighters fight?
28. If love is blind, why is Lingerie so popular?

Believe it or not

When everything's coming your way, you're in the wrong lane.

How do you tell when you run out of invisible ink?

Everyone has a photographic memory. Some don't have the film.

Laughing stock: cattle with a sense of humor

Wear short sleeves! Support your right to bare arms.

Corduroy pillows: They're making headlines!

Bigger Turkeys

A lady was picking through the frozen turkeys at the grocery store, but couldn't find one big enough for her family. She asked a stock boy, "Do these turkeys get any bigger?"

The stock boy replied, "No ma'am, they're dead."

Caterpillar on the Lettuce

Johnny: "Daddy, are caterpillars good to eat?"

Father: "Have I not told you never to mention such things during meals!"

Mother: "Why did you say that, Junior? Why did you ask the question?"

Johnny: "It's because I saw one on daddy's lettuce, but now it's gone."

Dinner for Four

My doctor told me to stop having intimate dinners for four; unless there are three other people.

Orson Welles

Do You Serve Lawyers?

A man walked into a bar, leading an alligator by a leash. He asked the bartender, "Do you serve lawyers here?"

"Sure do," said the bartender.

"Good," replied the man. "Give me a beer, and I'll have a lawyer for my 'gator."

Funeral Procession Passing By

Two guys were standing on the street corner as the funeral procession passed by and one said to the other, "I wonder who died." His friend said, "I'm not sure, but I think it's the one in the coffin."

George Carlin Quotes

1. Don't sweat the petty things and don't pet the sweaty things.

2. One tequila, two tequila, three tequila, floor.

3. Atheism is a non-prophet organization.

4. If man evolved from monkeys and apes, why do we still have monkeys and apes?

5. I went to a bookstore and asked the saleswoman,
"Where's the self-help section?"
She said if she told me, it would defeat the purpose.

6. What if there were no hypothetical questions?

7. If a deaf person swears, does his mother wash his hands with soap?

8. If a man is standing in the middle of the forest speaking and there is no woman around to hear him... is he still wrong?

9. If someone with multiple personalities threatens to kill himself, is it considered a hostage situation?

10. Is there another word for synonym?

11. Isn't it a bit unnerving that doctors call what they do "practice"?

12. Where do forest rangers go to "get away from it all?"

13. What do you do when you see an endangered animal eating an endangered plant?

14. If a parsley farmer is sued, can they garnish his wages?

15. Would a fly without wings be called a walk?

16. Why do they lock gas station bathrooms? Are they afraid someone will clean them?

17. If a turtle doesn't have a shell, is he homeless or naked?

18. Why don't sheep shrink when it rains?

19. Can vegetarians eat animal crackers?

20. If the police arrest a mime, do they tell him he has the right to remain silent?

21. Why do they put Braille on the drive-through bank machines?

22. How do they get the deer to cross at that yellow road sign?

23. What was the best thing before sliced bread?

24. One nice thing about egotists: they don't talk about other people.

25. How is it possible to have a civil war?

26. If one synchronized swimmer drowns, do the rest drown, too?

27. If you ate pasta and antipasto, would you still be hungry?

28. If you try to fail, and succeed, which have you done?

29. Whose cruel idea was it for the word "lisp" to have a "S" in it?

30. Why is the alphabet in that order? Is it because of that song?

31. If the "black box" flight recorder is never damaged during a plane crash, why isn't the whole airplane made out of that stuff?

32. Why is there an expiration date on sour cream?

33. If you spin an oriental man in a circle three times, does he become disoriented?

I Had A Dream

I had a dream last night, I was eating a ten pound marshmallow. I woke up this morning and the pillow was gone. I felt full but was light as a feather.

Jack in the Nude

"It's just too hot to wear clothes today," Jack says as he stepped out of the shower, "Honey, what do you think the neighbors would think if I mowed the lawn like this?" To which she replied "Probably that I married you for your money."

Ketchup

A family of three tomatoes were walking downtown one day when the little baby tomato started lagging behind. The big father tomato walks back to the baby tomato, stomps on her, squashing her into a red paste, and says, "Ketchup!"

Lessons Learned

Lessons I've learned...

I've learned that you cannot make someone love you. All you can do is stalk them and hope they panic and give in.

I've learned that no matter how much I care, some people are just assholes.

I've learned that it takes years to build up trust, and only suspicion, not proof, to destroy it.

I've learned that you can get by on charm for about fifteen minutes. After that, you'd better have a big dick or huge tits.

I've learned that you shouldn't compare yourself to others - they are more fucked up than you think.

I've learned that you can keep puking long after you think you're finished.

I've learned that we are responsible for what we do, unless we are celebrities.

I've learned that regardless of how hot and steamy a relationship is at first, the passion fades, and there had better be a lot of money to take its place.

I've learned that sometimes the people you expect to kick you when you're down will be the ones who do.

I've learned that we don't have to ditch bad friends because their dysfunction makes us feel better about ourselves.

I've learned that no matter how you try to protect your children, they will eventually get arrested and end up in the local paper.

I've learned that the people you care most about in life are taken from you too soon and all the less important ones just never go away.

I've learned to say "Fuck 'em if they can't take a joke" in 6 languages.

Let's Offend Everybody

Q. What's the Cuban National Anthem?
A. Row, Row, Row Your Boat

Q. Where does an Irish family go on vacation?
A. A different bar

Q. What did the Chinese couple name their tan, curly-haired baby?

A. Sum Ting Wong

Q. What do you call it when an Italian has one arm shorter than the other?
A. A speech impediment

Q. What does it mean when the Post Office's flag is flying at half-mast?
A. They're hiring

Q. Why aren't there any Puerto Ricans on Star Trek?
A. Because they're not going to work in the future either

Q. What do you call a Mississippi farmer with a sheep under each arm?
A. A pimp

Q. Why do Driver Ed classes in redneck schools use the car only on

Mondays, Wednesdays and Fridays?
A. Because on Tuesday and Thursday, the Sex Ed class uses it.

Q. What's the difference between a southern zoo and a northern zoo?
A. The southern zoo has a description of the animal on the front of the cage along with a recipe.

Q How do you get a sweet little 80-year-old lady to say the "F" word?
A. Get another sweet little 80-year-old lady to yell "BINGO!"

Q. What's the difference between a northern fairytale and a southern fairytale???
A. A northern fairytale begins, "Once upon a time..."
A southern fairytale begins, "Y'all ain't gonna believe this shit."

Q. Why doesn't Mexico have an Olympic team?
A. Because all the Mexicans who can run, jump or swim are already in the United States.

Michael Jackson Shops

Q. How did Michael Jackson pick his nose?
Ans. From a catalogue.

Misc Short Jokes

Q Why do golfers carry two pairs of trousers with them?

Ans. Just in case they get a hole in one.

Q What lies at the bottom of the ocean and twitches?

Ans. A nervous wreck

What do you get when you mix holy water with castor oil?

Ans. A religious movement!

Q. What did one saggy boob say to the other saggy boob?

Ans. We better get some support or people will think we're nuts.

Mommy, Mommy! Why do other kids tell me I have a long nose?

Ans. You don't, but lift your head up or you'll scrape the floor.

Did you hear about the blind prostitute?

Ans. Well, you got to hand it to her.

A bill collector came to my house the other day, so I gave him a huge stack of old bills

---

When I came back to Dublin I was court marshaled in my absence and sentenced to death in my absence, so I said they could shoot me in my absence.

Sex is like poker... if you don't have a good partner you better have a good hand.

Q: What is your date of birth?
Ans. July fifteenth.
Q: What year?
Ans. Every year.

Who is the most popular guy at the nudist colony?
Ans. The guy who can carry a cup of coffee in each hand and a dozen donuts.

Who is the most popular girl at the nudist colony?
Ans. She is the one who can eat the last donut!

What's the difference between a pick pocket and a peeping Tom?
Ans. A pick pocket snatches watches.

Questions

1. How do you catch a unique rabbit?
Ans. Unique up on it.

2. How do you catch a tame rabbit?
Ans. Tame way.

3. How do crazy people go through the forest ?
Ans. They take the psychopath.

4. How do you get holy water?
Ans. You boil the hell out of it.

5. What do fish say when they hit a concrete wall?
Ans. Dam!

6. What do Eskimos get from sitting on the ice too Long?
Ans. Polaroids

7. What do you call a boomerang that doesn't work?
Ans. A stick

8. What do you call cheese that isn't yours?
Ans. Nacho Cheese.

9. What do you call four bullfighters in quicksand?

Ans. Quatro Cinco.

10. What's the difference between roast beef and pea soup?
Ans. Anyone can roast beef.

11. Where do you find a dog with no legs?
Ans. Right where you left him.

12. Why do gorillas have big nostrils?
Ans. Because they have big fingers.

13. Why don't blind people like to sky dive?
Ans. Because it scares their dog.

14. What kind of coffee was served on the Titanic?
Ans. Sanka.

15. What is the difference between a Harley and a Hoover?
Ans. The location of the dirt bag.

16. Why did pilgrims' pants always fall down?
Ans. Because they wore their belt buckles on their hats.

17. What's the difference between a bad golfer and a bad skydiver?
Ans. A bad golfer goes, whack, dang! A bad skydiver goes dang! whack.

18. How is a Texas tornado and a Tennessee divorce the same?
Ans. Somebody's gonna lose a trailer.

19. How do you catch a fish with a computer?
Ans. With the Internet.

Quick Jokes

Q. Did you hear about the guy who lost his left arm and leg in a car crash?
A. He's all right now.

Q. Where do you get virgin wool from?
A. Ugly sheep.

Q. How do you double the value of a Geo Metro?
A. Fill it with gas.

Q. What's the definition of mixed emotions?
A. When you see your mother-in-law backing off a cliff in your new car.

Q. Why do chicken coops have two doors?
A. Because if it had four doors it's be a chicken sedan.

Q. What do you call a cow with no legs?
A. Ground beef.

Q. What's the difference between an oral and a rectal thermometer?
A. The taste!

Q. Did you hear about the new "divorced" Barbie doll that they're selling in stores now?
A. It comes with all of Ken's stuff.

Q. What's a Hindu?
A. Lays eggs.

Q. What's the difference between a porcupine and a Porsche?
A. The porcupine has the pricks on the outside.

Q. Why did the leper crash his car?
A. He left his foot on the accelerator.

Q. What do you do if you come across a tiger in the jungle?
A. Wipe him off, apologize and RUN!

Q. Why did the Leper go back into the shower?
A. He forgot his Head and Shoulders.

Q. Why did the ref call a penalty during the Leper Hockey game?
A. Because there was a face off in the corner.

Q. What is Osama bin Laden's idea of safe sex?
A. Marking the camels that kick.

Q. What should Kabul get for its air defense system?
A. A refund.

Q. What do you do if a bird shits on your car?
A. Don't ask her out again

Q. Why are women like condoms?
A. They spend 90% of their time in your wallet, and 10% on your dick.

Q. Who is the poorest guy in West Virginia?
A. The Tooth Fairy

Q. Did you hear that Fed Ex and UPS are going to merge?
A. Yeah. They're going to call it FED UP!

Q. What do your boss and a slinky have in common?
A. They're both fun to watch tumble down the stairs.

Two cannibals were eating a clown and one cannibal says to the other, "Does this taste funny to you?" He must not have gotten the funny bone yet.

Two cannibals were eating their dinner and one cannibal says to the other, "I don't like my mother-in-law much." The other cannibal replies, "Well, just eat your chips."

Little Johnny catches his parents going at it. He yells in, "Hey, Pop! What are you doin'?"
His father says, "Son, I'm filling your mother's tank."

Johnny says, "Oh, yeah? Well, you better get a model that gets better mileage. The postman filled her this morning."

A guy steps into an elevator and there's just one attractive woman in it. He turns around to push the button for his floor and his elbow bumps right into her breast. He says, "Oh, I'm so sorry. If your heart is as soft as your breast, I hope you'll be able to forgive me." She looks at him a few seconds and says, "That's all right. If your penis is as hard as your elbow, I'm in room 204."

A Man and His Dog

A man walked into a bar and sat down next to a man with a dog at his feet. "Does your dog bite?" he asked. "No," was the reply. So he reaches down to pet the dog, and the dog bites him. "I thought you said your dog doesn't bite!" he said. "That's not my dog!"

Discussion

A woman has the last word in any argument. Anything a man says after that is the beginning of a new argument.

Wrong Pants

Teacher: Joey, if you put your hand in one pants pocket and found 75 cents, then you put your other hand in your other pants pocket and found 50 cents, what would you have?

Joey: I'd have somebody else's pants on!

Two lawyers were walking down Rodeo Drive, and saw a beautiful model walking towards them. "What a babe," one said, "I'd sure like to fuck her!"

"Really?" the other responded, "Out of what?"

I am in shape. Round IS a shape!

Wine Does NOT Make You FAT

It Makes You LEAN...
Against Tables, Chairs, Floors, Walls and Ugly People.

You should always give 100% at work...
12% Monday; 23% Tuesday; 40% Wednesday; 20% Thursday; 5% Friday

---

Sex Before You're Married

Do you think it's okay to have sex before you're married, Father?

Not if it delays the ceremony.

Smart Ass Answers

Smart Ass Answer #1
A college teacher reminds her class of tomorrow's final exam. "Now class, I won't tolerate any excuses for you not being here tomorrow. I might consider a nuclear attach or a serious personal injury, illness, or a death in your immediate family, but that's it, no other excuses whatsoever!"

A smart-ass guy in the back of the room raised his hand and asked, "What would you say if tomorrow I said I was suffering from complete and utter sexual exhaustion?"

The entire class is reduced to laughter and snickering. When silence is restored, the teacher smiles knowingly at the student, shakes her head and sweetly says, "Well, I guess you'd have to write the exam with your other hand "

Smart Ass Answer #2
A truck driver was driving along on the freeway. A sign comes up that reads, "Low Bridge Ahead." Before he knows it, the bridge is right ahead of him and he gets stuck under the bridge. Cars are backed up for miles.

Finally, a police car comes up. The cop gets out of his car and walks to the truck driver, puts his hands on his hips and says, "Got stuck, huh?" The truck driver says, "No, I was delivering this bridge and ran out of gas."

Smart Ass Answer #3
The cop got out of his car and the kid who was stopped for speeding rolled down his window. "I've been waiting for you all day," the cop said. The kid replied, "Yeah, well I got here as fast as I could." When the cop finally stopped laughing, he sent the kid on his way without a ticket.

Smart Ass Answer #4
A lady was picking through the frozen turkeys at the grocery store but she couldn't find one big enough for her family. She asked a stock boy, "Do these turkeys get any bigger?" The stock boy replied, "No ma'am, they're dead."

Smart Ass Answer #6
It was mealtime during a flight on Hooters Airline. "Would you like dinner?" the flight attendant asked John, seated in front. "What are my choices?" John asked. "Yes or no," she replied.

Sometimes it's Just a Matter of Semantics.................

1) I'd just come out of the shop with a meat and potato pie, large chips, mushy peas & a jumbo sausage. A poor homeless man sat

there and said "I haven't eaten for two days" I told him "I wish I had your f**king will power."

2) Top tip; if you're camping in the summer and the attractive girl in the next tent tells you that because it's so hot she will be sleeping with her flaps open, it's not necessarily an invitation to casual sex............. Wish me luck; I appear in court next Monday.

3) I got fired on my first day as a male masseuse today. Apparently the instruction "finish off on her face" didn't mean what I thought it did.

4) A fat girl served me food in McDonald's at lunch time. She said "sorry about the wait." I said "Don't worry Chubby, you're bound to lose it eventually."

5) Snow in the forecast! The TV weather gal said she was expecting 8 inches tonight, I thought to myself "fat chance with a face like that!"

6) I have a new pick up line that works every time. It doesn't matter how gorgeous or out of my league a woman might be, this line is a winner & I always end up in bed with them. Here's how it goes "Excuse me love, could I ask your opinion? Does this damp cloth smell like chloroform to you?"

7) Years ago it was suggested that an apple a day kept the doctor away. But since almost all the doctors are now Muslim, I've found that a bacon sandwich works best!

8) I took my Biology exam last Friday. I was asked to name two things commonly found in cells. Apparently "Blacks" and "Mexicans" were not the correct answers.

Spread the Stupidity

Only in America ....do drugstores make the sick walk all the way to the back of the store to get their prescriptions while healthy people can buy cigarettes at the front.

Only in America ......do people order double cheeseburgers, large fries, and a diet coke.

Only in America .....do banks leave vault doors open and then chain the pens to the counters.

Only in America .....do we leave cars worth thousands of dollars in the driveway and put our useless junk in the garage.

Only in America ....do we buy hot dogs in packages of ten and buns in packages of eight

Only in America ......do they have drive-up ATM machines with Braille lettering.

EVER WONDER ....

Why the sun lightens our hair, but darkens our skin?

Why can't women put on mascara with their mouth closed?

Why don't you ever see the headline 'Psychic Wins Lottery'?

Why is it that doctors call what they do 'practice'?

Why is lemon juice made with artificial flavor, and dishwashing liquid made with real lemons?

Why is the man who invests all your money called a broker?

Why is the time of day with the slowest traffic called rush hour?

Why isn't there mouse-flavored cat food?

Why didn't Noah swat those two mosquitoes?

Why do they sterilize the needle for lethal injections?

You know that indestructible black box that is used on airplanes? Why don't they make the whole plane out of that stuff?

Why are they called apartments when they are all ctuok together?

If con is the opposite of pro, is Congress the opposite of progress?

If flying is so safe, why do they call the airport the terminal?

They Walk Among Us

They Walk Among Us and Many Work Retail
I was at the checkout of a K-Mart. The clerk rang up $46.64 charge. I gave her a fifty dollar bill. She gave me back $46.64. I gave the money back to her and told her that she had made a mistake in MY favor. She became indignant and informed me she was Educated and knew what she was doing, and returned the money again. I gave her the Money back....same scenario! I departed the store with the $46.64.

They Walk Among Us and Many Work Retail
I walked into a Starbucks with a buy-one-get-one-free coupon for a Grande Latte. I handed it to the girl and she looked over at a little chalkboard that said "buy one-get one free." "They're already buy-one-get-one-free," she said, "so I guess they're both free." She handed me my free lattes and I walked out the door.

They Walk Among Us!

One day I was walking down the beach with some friends when one of them shouted, 'Look at that dead bird!' Someone looked up at the sky and said,.............."Where"?

They Walk Among Us!
While looking at a house, my brother asked the real estate agent which direction was North because, he explained, he didn't want the sun waking him up every morning. She asked, "Does the sun rise in the North?" When my brother explained that the sun rises in the East, and has for sometime, she shook her head and said, "Oh I don't keep up with all that stuff."

They Walk Among Us!
I used to work in technical support for a 24/7 call center. One day I got a call from an individual who asked what hours the call center was open. I told him, "The number you dialed is open 24 hours a day, 7 days a week" He responded, "Is that Eastern or Pacific time?" Wanting to end the call quickly, I said, "Uh, Pacific."

They Walk Among Us!
My sister has a life-saving tool in her car designed to cut through a seat belt if she gets trapped. She keeps it in the trunk.

They Walk Among Us!
My friends and I were on a beer run and noticed that the cases were discounted 10%. Since it was a big party, we bought 2 cases. The cashier multiplied 2 times 10% and gave us a.....20% discount.

They Walk Among Us!
I couldn't find my luggage at the airport baggage area, so I went to the lost luggage office and told the woman there that my bags never showed up. She smiled and told me not to worry because she was a trained professional and I was in good hands.   "Now," she asked me, "has your plane arrived yet?"

Yep, They Walk Among Us!

They Walk Among Us--- and they Reproduce.

Two guys are drinking in a bar.

Two guys are drinking in a bar.

One says, "Did you know that lions have sex 10 to 15 times a night?"

"Shit," says his friend, "and I just joined the Elks!!"

Two Guys in a Bar

Two guys walk into a bar and sit down to eat their lunches. Then the bartender says, "Sorry, but you can't eat your own food in here." So the two guys look at each other and swap lunches.

Washing a Sweatshirt

One day my housework-challenged husband decided to wash his Sweatshirt. Seconds after he stepped into the laundry room, he shouted to me, "What setting do I use on the washing machine?" "It depends," I replied. "What does it say on your shirt?" He yelled back, OHIO STATE!" And they say blondes are dumb!

Westinghouse Easter Bunny

A lady opened her refrigerator and saw the Easter Bunny sitting on one of the shelves. "What are you doing in there?" she asked. The bunny replied, "This is a Westinghouse, isn't it?" To which the lady replied, "Yes" "Well" the bunny explained, "I'm westing."

Sports

A Guy Out on the Golf Course

A guy out on the golf course takes a high speed ball right in the crotch. Writhing in agony, he falls to the ground, when he finally gets himself to the doctor.

He says, "How bad is it doc? I'm going on my honeymoon next week and my fiancé is still a virgin in every way."

The doc said, "I'll have to put your penis in a splint to let it heal and keep it straight. It should be okay next week."

So he took four tongue depressors and formed a neat little 4-sided bandage, and wired it all together; an impressive work of art.

The guy mentions none of this to his girl, marries, and on his honeymoon night in the motel room, she rips open her blouse to reveal a gorgeous set of breasts. This was the first time he saw them.

She says, "You are my FIRST, no one has ever touched these breasts."

He whips down his pants and says... "Look at this, it's still in the CRATE!"

Ask Me – I know the Answer

All the children are restless and the teacher decides to have an early dismissal.

Teacher: "Whoever answers the questions I ask, first and correctly can leave early today."

Little Johnny says to himself "Good, I want to get outta here. I'm smart and will answer the question."

Teacher: "Who said ' Four Score and Seven Years Ago'?"

Before Johnny can open his mouth, Susie says, "Abraham Lincoln."

Teacher: "That's right Susie, you can go home."

Johnny is mad that Susie answered the question first.

Teacher: "Who said 'I Have a Dream'?"

Before Johnny can open his mouth, Mary says, "Martin Luther King."

Teacher: "That's right Mary, you can go."

Johnny is even madder than before.

Teacher: "Who said 'Ask not, what your country can do for you'?"

Before Johnny can open his mouth, Nancy says, "John F. Kennedy."

Teacher: "That's right Nancy, you may also leave."

Johnny is boiling mad that he has not been able to answer any of the questions.

When the teacher turns her back Johnny says, "I wish these bitches would keep their mouths shut!"

The teacher turns around: "NOW WHO SAID THAT?"

Johnny: "TIGER WOODS. CAN I GO NOW?"

Bill Goes Golfing

Bill goes golfing every Saturday. One Saturday, he comes home three hours late. His wife asks him, "What took you so long?"
Bill says, "That was the worst game of golf I've ever had. We got up to the first tee, and Jim hit a hole-in-one and immediately dropped

dead of a heart attack."

Bill's wife says, "That's terrible!"

Bill says, "I know. Then, for the rest of the game, it was hit the ball, drag Jim, hit the ball, drag Jim, hit the ball, drag Jim. . ."

Could Have Been Worse

Frank always looked on the bright side. He would constantly irritate his friends with his eternal optimism. No matter how horrible the circumstance, he would always reply, "It could have been worse." To cure him of his annoying habit, his friends decided to invent a situation so completely bad, so terrible, that even Frank could find no hope in it.

On the golf course one day, one of them said, "Frank, did you hear about Tom? He came home last night, found his wife in bed with another man, shot them both and then turned the gun on himself!"

"That`s awful," said Frank, "But it could have been worse."

"How in the hell," asked his bewildered friend, "Could it have been worse?"

"Well," replied Frank, "If it happened the night before, I`d be dead now!"

Female Hockey Player

There was a boy who worked in the produce section of a super market. A man came in and asked to buy half a head of lettuce. The boy told him that they only sold whole heads of lettuce, but the man replied that he did not need a whole head, only half. The boy explained that he would have to ask the manager and so he walked into the back room and said, "There is some jerk out there who wants to buy only a half a head of lettuce." As he finished saying this, he turned around to find the man standing right behind him, so he quickly added, "And this gentleman wants to buy the other half." The manager okayed the request and the man went on his way.

Later on the manager said to the boy, "You almost got yourself in a lot of trouble earlier, but I must say I was impressed with the way you got out of it. You think on your feet and we like that around here. Where are you from, son?"

The boy replied, "Minnesota, sir."

"Oh, really? Why did you leave Minnesota?" inquired the manager.

The boy replied, "They're all just whores and hockey players up there."

"My wife is from Minnesota", exclaimed the manager.

The boy instantly replied, "Really! What team did she play for?"

Fish What Fish?

A redneck was stopped by a game warden in Central Mississippi recently with two ice chests full of fish. He was leavin' a cove well-known for its fishing.

The game warden asked the man, "Do you have a license to catch those fish?"

"Naw, sir", replied the redneck. "I ain't got none of them there licenses. You must understand, these here are my pet fish."

"Pet fish?"

"Yeah. Every night, I take these here fish down to the lake and let 'em swim 'round for awhile. Then, when I whistle, they jump right back into these here ice chests and I take 'em home."

"That's a bunch of hooey! Fish can't do that."

The redneck looked at the warden for a moment and then said, "It's the truth, Mr. Government Man. I'll show ya. It really works."

"O. K.", said the warden. "I've got to see this!"

The redneck poured the fish into the lake and stood and waited.

After several minutes, the warden says, "Well?"

"Well, what?" says the redneck.

The warden says, "When are you going to call them back?"

"Call who back?"

"The FISH" replied the warden!

"What fish?" replied the redneck.

Moral of the story: We may not be as smart as some city slickers, but we ain't as dumb as some government employees.

You can say what you want about the South, but you never hear of anyone retiring and moving north.

Fishing Trip

A man phones home from the office and tells his wife, "Something has just come up. I have the chance to go fishing for a week. It's the opportunity of a lifetime. We leave right away, so can you pack my clothes, my fishing equipment, and especially my blue silk pajamas? I'll be home in an hour to pick them up."

He hurries home, grabs everything and rushes off. A week later he returns. His wife asks, "Did you have a good trip?"

"Oh yes, great! But you forgot to pack my silk pajamas."

"Oh no I didn't. I put them in your tackle box."

Golf Courses in Heaven

An avid golfer goes to a fortune teller and asks, "Madame fortune teller, tell me, are there any golf courses in heaven?" She says, "I have good news and bad news."

"What's the good news?"

"The good news is that the golf courses in heaven are beautiful beyond anything you could imagine,"

"That's wonderful."

"And you'll be teeing off at 8:30 tomorrow morning."

Golf Enthusiast

A woman arrived at a party. While scanning the guests, she spotted an attractive man standing alone.

She approached him, smiled and said, "Hello. My name is Carmen." "That's a beautiful name," he replied. "Is it a family name?"

"No," she replied. As a matter of fact I gave it to myself. It represents the things that I enjoy the most - cars and men. Therefore I chose "Carmen". "What's your name?" she asked.

He answered "B.J. Titsengolf."

Golf Tees

A man and his wife were driving through country on his way from New York to California. Looking at his fuel gauge, he decided to stop at the next gasoline station and fill up. About 15 minutes later, he spots a Mobil station and pulls over to the high octane pump.

"What can I do for y'all?" asks the attendant. "Fill `er up with high test," replies the driver. While the attendant is filling up the tank, he's looking the car up and down. "What kinda car is this?" he asks. "I never seen one like it before." "Well," responds the driver, his chest swelling up with pride, "this, my boy is a 1999 Cadillac DeVille."

"What all's it got in it?" asks the attendant. "Well," says the driver, "it has everything. It's loaded with power steering, power seats, power sun roof, power mirrors, AM/FM radio with a 10 deck CD player in the trunk with 100 watts per channel, 8 speaker stereo, rack and pinion steering, disk brakes all around, leather interior, digital instrument package, and best of all, a 8.8 liter V12 engine."

"Wow," says the attendant, "that's really something!" "How much do I owe you for the gasoline?" asks the driver. "That'll be $30.17," says the attendant.

The driver pulls out his money clip and peels off a $20 and a $10. He goes into his other pocket and pulls out a handful of change. Mixed up with the change are a few golf tees. "What are those little wooden things?" asks the attendant. "That's what I put my balls on when I drive," says the driver. "Wow," says the attendant, "those Cadillac people think of everything!"

Golfing Groom

The bride came down the aisle and when she reached the altar, the groom was standing there with his golf bag and clubs at his side.

She said:" What are your golf clubs doing here"?

He looked her right in the eye and said, "This isn't going to take all day, is it?"

Golfing With The Mob

One morning, a man approached the first tee, only to find another guy approaching from the other side. They began talking and decided to play 9 holes together. After teeing off, they set off down the fairway, continuing their chat.

"What do you do?" the first man asked.

"I'm a salesman. What about you?"

"I'm a hit man for the mob," replied the second man.

The hit man noticed that the 1st guy started getting a little nervous and continued, "Yeah, I'm the highest paid guy in the business. I'm the best."

He stopped, sat down his bag of clubs, and pulled out a fancy, high powered rifle that was loaded with all types of scopes and sights. He then asked the man where he lived.

Still nervous the man replied, "In a subdivision just west of here."

The hit man placed the gun against his shoulder, faced west, peered into a scope and asked "What color roof ya' got?"

"Gray."

Then he asked "What color siding?"

"Yellow."

"You got a silver Toyota?"

"Yeah," replied the first man who was now completely amazed by the accuracy of the hit man's equipment. "That's my wife's car."

"That your red pickup next to it?"

Looking baffled the man asked if he could look through the scope. Looking through the sights, he said "Hell. That's my buddy Jeff's truck. What the hell is he doing there if I'm..?"

The hit man looked through the scope once more. "Your wife a blond and your buddy got black hair?"

The man nodded.

"Well, I don't know how to tell you, but I think you've got a problem. They're going at it like a couple of teenagers in there." said the hit man.

"Problem??! THEY'VE got the problem! I want you to shoot both of them! Right now!"

The hit man paused and said, "Sure. But it'll cost you. Like I said, I'm the best. I get paid $5,000 per shot."

"I don't care! Just do it! I want you to shoot her right in the head, and shoot him in the balls."

The hit man agreed, turned, and took firing position. He carefully stared into the sights, taking careful aim. He then said, "You know what buddy; this is your lucky day. I think I can save you $5,000!"

Instructions

Teacher asks the football player: "Sam, what is the outside of a tree called?"

Sam: "I don't know."

Teacher: "Bark, Sam, bark."

Sam: "Bow, wow, wow!"

Two Nuns at a Football Game

Three men went to their seats at the football game and there were a couple of nuns sitting ahead of them. The men wanted to drink beer and swear at the referees and not be scolded by nuns, so they decided to badger the nuns and get them to move. One guy said, "I think I'm going to move to Utah, there are only 100 Catholics living there." The second guy said, "I want to go to Montana, there are only 50 Catholics there." The third guy said, "I want to go to Idaho, there are only 25 Catholics living there."

One of the nuns turned around and said, "Why don't you go to hell? There aren't any Catholics there."

St. Peter

A COWBOY FROM MONTANA

A cowboy appeared before St. Peter at the Pearly Gates. "Have you ever done anything of particular merit?" St. Peter asked.

"Well, I can think of one thing," the cowboy offered.

"On a trip to the Black Hills out in South Dakota, I came upon a gang of bikers who were threatening a young woman.

I directed them to leave her alone, but they wouldn't listen. So, I approached the largest and most tattooed biker and smacked him in the face, kicked his bike over, ripped out his nose ring, and threw it on the ground.

I yelled, Now, back off or I'll kick the crap out of all of you!"

St. Peter was impressed, "When did this happen?"

"Couple of minutes ago."

George Bush and Saint Peter

Einstein dies and goes to heaven. At the Pearly Gates, Saint Peter tells him, "You look like Einstein, but you have no idea the lengths that some people will go t, in order to sneak into Heaven. Can you prove who you really are?" Einstein ponders for a few seconds and asks, "Could I have a blackboard and some chalk?" Saint Peter snaps his fingers and a blackboard and chalk instantly appear. Einstein proceeds to describe with arcane mathematics and symbols his Theory of Relativity. Saint Peter is suitably impressed, "You really are Einstein!" he says. "Welcome to Heaven!"

The next to arrive is Picasso. Once again, Saint Peter asks for credentials. Picasso asks, "Mind if I use that blackboard and chalk?" Saint Peter says, "Go ahead." Picasso erases Einstein's equations and sketches a truly stunning mural with just a few strokes of chalk. Saint Peter claps, "Surely you are the great artist you claim to be!" he says. "Come on in"

Then Saint Peter looks up and sees George Bush. Saint Peter scratches his head and says, "Einstein and Picasso both managed to prove their identity. How can you prove yours?" George looks bewildered and says, "Who are Einstein and Picasso?" Saint Peter sighs and says, "Come on in, George."

I HAD A BAD DAY

It was getting a little crowded in Heaven, so God decided to change the admittance policy. The new law was that, in order to get into Heaven, you had to have a really bad day the day you died. The policy would go into effect at noon the following day. So the next day at 12:01 the first person came to the gates of Heaven. St. Peter at the gate, remembering about the new law, promptly told the man, "Before I can let you in, I need you to tell me about the day you died."

"No problem." said the man. "Well, for some time now, I've thought my wife was having an affair. I believed that each day on her lunch hour, she'd bring her lover home to our 25th floor apartment and have sex with him. So today I was going to come home too and catch them. Well, I got there and busted in and immediately began searching for this guy. My wife was half-naked and yelling at me as I searched the entire apartment. But, damn it, I couldn't find him! Just as I was going to give up, I happened to glance out onto the balcony and noticed that there was a man hanging off the edge by his fingertips! The nerve of that guy to think he could hide from me! Well, I ran out there and promptly stomped on his fingers until he fell to the ground. But wouldn't you know it, he landed in some bushes that broke his fall and he didn't die. This pissed me off even more, so in a rage I went back inside to get the first thing I could get my hands on to throw at him. And oddly enough, the first thing I could grab was the refrigerator. I unplugged it, pushed it out onto the balcony and heaved it over the side. It plummeted 25 stories and crushed him! The excitement of the moment was so great that right after that I had a heart attack and died almost instantly."

St. Peter sat back and thought for a moment. Technically, the guy DID have a bad day, and it was a crime of passion, so he announced, "OK, Sir. Welcome to the Kingdom of Heaven," and let him in.

A few seconds later the next guy came up. "OK, here's the rule. Before I can let you in, I need to hear about the day you died."

"Sure thing" the man replied. "But you're not gonna believe this. I was out on the balcony of my 26th floor apartment doing my daily exercises when I got a little carried away and accidentally fell over the side! Luckily however, I was able to catch myself by my fingertips on the balcony directly beneath mine. When all of a sudden this crazy man comes running out of his apartment and starts cussing and stomping on my fingers! Well, of course I fell. I hit some trees and bushes on the way down which broke my fall so I didn't die right away. As I'm laying there face up on the ground, unable to move and in excruciating pain, I see the man push his refrigerator, of all things, over the ledge and it falls directly on top of me and kills me!"

St. Peter is quietly laughing to himself as the man finishes his story. "I could get used to this new policy," he thinks to himself. "Very well," St. Peter announces. "Welcome to the Kingdom of Heaven," and he lets the man enter.

A few seconds later the third man in line comes up to the gate. "Tell me about the day you died," said St. Peter.

"OK, picture this," says the man. "I'm naked inside a Refrigerator......."

Nuns At The Gates of Heaven

Four nuns were standing in line at the gates of heaven. Peter asks the first if she has ever sinned. "Well, once I looked at a man's penis," she said. "Put some of this holy water on your eyes and you may enter heaven," Peter told her. Peter then asked the second nun if she had ever sinned. "Well, once I held a man's penis," she replied. "Put your hand in this holy water and you may enter heaven," he said. Just then the fourth nun pushed ahead of the third nun. Peter asked her,

"Why did you push ahead in line?" She said, "Because I want to gargle before she sits in it!"

Pearly Gates Missing

One day at the entrance to heaven, St. Peter saw a New York street gang walk up to the Pearly Gates. This being a first, St. Peter ran to God and said, "God, there are some evil, thieving New Yorkers at the Pearly Gates. What do I do?"

God replied, "Just do what you normally do with that type. Re-direct them down to hell."

St. Peter went back to carry out the order and all of a sudden he comes running back yelling "God, God, they're gone, they're gone!"

"Who, the New Yorkers?"

"No, the Pearly Gates."

Three People

The Chinese Construction Worker

A foreman at a construction site gathers three of his workers: an Irishman, an Italian and a Chinese. He says to the Irishman, "you're in charge of sweeping, I want this whole area swept up before I get back."

He says to the Italian, "You're in charge of shoveling. I want that pile shoveled into the truck so they can haul it away."

He says to the Chinaman, "You're in charge of supplies. Now make sure that all gets done before I get back."

Three hours later, he returns and none of the work is done. The Irishman says, "I couldn't find a broom. You left the Chinaman in charge of supplies and he disappeared."

The Italian says "And I couldn't find a shovel." So the foreman starts walking and looking for the Chinaman.

Just then, the Chinaman jumps out from behind a pillar and screams "SUPPLIES!"

The Three Stars

One day avant-garde violinist, Malcolm Goldstein, US Ambassador to Spain, Eduardo Aguirre, and television's Tony Danza were on a jungle vacation together when they were caught by a tribal group.

Before they were about to be executed, they pleaded to the Queen of the Tribe for mercy. She said, "Get me something good to eat. If I like it, you will be freed." The three men looked at each other and agreed. They then went into the jungle to look for some food

Malcolm Goldstein was the first to come back. He came up to the altar and offered grapes. The Queen tasted one and immediately spat it out. She ordered her servants to shove the rest of the grapes up Malcolm Goldstein's ass. The servants did their duty, and left Malcolm Goldstein lying on the ground screaming.

Eduardo Aguirre was the next to arrive with some yummy apples. The same thing happened to him, but curiously he laughed as the apples were shoved up his ass. Malcolm Goldstein was shocked. Here he was with grapes up his ass howling in pain, but Eduardo Aguirre had several apples in his ass and he was laughing. He asked him "What the hell are you laughing about?"

A laughing Eduardo Aguirre replied "Tony Danza's coming back with a watermelon."

You Get What You Ask For

There were these three guys. They had been walking for 3 days and were very tired. They found a hotel, rented a room and went to sleep. Then, this old guy comes in out of nowhere, and says there is a magic pool just outside their hotel room. He tells them "Ok, you must jump off the diving board, and yell out what you wanna land in."

So the three guys go over to the pool. The first guy, a vegetarian, yells out "Bananas!" and lands in a pool of bananas.

The second guy was money hungry and yelled out "Money!" and lands in a pile of money.

The third guy jumps, when a bird shits on his head, and he yells "Oh Shit!"

13578831R00214

Made in the USA
Charleston, SC
18 July 2012